Avenging Lincoln's Death

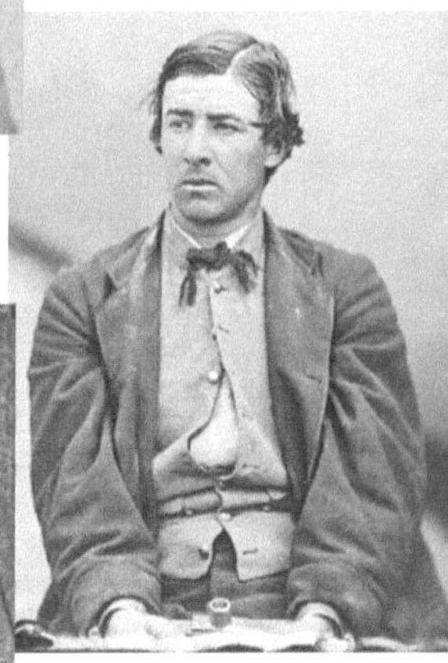

Avenging Lincoln's Death

The Trial of John Wilkes Booth's Accomplices

Thomas J. Reed

FAIRLEIGH DICKINSON UNIVERSITY PRESS
Madison • Teaneck

Published by Fairleigh Dickinson University Press
Copublished by The Rowman & Littlefield Publishing Group, Inc.
4501 Forbes Boulevard, Suite 200, Lanham, Maryland 20706
www.rowman.com

Unit A, Whitacre Mews, 26-34 Stannary Street, London SE11 4AB

British Library Cataloguing in Publication Information Available

Library of Congress Cataloging-in-Publication Data

Reed, Thomas J. (Thomas James), 1940- author.
Avenging Lincoln's death : the trial of John Wilkes Booth's accomplices / Thomas J. Reed.
p. cm.
Includes bibliographical references and index.
ISBN 978-1-61147-827-3 (cloth : alk. paper) – ISBN 978-1-61147-828-0 (ebook)
1. Lincoln Assassination Conspiracy Trial, Washington, D.C., 1865. I. Title.
KF223.L47R44 2016
345.73'02524–dc23
2015029166

∞™ The paper used in this publication meets the minimum requirements of American National Standard for Information Sciences Permanence of Paper for Printed Library Materials, ANSI/NISO Z39.48-1992.

Printed in the United States of America

Contents

List of Illustrations

Prelude

> Don't know the manners of good society, eh? Well, I guess I know enough to turn you inside out, old gal—you sockdologizing old man-trap.—Tom Taylor, *Our American Cousin*

Ford's Theatre was packed on Good Friday, April 14, 1865. The talented Laura Keene was starring in *Our American Cousin*, a light farce that had been an audience favorite since its debut in 1858. Harry Hawks, her leading man, played Asa Trenchard, the rustic from Vermont who had traveled to England to claim his estate and to meet his titled relatives.[1] President Abraham Lincoln occupied the presidential box in the dress circle overlooking the stage from stage left. His party consisted of Mrs. Lincoln, Miss Clara Harris, daughter of Senator Ira Harris, and her fiancé, Maj. Henry Rathbone.[2] The Lincoln party arrived after the play started. When the president walked to his box, the play stopped and the house orchestra struck up *Hail to the Chief.*[3] The audience had seen playbills printed that afternoon by the Ford brothers announcing that President Lincoln and General Grant would be attending the play that night. General and Mrs. Grant had politely declined to attend the theater that night. Instead the Grants were in the Union Railroad Station waiting to board a train for Philadelphia so that they could rejoin their children.

The audience had good reason to be joyous that night. The Confederate Army of Northern Virginia surrendered on April 9. General Grant and General Lee met at the Wilmer McLean house in Appomattox Court House to settle on surrender terms. Although hundreds of thousands of Confederate soldiers were in the field and the last engagement of the Civil War at Palmetto Ranch in Texas would not take place until June, the end of the Civil War was in sight.

Figure 0.1. Ford's Theatre. *Source:* Library of Congress.

The Lincoln party was screened from view by draperies. The play rolled on to act 3, scene 2, where Asa Trenchard speaks up to Mrs. Mountchessington. She attacks Trenchard as a man with no manners. As the insulted aristocrat flounced off stage, Harry Hawks spoke the lines that usually got the most laughter: "Don't know the manners of good society, eh? Well, I guess I know enough to turn you inside out, old gal—you sockdologizing old man-trap." As the audience broke into gales of laughter, a popping noise came from the presidential box. Presently, a man holding a dagger leaped from the box twelve feet to the stage below. Before the man ran off the stage to stage right, he said something, variously reported by audience members as "Sic semper tyrannis"[4] or "The South is avenged!"[5]

A woman's screams emanated from the presidential box. Another voice from the box shouted, "Stop that man!" The audience, slow to react to this assault, did not impede the flight of the assailant. The cast of *Our American Cousin* and several people in the audience almost immediately identified the assailant as the popular tragedian John Wilkes Booth. Someone called out for a doctor. Young army surgeon Charles Leale recovered from shock and went upstairs to the dress circle and ran to the presidential box. Leale found a grisly scene in the box. President Lincoln was slumped over unconscious in the rocking chair provided by the Ford brothers for his personal comfort. Mrs. Lincoln, dissolved in tears, held her husband up in the chair.[6] Major Rathbone's right arm had been slashed by the assailant's dagger. He was bleeding from the wound.[7] Leale did an immediate triage and went to Lincoln. Lincoln was unconscious. He was breathing stertorously. Surgeon Leale performed a quick head-to-toe examination of the victim. He felt for a pulse and found none. There were no obvious wounds on the president's head or chest. Leale felt the president's head and found an entry wound plugged by clotted blood. Leale pulled out the clot with his finger, and the president's breathing became more regular. Leale gave the victim a drink of brandy, which was retained.[8]

By this time Dr. C. F. Taft and Dr. A. F. A. King had joined Leale in the box. All three concurred that the president was mortally wounded and would not survive a trip to the White House.[9] Leale corralled several soldiers who had squeezed into the box to take up the president and carry him from the theater across the street to one of the row houses opposite the theater.

Other soldiers cleared the way through the crowd that had gathered outside Ford's Theatre. The president was taken to the house of William Petersen, an immigrant tailor, and laid on a spool bed in the back room, a room that had been rented out to a boarder. Lincoln was too long for the bed so the soldiers laid him down across the bed.[10] The death watch began.

Within minutes of the attack upon President Lincoln, six blocks away on Lafayette Square, a tall young man in a white coat knocked on the door of Secretary of State William Seward's residence. The secretary had been badly injured in a carriage accident on April 5. He broke his right arm and fractured his right jaw.[11] He was confined to bed, his jaw wired in place, wearing an iron brace on his right arm. The young man said he was sent by Dr. Verdi, Seward's doctor, with medicine to deliver to Seward personally. He talked his way past Daniel Bell, Seward's butler, and climbed the stairs to the second floor where he was confronted by Frederick Seward, Seward's eldest son.[12] The man in the white coat insisted that he had to give the medicine to Secretary Seward. Fred told the man that his father was sleeping in the bedroom to the right of the head of the stairs and could not be disturbed. The man in the white coat turned around as if to go downstairs and out the door. Suddenly, he produced a revolver and whirled about, facing Fred Seward. He pulled the trigger and got only a snap as the revolver misfired.[13] The man then slugged Fred Seward about the head with the barrel of his weapon, fracturing Fred's skull in two places. Seward went down. Secretary Seward's daughter Fanny and male nurse George Robinson were inside. The commotion outside the bedroom caught their attention, and they opened the door to see what was causing the uproar. The man in the white coat stood in the hallway.[14] Fred Seward, who had regained his feet, was conscious and bleeding profusely, swaying back and forth before his attacker. The man in the white coat pushed past Robinson and Fanny Seward, leaped on the bed, and began stabbing the secretary about the head and shoulders with a bowie knife. The assailant inflicted painful wounds on Seward's face, slicing open his left jaw, but the attacker missed the jugular vein because of Seward's iron arm brace. Robinson and Fanny wrestled with him, trying to stop the attack. The attacker leaped off the bed, knocking Fanny to the floor and stabbing Robinson as he tried to flee. Augustus Seward, the secretary's youngest son, joined the scuffle in his father's bedroom. Robinson and Augustus were able to pin down the attacker. Seward went to get his revolver while Robinson held on to the struggling man in the white coat. The attacker broke Robinson's hold. Still carrying his knife, he ran downstairs passing State Department messenger Emrick Hansell. The attacker stabbed Hansell in the back and pushed his way out the door. As the assailant ran downstairs, he shouted, "I'm mad, I'm mad!"[15] The assailant was Lewis Powell, a former member of the First Florida Infantry, CSA and Mosby's Rangers, also known as "Lewis Paine" (also spelled "Payne") and "Mr. Wood."[16]

Around 10:00 p.m. Michael Henry, the bartender at the Kirkwood House, the hotel in which Vice President Andrew Johnson had taken a room, saw a shabby-looking man who had registered at the hotel the day before drinking at the bar. The individual slunk out of the bar as if on his way to do someone a bad turn. Around 10:30 John Lee, the chief detective for Washington, D.C., and D.C. provost marshal Maj. James O'Beirne entered Kirkwood House with the news that President Lincoln had been shot. Michael Henry told Lee about the lowlife whom he had observed earlier. He mentioned that the man had a thick German accent. Lyman Sprague, the hotel manager, was called in and Lee checked the hotel's guest register. "G. A. Atzerodt" was registered for room 126. Lee, accompanied by the bartender and the manager, ran up the main staircase to the second floor and pounded on the door of room 126.[17] When no one answered, the manager opened the door. Lee found a loaded and capped revolver and a bowie knife in the room. Lee removed an overcoat from the room. Searching its pockets, Lee turned up a map of the Southern states, a handkerchief marked "Mary A. H. Booth," another marked "F. M. Nelson," and a Bank of Ontario bankbook for the account of John Wilkes Booth.[18] The Washington detectives and the military marked Atzerodt for arrest as one of Booth's accomplices.[19]

Secretary of War Edwin M. Stanton got word that someone had attacked Secretary Seward shortly after 10:00 p.m. Stanton went to Seward's house in the company of Secretary of the Navy Gideon Welles. They discovered the attack on Secretary Seward. Rumors that the president was shot at Ford's Theatre reached the Seward house. Stanton and Welles climbed back in their carriage and made for Tenth Street and Ford's Theatre. Immediately upon arriving at the Petersen house, Stanton went to the bedroom where the president lay dying. He broke down and wept, knowing that the president would not live. When Stanton regained his composure, he left the bedroom and made his way to the rear parlor of the Petersen house where he set up a command post.[20] From 11:00 p.m. until Lincoln's death at 7:34 a.m. on April 15, Secretary Stanton organized the vast task of pursuing the assassins and capturing them. First, the secretary of war ordered all roads leading out of Washington closed. He also ordered that the Washington garrison stand to in case the assassinations were part of a general uprising.[21] A relay chain of soldiers took Stanton's messages from the Petersen house to the War Department on Fifteenth Street, where Maj. T. T. Eckhart, the chief telegrapher for the War Department, had the messages sent from the telegraph office. Stanton sent a midnight telegram to General Grant, recalling him from leave.[22] District of Columbia judge David Cartter took charge of interrogating witnesses to the assassination in Ford's Theatre. Corporal James Tanner, a wounded veteran who had learned shorthand and who lived next door to the Petersen house, volunteered his services as ad hoc court reporter for the judge. By 1:00 a.m. Judge Cartter had interviewed six witnesses who identified Lincoln's assailant as John Wilkes Booth. He informed Stanton who dashed off a message to New York City police chief Kennedy shortly after 1:00 a.m.[23] By 1:30 Stanton knew that Lincoln's assassination had been perpetrated by John Wilkes Booth, but Stanton did not inform military or civilian offices of the identity of the killer until 3:00 a.m.[24] Meanwhile, he mobilized the National Detective Police, the provost marshal's offices in Washington and Baltimore, and Maj. Gen. Christopher C. Auger's cavalry units to commence a dragnet search for the killer and his accomplices.

On April 26, 1865, a detachment of the Sixteenth New York Cavalry escorting National Detective Police agent Luther Baker and Lt. Col. Everton Conger of the First District of Columbia Cavalry, appointed by National Detective Police chief Lafayette Baker to run down Booth, caught up with John Wilkes Booth and his traveling companion, David Herold, at the farm of Richard Garrett located near Bowling Green, Virginia. Booth and Herold were trapped in Garrett's tobacco barn. When they refused to give themselves up, Colonel Conger ordered that the barn be set on fire. Herold surrendered, but Booth resisted and was shot and mortally wounded by Sgt. Boston Corbett. Booth died around 7:00 a.m. on April 26.[25]

Secretary Stanton's dragnet caught more than two hundred individuals suspected of aiding and abetting John Wilkes Booth. The government chose to try eight alleged accomplices from among its prisoners: George Atzerodt, identified as the man who hung around the bar at Kirkwood House on the night of April 14; Samuel Arnold, whose letter to John Wilkes Booth requesting Booth to check with Richmond about his plans was found in Booth's trunk; David Herold, who traveled with Booth from Washington to the Garrett farm where Booth was killed; Dr. Samuel Mudd, a Maryland physician who treated Booth's broken leg on April 15, 1865; Michael O'Loughlen, a boyhood friend of Booth identified by at least one witness as a man who attended Secretary Stanton's soirée for General Grant on April 13; Lewis Powell, identified as Secretary Seward's assailant; Edman Spangler, a friend of the Booth family who worked at Ford's Theatre whom Booth asked to hold his horse on the night of April 14; and Mary Surratt, the proprietor of an H Street boardinghouse where Booth was a frequent visitor. Booth consorted with her son John Surratt and other alleged accomplices at Mrs. Surratt's boardinghouse in the winter of 1864–1865. This book is the story of the trial of Booth's alleged accomplices. It is also a legal and constitutional analysis of the trial.

NOTES

1. Tom Taylor, *Our American Cousin*, 1858, available at http://www.gutenberg.org/ebooks/3158.
2. James Swanson, *Manhunt: The Twelve-Day Chase for Lincoln's Killer* (New York: Harper Perennial, 2007), 32–33.
3. Swanson, *Manhunt*, 33.
4. Swanson, *Manhunt*, 48; Edward Steers Jr., *Blood on the Moon: The Assassination of Abraham Lincoln* (Lexington: University Press of Kentucky, 2001), 118.
5. David Herbert Donald, *Lincoln* (New York: Simon & Schuster, 1995), 597.
6. Charles A. Leale, " Lincoln's Last Hours," address delivered before the Commandery of the State of New York Military Order of the Loyal Legion of the United States at its regular meeting February 1909, available at Project Gutenberg, http://www.gutenberg.org/files/24088/24088.txt. Dr. Leale's original report dated April 15, 1865, had been mislaid during the investigation of the assassination and surfaced in 2011 in papers collected for the Abraham Lincoln Library and Museum in Springfield, Illinois.
7. Steers, *Blood on the Moon*, 120.
8. Leale, "Lincoln's Last Hours."
9. Leale, "Lincoln's Last Hours."
10. Michael W. Kauffman, *American Brutus: John Wilkes Booth and the Lincoln Conspiracies* (New York: Random House, 2004), 19; Leale, "Lincoln's Last Hours."
11. Margaret Leech, *Reveille in Washington 1860–1865* (New York: Harper & Bros., 1941; New York: Time, 1962), 468. Citations refer to the Time edition.
12. Kauffman, *American Brutus*, 22–23.
13. Kauffman, *American Brutus*, 22–23.
14. Kauffman, *American Brutus*, 22–23.
15. Patricia Carley Johnson, transcriber, *The Selected Diaries and Papers, 1858–1866, of Frances Adeline (Fanny) Seward*, April 14, 1865, available at http://www.lib.rochester.edu/index.cfm?page=1420&Print=436. See also Kaufmann, *American Brutus*, 24.

16. Steers, *Blood on the Moon*, 82–83, 126.
17. Kauffman, *American Brutus*, 30–31.
18. Kauffman, *American Brutus*, 32.
19. The seven men and one woman who were tried by military commission are often loosely referred to as "the Lincoln conspirators," which is a legal conclusion. These individuals and many others not charged with crimes were alleged to be Booth's accomplices and throughout this book they will be referred to as "alleged accomplices" or "accomplices."
20. Swanson, *Manhunt*, 110.
21. U.S. War Department, "Maj. Gen. M. J. Meigs to Maj. Gen. C. C. Augur Midnight Apr. 14, 1865," in *The War of the Rebellion: A Compilation of the Official Records of the Union and Confederate Armies* [also known as *The Official Record of the War of the Rebellion,* hereafter "OR"], series 1, vol. 46, part 3 (Washington, D.C.: Government Printing Office, 1880–1901), 756. See also Kauffman, *American Brutus,* 112. Quartermaster General Montgomery Meigs alerted Maj. Gen. Christopher Columbus Augur, commanding general of the District of Columbia garrison, shortly after midnight by a hand-carried message.
22. OR, series 1, vol. 46, part 3, 757; Swanson, *Manhunt*, 111.
23. Kauffman, *American Brutus*, 114. Stanton requested that Kennedy send three or four detectives to Washington to assist in the investigation.
24. Kaufmann, *American Brutus*, 116.
25. Swanson, *Manhunt*, 333–43.

Acknowledgments

The impetus for *Avenging Lincoln's Death* dates back to 1997 when I assisted Candida Ewing Steel, Esq., of Baltimore in the effort to rectify the record for Dr. Samuel Mudd. I was able to put together a research team headed by one of my students, John Benson, to work with me on legal issues. We pursued a project to attack Dr. Mudd's unlawful conviction by an extraordinary writ petition or by an appeal from the assistant secretary of the army's decision to disregard the Army Board for Correction of Military Records' decision setting aside Dr. Mudd's conviction. I mined the mass of material accumulated in support of Dr. Mudd's case for a talk called "Abraham Lincoln and the Simple-Minded Soldier Boy" that was presented several times from 2002 to 2013 to the Abraham Lincoln Club of Delaware and to Civil War roundtables in the eastern United States. In 2011 I incorporated some of the 1997 research in a course on the Lincoln assassination for the Osher Institute of the University of Delaware. My students encouraged me to put my course materials into book form.

I owe a great deal to the people who assisted me in the development of this book from my Lincoln assassination course materials. The men and women who reviewed my work would include my colleagues at Widener University School of Law who commented on the first draft of the book and contributed thoughtful comments and suggestions: Vice Dean Erin Daly, a notable constitutional law scholar; Associate Dean Michael Slinger, who teaches a seminar on civil liberties in the Civil War; and Professor Emeritus John F. Nivala. Professor Emeritus John P. Jones of T. C. Williams School of Law, University of Richmond, drafted a critique that helped to produce the last chapter of the book. Professor Jones sponsored a daylong moot court program in 1993 on the Mudd case (published by Combined Books in 1995) that contained valuable articles on Dr. Mudd's case and the law pertaining to conspiracy.

Candida Ewing Steel read the chapters pertaining to Mary Surratt and Dr. Mudd. Michael Wims, Esq., author of the American Bar Association's *How to Try a Murder Case* and an authority on military law and procedure, made many useful suggestions that improved this work, as did my cousin Elizabeth Hatle, a high school history teacher in St. Paul, Minnesota.

The staff of Widener University School of Law Legal Information Center has assisted in procuring rare sourcebooks for this project over the past eighteen years. David King, Janet Lindenmuth, and Mary Jane Mallonee in particular assisted my team in our 1997 project.

I am especially grateful for the editorial work done by Kalman Goldstein of Fairleigh Dickinson University Press, which has resulted in the present text, and suggestions made by Dr. Harry Keyishian, the director of Fairleigh Dickinson University Press. Lynn Weber reviewed and edited this work for publication. She was an invaluable asset to this work, Finally, my wife, Emily A. Reed, PhD, has been very supportive and very patient, accompanying me on expeditions to the Surratt Society and Dr. Mudd's house in search of obscure information on these alleged accomplices. She has also used her artistic and computer skills to prepare the illustrations for this book.

Introduction

This book examines the trial transcripts and other evidence relating to the trial of the Lincoln assassination accomplices from the viewpoint of a lawyer and legal historian. The book's thesis is that the trial of the alleged accomplices by military commission was unfair and unconstitutional for the following reasons:

- Congress did not authorize President Johnson to try Booth's alleged accomplices by military commission according to Article I § 8 of the Constitution, and the president's authority as commander-in-chief under Article II § 2 did not authorize him to order civilians to be tried by military commission.
- President Johnson and Secretary Stanton failed to comply with the mandatory requirements of the Habeas Corpus Act of 1863 that required them to turn over the names of the accomplices to the civilian authorities to be treated as common criminals and to be indicted, tried, and perhaps convicted by a jury of their peers (a constitutional violation of the misuse of executive power).
- The accomplices were convicted in part on perjured testimony, a violation of the Fifth Amendment.
- The accomplices were charged with treason, and Article III § 3 of the Constitution requires that at least one treasonable act be proved by two eyewitnesses. The government failed to prove a treasonable act by two witnesses in the cases of Samuel Arnold, Samuel Mudd, Michael O'Loughlen, Mary Surratt, and Edman Spangler.
- In the case of Mary Surratt and Samuel Mudd, the evidence admitted at trial failed to prove that Surratt knowingly acted as an accessory before

the fact to murder or that Mudd knowingly assisted John Wilkes Booth and David Herold in their flight from justice.

- The government introduced irrelevant testimony relating to atrocities committed by the Confederate States (e.g., the use of clothing from yellow fever victims to spread an epidemic among Union-held cities, maltreatment of Union prisoners of war by Confederate jailors).

The seven men and one woman selected by the secretary of war and Joseph Holt, the judge advocate general of the army, to be charged with aiding and abetting John Wilkes Booth's assassination plot were tried by a military commission authorized by President Andrew Johnson on May 1, 1865.[1] The alleged accomplices were charged with treason, conspiracy, attempted murder, and aiding and abetting Booth before and after Lincoln's assassination.[2] Attorney General James Speed gave the president verbal assurance that he had the inherent authority to appoint a military commission to try the alleged accomplices. Speed later produced a written opinion justifying trial by military commission after the Hunter Commission had passed sentences on the alleged accomplices, sending four of them to the gallows and the rest to prison.[3] There is no record of the oral advice Speed gave to President Johnson and Secretary Stanton. Speed's predecessor Judge Edward Bates and Navy Secretary Gideon Welles disagreed with Speed and opposed trial by military commission.[4] The cabinet was convened to ponder the impact of trying the accused accomplices by military commission on May 9, 1865. Secretary Stanton and Attorney General Speed argued in favor of a secret trial by military commission, but no formal vote was taken.[5] The reaction of the press to trial by military commission was generally favorable, although the *New York Times* editorialized against a secret trial.[6] The accomplices of John Wilkes Booth would be tried on the third floor of the Washington Arsenal Penitentiary by a military commission consisting of very loyal, high-ranking Union officers.[7]

The trial of Booth's alleged accomplices has fascinated lay historians and scholars since 1865. Some of the men involved in the trial published articles and books espousing their view of the fairness of the Hunter Commission trial. In 1880 John W. Clampitt, one of Mary Surratt's lawyers, published his version of the Hunter Commission trial, condemning it as a travesty of justice because the commission was prejudiced against the defendants and consistently allowed inadmissible evidence to be admitted against Mrs. Surratt and the other defendants.[8] William E. Doster, Lewis Powell's lawyer, published his memoir in 1915.[9] He devoted one chapter in his 1915 *Lincoln and Episodes of the Civil War* to the trial of Booth's alleged accomplices.[10] Doster adopted the argument of Senator Reverdy Johnson made to the Hunter Commission during trial that the commission was without jurisdiction to try the eight defendants because the Constitution required that the defendants be tried by a fair and impartial jury. Doster had the benefit of *Ex parte Milligan* decided in 1866 that held that when civilian courts were open and the venue was under no threat of attack, civilians could not be tried by a military commission.[11] Hunter Commission member Brig. Gen. Thomas Harris produced two books relating to the trial. His first was a relatively dispassionate defense of the trial and its conduct. Harris did not question the constitutionality of the Hunter Commission and the trial. He maintained that the alleged accomplices were properly tried by a military commission according to the law of war because Washington, D.C., was under martial law at the time of Lincoln's assassination.[12] Harris's second work was an inflammatory attack on the alleged accomplices as a Jesuit-managed plot to remove President Lincoln because of his opposition to the Vatican's plan to take over the United States.[13] Henry Burnett, the junior judge advocate at the trial, published two papers read to the Military Order of the Loyal Legion of the United States on the trial and on the controversy over the clemency recommendation for Mary Surratt submitted to President Johnson in July 1865. Neither paper was concerned with the constitutionality of the Hunter Commission trial.

Professional writers and amateur historians published their comments on the trial within days after the execution of Atzerodt, Herold, Powell, and Mrs. Surratt. George Alfred Townsend, America's premier news correspondent, republished many of his articles on the Lincoln assassination in 1865.[14] Townsend produced a trenchant literary description of the trial, the lawyers, and the defendants but never analyzed the law supporting the trial of the alleged accomplices by military commission. Osborn Oldroyd published his story of Lincoln's assassination in 1891.[15] He devoted several chapters to the trial of Booth's alleged accomplices including biographical sketches of the eight accomplices. Oldroyd did not challenge the lawfulness of the commission nor the fairness of the trial.[16] He carefully avoided analyzing the constitutionality of trial by military commission. Former congressman David DeWitt denounced the conviction of Mary Surratt as "judicial murder" in his 1895 *The Judicial Murder of Mary E. Surratt*.[17] DeWitt, like William E. Doster, cited *Ex parte Milligan* as the basis for his argument that Mrs. Surratt's trial was unconstitutional.[18] DeWitt did not analyze the evidence and the existence of one or two conspiracies. It was sufficient for his case to show that Mrs. Surratt had been denied a fair trial.

No one questioned the legality of nor reexamined the legal implications of the trial of Booth's alleged accomplices until the late twentieth century. In 1993, law professor John P. Jones of the University of Richmond School of Law held a mock appellate argument challenging the conviction of Dr. Samuel Mudd on constitutional grounds. Jones edited and contributed to a book summarizing the mock argument.[19] The brief of the appellant included a constitutional argument based on *Ex parte Milligan*, but did not address the

Habeas Corpus Act of 1863, Congress's failure to pass a statute authorizing trial by military commission, nor the limitations on the presidential war power. The answering brief for the United States claimed military necessity in time of war justified the trial of Booth's alleged accomplices, essentially asserting that the president's war power under Article II included the inherent power to try civilians by military commission.[20]

Jones's mock argument exercise was the result of a determined effort by Dr. Samuel A. Mudd's grandson, Dr. Richard Mudd, to clear the name of his grandfather by showing that Samuel A. Mudd was not guilty of conspiracy to commit treason, nor of aiding and abetting the escape of John Wilkes Booth. By 1992 Dr. Mudd had enlisted the volunteer aid of very able lawyers including Candida Ewing Steel, a direct descendant of Brig. Gen. Thomas Ewing, Mudd's defense counsel in 1865. Steel and her associates filed a petition in 1992 with the Army Board for Correction of Military Records that resulted in a unanimous decision that Dr. Mudd was wrongfully convicted, based on the majority decision in *Ex parte Milligan*. The secretary of the army overturned the board decision, resulting in a protracted court battle in the District of Columbia that ended with failure to perfect an appeal in 2001.[21]

The advocates who participated in Professor Jones's mock appellate argument did not argue that the president exceeded the scope of his power to wage war by unilaterally appointing a military commission to try Booth's alleged accomplices. They did not comment on President Johnson's and Secretary Stanton's failure to follow the Habeas Corpus Act of 1863, which mandated that the names of Booth's alleged accomplices be turned over to the civilian courts in the District of Columbia for indictment and trial. These advocates also implicitly treated Booth's conspiracies as a single conspiracy to assassinate President Lincoln and to decapitate the United States government, bypassing evidence that was available in May 1865 that showed that there were two distinct conspiracies: the first to kidnap the president as a bargaining chip for release of Confederate prisoners of war, the second to murder the president, the vice president, and the secretary of state.

Frederick B. Wiener, an eminent military lawyer and adjunct law professor, contributed a major article to Jones's book.[22] Wiener asserted that the original kidnapping conspiracy and the murder conspiracy was a single conspiracy, despite the contradictory purposes of the original conspiracy and the murder conspiracy.[23] He argued that in May 1865 Washington, D.C., was under military rule until President Johnson's amnesty proclamation issued May 26, 1865. The offenses with which Booth's alleged accomplices were charged were violations of the international law of war, not domestic crimes.[24] Wiener's piece was the best argument for trial of Booth's alleged accomplices by military commission. He asserted that Booth's alleged accomplices were properly tried by a military court because *Ex parte Milligan* applied to Indiana conditions, removed from any threat of invasion, but

Washington was still under the threat of potential enemy action. Using twentieth-century cases he argued that in time of war the president may convene military commissions to try civilians. Wiener did not analyze the source of presidential authority under Article II of the Constitution. Wiener never contended that Article II gave President Johnson plenary power to order civilians to be tried by a military tribunal for violating the law of war.[25] The doctrine of inherent authority to appoint military tribunals was implicit support for his argument. Professor John Yoo articulated the case for presidential authority to try civilians before military tribunals in his 1996 seminal article appearing in the University of California's law review.[26] Yoo asserted that Article II of the Constitution conferred upon the president authority as commander-in-chief to carry out unilateral actions furthering the general purposes of any particular war.[27] Chief Justice William Rehnquist articulated this standard, basing his analysis on military necessity in *All the Laws but One*, published in 1998. Rehnquist argued that the president had a constitutional duty to preserve the union that permitted the president to act unilaterally in time of emergency.[28] He analyzed the trial of Booth's alleged accomplices and concluded that the accomplices could be tried by military commission, adopting Judge Boynton's argument from *Ex parte Mudd*.[29]

Wiener's single conspiracy argument was picked up by Edward Steers Jr., the author of *Blood on the Moon*, the most widely read account of Lincoln's assassination and the trial of Booth's alleged accomplices.[30] Steers followed Wiener, asserting that the original kidnapping conspiracy morphed into a murder conspiracy, making all who were a party to the kidnapping conspiracy legally responsible for the murder of President Lincoln and the attempted murder of Secretary Seward, although they were unaware of the murder plot. Steers's analysis also accepted Wiener's conclusion that the president had inherent power to appoint military tribunals without congressional authorization. Steers did not try to avoid the government's failure to follow the Habeas Corpus Act of 1863 on the trial of Booth's alleged accomplices. He said nothing about this failure. Steers did not comment on the government's use of perjured testimony, or the government's introduction of Confederate atrocities unrelated to the assassination of President Lincoln. He also failed to comment on the bias and prejudice of commission members who were personal friends of President Lincoln, or were involved in his funeral and burial, nor did he comment on Gen. Thomas Harris's virulent anti-Catholicism.

The facts do not support Wiener's and Steers's conclusion that one great conspiracy included the kidnapping plot and the assassination plot. The primary purpose of Booth's kidnapping conspiracy was to take President Lincoln hostage and use him as a bargaining chip to free Confederate prisoners of war. That conspiracy ended on March 17, 1865, when Booth and his accomplices failed to take Lincoln prisoner on the Seventh Street road as they had planned. Samuel Arnold, Michael O'Loughlen, and John Surratt withdrew from the Booth conspiracy at the time. The murder conspiracy was formed sometime between late March and April 14, 1865. Booth was able to recruit Lewis Powell, David Herold, and George Atzerodt for the murder plot. Steers's argument fails to note that the kidnapping conspiracy's primary purpose would be defeated if Lincoln was killed—no more bargaining chip.

Other authors, notably Kate Clifford Larson who authored *The Assassin's Accomplice*,[31] the historical and literary basis for Robert Redford's 2011 motion picture *Conspirator*, use posttrial disclosures of evidence to assure the reader that the guilt of one of Booth's alleged accomplices was properly assessed at trial. Larson depended upon Richard Smoot's biography written forty-three years after the events of April 1865 to prove that Mrs. Surratt was a member of or aware of the kidnapping conspiracy.[32] Implicitly accepting the Wiener-Steers argument, she treats this disclosure as evidence of Mrs. Surratt's complicity in the assassination plot. She failed to note that Smoot's story was not offered by the government at the Hunter Commission trial. Such ex post facto evidence could not be used to support her conviction. The same analysis would apply to using Capt. George W. Dutton's claim that Samuel Mudd confessed to knowingly harboring John Wilkes Booth on the way to incarceration in Dry Tortuga, or his alleged confidential statement to Samuel Cox Jr. that he knew that Booth was the man he treated for a broken leg. Careful examination of these "disclosures" shows that the "disclosures" fail to confirm the convictions of Mrs. Surratt and Dr. Mudd for taking part in the murder conspiracy. These "disclosures" are suspect due to the age of the disclosures and the bias and interest of the men who reported these occurrences.

This book focuses on the trial of Booth's alleged accomplices. Chapter 1 examines the multiple assassination and kidnap conspiracies known to historians that began with the February 1861 Baltimore conspiracy to murder President-Elect Lincoln and culminated with John Wilkes Booth's March 1865 assassination conspiracy. It also examines the probable motive for any assassination attempt. Chapter 2 examines the men who were appointed by the secretary of war to the military commission chaired by President Lincoln's friend Maj. Gen. David M. Hunter; at least three of the commission members were biased in favor of conviction or so prejudiced against some or all of the alleged accomplices that they would not have been seated as jurors in a civilian trial. Chapter 3 turns to the lawyers. Popular mythology exaggerates the competence and the hostility of the three very highly qualified members of the prosecution team and the perceived inadequacy of individual defense counsel. With two exceptions, individual defense counsel were as qualified to handle the defense in a high-profile trial as the prosecution. However, defense counsel lacked a common strategy to counter the prosecution's carefully crafted plan to present evidence showing that Confederate president Jefferson Davis, and Confederate commissioners Clement C. Clay and Jacob Thompson conspired with Booth and his band to murder President Lincoln as part of a grand strategy to commit atrocities upon Union civilians and Union prisoners of war.

Chapter 4 examines the conduct of the trial, emphasizing the prosecution's use of perjured testimony to convict Booth's alleged accomplices and to show the nature and extent of the prosecution's grand conspiracy theory. This chapter also reviews the prosecution's use of unrelated atrocity testimony to prove the evil character of the men who were allegedly associated with Booth's putative accomplices. Chapter 5 details the case against Mary Surratt. The strongest evidence given at trial against Mrs. Surratt came from two individuals who agreed to testify against Mrs. Surratt to save themselves from appearing on the docket as a "coconspirator," Louis Weichmann and John Lloyd. The evidence put in by defense counsel in Mrs. Surratt's case consisted of proof of her good moral character and eyewitnesses who discredited John Lloyd's evidence of Mrs. Surratt's complicity. Chapter 6 reviews the case against Samuel Mudd. The most serious substantive charge against Mudd was knowingly assisting John Wilkes Booth and David Herold in their flight from justice. The prosecution had no direct evidence that Mudd knew that Booth had assassinated President Lincoln when he set Booth's broken left leg and kept him overnight. The government also had practically no circumstantial evidence of Dr. Mudd's guilty knowledge. The government was able to prove that Mudd was evasive and a liar. Had Mudd been tried by a civilian court, he would have been entitled to a directed verdict of acquittal.

The seventh and last chapter is a summary of the constitutional and legal flaws committed during the Hunter Commission trial. First, the commission had no jurisdiction to try Booth's alleged accomplices because the president's war powers did not include unilateral establishment of a military tribunal to try civilians. Second, the president had no constitutional basis for failing to follow the Habeas Corpus Act of 1863 by turning over Booth's alleged accomplices to civilian authorities for indictment and trial. Third, the prosecution put in perjured testimony, and knew that the testimony of Sanford Conover was perjurious before the trial closed. This also made the trial unconstitutional. Fourth, the prosecution put in testimony relating to the Confederate incendiary raid on New York City, the St. Albans bank robbery, and the yellow fever plot. None of these events were in any way related to the charges and specifications against the alleged accomplices. They were irrelevant and inflammatory. The only purpose this evidence served was to prejudice the Hunter Commission against Jefferson Davis, Clement Clay, Jacob Thompson, and the alleged accomplices. Given all these major infirmities, the trial of Booth's alleged accomplices was unfair, unconstitutional, and a travesty of justice that served only to wreak retribution on the eight alleged accomplices for the loss of President Lincoln.

In respect to the evidence admitted by the prosecution during the trial, the evidence relating to Samuel Arnold, Michael O'Loughlen, Edman Spangler, Mary Surratt, and Samuel Mudd was insufficient to prove guilt beyond a reasonable doubt. The military commission was not bound to the presumption of innocence and proof beyond a reasonable doubt. Therefore it could convict the alleged accomplices if two-thirds of the commission members decided it was as likely as not that they were guilty as charged. The prosecution also was permitted to drag in evidence of alleged Confederate maltreatment of Union prisoners of war, and of Confederate atrocities such as the insertion of the clothing of yellow fever victims into several U.S. cities in an attempt to start a yellow fever epidemic, the robbing of banks at St. Albans, Vermont, by Confederate special agents, and the attempt to burn down New York City, none of which was remotely related to the guilt of Booth's accomplices. A civilian court would not have permitted irrelevant evidence of uncharged misconduct to be admitted.

Were these people tried by a civilian court, the trial court could very well have granted a motion for directed verdict of acquittal at the close of the government's case. That may explain why Stanton, Holt, and President Johnson decided to try the alleged accomplices by military commission. The remainder of this book will examine the trial from a historical and legal perspective.

NOTES

1. See Douglas Linder, ed., "Order of the President: Proceedings of a Military Commission," May 1, 1865, available at Famous Trials Project, University of Missouri, Kansas City, http://law2.umkc.edu/faculty/projects/ftrials/lincolnconspiracy/commissionorder.html.
2. See Douglas Linder, ed., "Chronology of Lincoln Assassination Conspirators Trial," available at Famous Trials Project, University of Missouri, Kansas City, http://law2.umkc.edu/faculty/projects/ftrials/lincolnconspiracy/lincolnchronology.html.
3. See Douglas Linder, ed., "James Speed, Opinion on the Constitutional Power of the Military to Try and Execute the Assassins of the President," July 1865, Washington, D.C., available at Famous Trials Project, University of Missouri, Kansas City, http://law2.umkc.edu/faculty/projects/ftrials/lincolnconspiracy/commissionorder.html.
4. See entry for May 25, 1865, in Edward Bates, *The Diary of Edward Bates 1859–1866,* ed. Howard K. Beale (Washington, D.C.: Government Printing Office, 1933), 483 and 498–503 (Bates's analysis of Speed opinion); see also entry for May 9, 1865, in Gideon Welles, *Diary of Gideon Welles, Secretary of the Navy under Lincoln and Johnson*, vol. 2 (Boston: Houghton Mifflin, 1911), 203–4.
5. Welles, *Diary*, 2:304.
6. See editorial, *New York Times*, May 15, 1865, 4; see also *New York Times*, August 1, 1865, 2, quoting the *London Times*, July 17, 1865 (highly favorable to military commission).
7. See Barry Cauchon, "The Washington, D.C. Arsenal Penitentiary (Part 1 of 3)," *A Little Touch of History* (blog), July 2, 2009, https://awesometalks.wordpress.com/2009/08/02/the-washington-d-c-arsenal-penitentiary-part-1-of-3/ . The building remains standing today as Fort Lesley McNair's Building 20.
8. John W. Clampitt, "The Trial of Mrs. Surratt," *North American Review* 131, 1880, 223.
9. William E. Doster, *Lincoln and Episodes of the Civil War* (New York: Putnam, 1915).

10. Doster, *Lincoln and Episodes of the Civil War*, 263.

11. Doster, *Lincoln and Episodes of the Civil War*, 261–63. When the Hunter Commission rejected Senator Johnson's plea to the jurisdiction, Doster said, "This was practically the end of my case, as far as any show of legal defense was concerned" (263).

12. Thomas M. Harris, *Assassination of Lincoln: A History of the Great Conspiracy; Trial of the Conspirators by a Military Commission and a Review of the Trial of John H. Surratt* (Boston: American Citizen, 1892). Harris glosses over the use of perjured testimony from Sanford Conover, James Merritt, and Richard Montgomery, treating their evidence as trustworthy. He notes that evidence of alleged Confederate atrocities (e.g., the attempt to burn New York City, the yellow fever plot, and ill treatment of Union prisoners of war) were part of the great conspiracy that included Booth's assassination plot (Harris, *Assassination of Lincoln*, 119–21). Harris defended the decision to try Booth's alleged accomplices, reprinting Attorney General James Speed's opinion in full. Harris opined that trial by military commission was appropriate according to the law of war because Washington, D.C., was under martial law at the time of Lincoln's assassination (82–95).

13. Thomas M. Harris, *Rome's Responsibility for the Assassination of Abraham Lincoln* (Pittsburgh: Williams, 1897).

14. George A. Townsend, *The Life, Crime, and Capture of John Wilkes Booth with a Full Sketch of the Conspiracy of Which He Was the Leader and the Pursuit, Trial and Execution of His Accomplices* (New York: Dick & Fitzgerald, 1865).

15. Osborn H. Oldroyd, *The Assassination of Abraham Lincoln: Flight, Pursuit, Capture, and Punishment of the Conspirators* (Washington, D.C.: By the author, 1891).

16. Oldroyd, *Assassination of Abraham Lincoln*, 115–212.

17. David Miller DeWitt, *The Judicial Murder of Mary E. Surratt* (Baltimore: John Murphy, 1895).

18. DeWitt, *Judicial Murder of Mary E. Surratt*, 127–44.

19. John P. Jones, ed., *Dr. Mudd and the Lincoln Assassination: The Case Re-opened—The Proceedings of a Moot Court of Military Appeal to Hear the Case of Dr. Samuel A. Mudd with contributions by F. Lee Bailey, John Jay Douglass, Candida Ewing Steel, John S. Jenkins and Others* (Conshohocken, Pa.: Combined Books, 1997).

20. Jones, *Dr. Mudd and the Lincoln Assassination*, 32–52.

21. For the story of the failed attempt to overturn Mudd's conviction through the Army Board for Correction of Military Records, see Jones, *Dr. Mudd and the Lincoln Assassination*, 259–74. For judicial review of the appeal from the Board see Mudd v. White, 309 F.3d 819 (D.C. App. 2002); Mudd v. Caldera, 26 F. Supp.2d113 (1998).

22. Frederick B. Wiener, "His Name Was Mudd," in Jones, *Dr. Mudd and the Lincoln Assassination*, 117.

23. Wiener, "His Name Was Mudd," 118–19.

24. Wiener, "His Name Was Mudd," 136–42. Wiener correctly asserts that the justices unanimously ruled that Congress had not authorized the trial of the Northwest Conspirators by military commission and the War Department had failed to comply with the Habeas Corpus Act of 1863.

25. Wiener, "His Name Was Mudd," 135–36. Wiener cites Francis Lieber's General Order 100 in support of his conclusion that the president had the power to convene military commissions to try civilians. He also cites Attorney General James Speed's opinion.

26. See John C. Yoo, "The Continuation of Politics by Other Means: The Original Understanding of War Powers," *California Law Review* 84, no. 2 (1996): 196–241. Professor Yoo later became an advisor to President Bush and authored a memo that was consistent with his 1996 law review article. See John Yoo, "Memorandum Opinion: The President's Constitutional Authority to Conduct Military Operations against Terrorists and Nations Supporting Them," U.S. Department of Justice, Opinions of the Office of Legal Counsel, September 25, 2001, http://www.justice.gov/sites/default/files/olc/opinions/2001/09/31/op-olc-v025-p0188_0.pdf ; a revised version was published as John Yoo and Robert J. Delahunty, "The President's Constitutional Authority to Conduct Military Operations against Terrorist Organizations and the Nations That Harbor or Support Them," *Harvard Journal of Law and Public Policy* 25 (2002).

27. Yoo, "Continuation of Politics by Other Means," 251–54, 296–99.

28. William H. Rehnquist, *All the Laws but* One: Civil Liberties in Wartime (New York: Knopf, 1998), 222–24.

29. Rehnquist, *All the Laws but One*, 167–68. Judge Boynton asserted that the crime committed was a crime against the law of war because Lincoln was commander-in-chief, and therefore anyone involved in the assassination of Lincoln committed a crime against the law of war, triable by military commission whether or not the civilian courts were open. Boynton did not address the Habeas Corpus Act of 1863 or the reach of presidential power to make war. See also opinion in Ex parte Mudd, Fed. Cas. 9899 D. Fl. 1868 (opinion recovered from Fifth Circuit Archives by Candida Ewing Steel, Esq., 1993).

30. Edward Steers Jr., *Blood on the Moon: The Assassination of Abraham Lincoln* (Lexington: University Press of Kentucky, 2001), 209–10.

31. Kate Clifford Larson, *The Assassin's Accomplice: Mary Surratt and the Plot to Kill Abraham Lincoln* (New York: Basic Books, 2008).

32. Larson, *Assassin's Accomplice,* 80–81.

Chapter One

The Conspiracies

> It was the purpose of the conspirators to kidnap and hold him [President Lincoln] in captivity, without injury to his person, until such concessions were made to the Southern leaders as their plan of compromise rendered necessary. The various schemes of abduction having proved futile, some of the more desperate among the conspirators, exasperated by these repeated failures, resolved to dispose of Mr. Lincoln by the dagger or the bullet.—Osborn H. Oldroyd, *The Assassination of Abraham Lincoln: The Flight, Pursuit, Capture, and Punishment of the Conspirators*

John Wilkes Booth, one of the three sons of actor Junius Brutus Booth who were among the best actors in the United States, was an audience member during President Lincoln's April 11, 1865, speech from the White House balcony. Lincoln told the crowd that the suffrage should be extended to those African Americans who served in the Union army and navy and to "intelligent" civilian African Americans. Booth was outraged by Lincoln's promise to give African Americans the right to vote. He muttered to his companion ex-Confederate soldier Lewis Powell, "That means Nigger suffrage, by God, I'll put him through!"[1]

THE KIDNAP PLOTS

Booth was not the only Confederate operative who planned to kidnap President Lincoln. Thomas Nelson Conrad, a member of the Confederate Secret Service and a Methodist lay minister, proposed to kidnap President Lincoln. Conrad presented his plan to Confederate secretary of war James Seddon in the summer of 1864. Conrad had made several trips to Washington on secret service missions. He knew that President Lincoln traveled alone to and from the Soldiers' Home on horseback. He put together a party of four men and planned to apprehend President Lincoln on his way to the Soldiers' Home. Conrad was promised assistance from Mosby's Rangers to capture the president and cross the Potomac by an escape route that passed through Charles County, Maryland. Just prior to Booth's meeting with the Confederate commissioners in the summer of 1864, Conrad reported to Richmond that his plan to kidnap Lincoln was now impossible because Lincoln was escorted around the city by a troop of Union cavalry.[2]

Booth was a Confederate sympathizer who was involved in Confederate Secret Service work during the war.[3] In the summer of 1864, Booth started to organize a second conspiracy to kidnap President Lincoln and hold the president as a bargaining chip for the release of Confederate prisoners of war. Booth met his old schoolmates, ex-Confederate soldiers Michael O'Loughlen and Samuel Arnold, in August 1864 in Baltimore. Arnold said in his memoirs that Booth broached the subject of a plot to kidnap President Lincoln.[4] In October 1864, Booth had traveled to Montreal to have talks with Confederate agents working out of Montreal. Booth met with Baltimore shipowner Charles Martin, former Baltimore police commissioner George Kane, and George Sanders, all of whom were Confederate Secret Service operatives. It is not clear that Booth met with Confederate commissioners Jacob Thompson and Clement Clay.[5] The discussion topics and substance of the discussions are unknown. Booth was evidently encouraged by the Confederate agents to move ahead with his plan.

Booth put together a group of ex-soldiers, Maryland planters, and blockade runners between August 1864 and March 1865. Booth recruited two childhood friends from Baltimore who were ex-Confederate soldiers, Michael O'Loughlen and Samuel Arnold, on his own in August 1864. Booth also obtained the services of Lewis Powell in February 1865; Powell, also known as "Lewis Paine" and "Mr. Wood," enlisted at age seventeen in the First Florida Infantry, CSA. Powell was wounded at Gettysburg in July 1863 and served for a time as male nurse for other wounded Confederate prisoners before escaping confinement and joining Maj. John S. Mosby's Forty-Third Virginia Battalion, commonly known as "Mosby's Rangers." Powell apparently deserted in early 1865, assumed the name of Lewis Paine, swore an oath of allegiance to the United States, and went to Baltimore. Booth made contact with Powell and included him in the band of accomplices who would physically seize the president.[6]

Booth had a letter of introduction from Confederate agent Charles Martin to present to two Maryland planters who were pro-Confederate: Dr. Samuel Mudd and Dr. William Queen. He consulted with both men in November in Charles County, Maryland, after Sunday Mass at St. Peter's Catholic Church. Booth stayed overnight in Dr. Queen's house.[7] Dr. Mudd met with Booth twice after the November meeting. In December 1864, Dr. Mudd traveled to Washington and met with Booth. He introduced Booth to John Surratt, a twenty-two-year-old Confederate blockade runner, whose mother Mary Surratt ran a boardinghouse on H Street NW in Washington. Surrat had his college friend Louis Weichmann in tow on that December afternoon. Surratt, Booth, and Mudd went to Booth's hotel room to talk over matters probably relating to the escape route that Booth would use once he captured President Lincoln. Weichmann, who was not included in the group and sat apart from them at the meeting, later testified that Booth had some kind of map in hand that he showed to Surratt and Mudd.[8] Booth visited Dr. Mudd later in December 1864, staying overnight and buying a one-eyed horse from one of Mudd's neighbors. Surratt recruited pharmacy clerk David Herold who hunted the backcountry in southeastern Maryland between Washington and Port Tobacco, and carriage maker and Potomac River blockade runner George Atzerodt to man the boat that would carry the Booth party across the Potomac.[9] It is likely that Surratt also recruited Maryland Confederate Secret Service operatives Thomas Jones and Samuel Cox on the north shore of the Potomac and Thomas Harbin, Mrs. Elizabeth Quesenberry, and Dr. Richard Stuart who worked with the Confederate Signal Service on the south side of the Potomac. There probably were other men involved in the plot to kidnap the president who have never been identified.

Booth continued to plan his mission through the early months of 1865. At first, he proposed capturing President Lincoln while the president was watching a play at Ford's Theatre. When his confederates balked at trying to take the president alive in a crowded theater, Booth fell back on Conrad's plan. The president often traveled by horseback or in a carriage with no military escort to the Soldiers' Home located off Sixteenth Street in Rock Creek on the outskirts of Washington. Booth discovered that the president was scheduled to make a personal appearance at a benefit performance of *Still Waters Run Deep* at Campbell Hospital located on the Seventh Street road on March 17.[10] Booth alerted the capture team, Arnold, O'Loughlen, Powell, and Surratt, and got word to David Herold, George Atzerodt, and other conspiracy members to be ready to receive the president and his carriage on the escape route through Charles County, Maryland, to the Potomac and into Confederate territory on the south bank of the Potomac.

President Lincoln decided on the morning of the seventeenth to go to a flag presentation ceremony for the 140th Indiana regiment in front of the National Hotel rather than to the Campbell Hospital.[11] Indiana's war governor, Oliver P. Morton, was in town and invited the president to attend the presentation. It was an offer Lincoln could not refuse, since the politically powerful Morton had backed the war effort by extralegal measures when the Democratically controlled Indiana General Assembly had tried to take Indiana out of the war by shutting off appropriations for equipment for new volunteer regiments.[12] Booth never learned of the change of plans. His capture team assembled on the Seventh Street road as planned. A carriage came clattering north on the road. Booth rode up to the carriage, discovered that the person occupying the vehicle was not President Lincoln, and returned to his fellow kidnappers. The attempt to capture the president was a dismal failure. Arnold and O'Loughlen, disgusted with Booth's planning, went home to Baltimore. Lewis Powell also left town for Baltimore to stay at the Branson boardinghouse where he had gotten into trouble with the local authorities for beating up an African American servant. John Surratt and Booth went to the Surratt boardinghouse where Louis Weichmann happened to be at the time of their entry. Booth and Surratt were agitated, according to Weichmann, and were also heavily armed. The two men ignored Weichmann and went upstairs to Surratt's bedroom. John Surratt left a few days later for Richmond, carrying dispatches for the Confederate government in company with Mrs. Sarah Slater, a Confederate agent. Booth went to New York City on March 20. The grand conspiracy to kidnap the president was for all intents and purposes over.[13]

THE ASSASSINATION PLOTS

At least two unsuccessful assassination plots threatened President Lincoln prior to April 14, 1865. In February 1861, a group of Confederate sympathizers led by Corsican barber Cipriano Ferrandini planned to murder President-Elect Lincoln as he changed trains in Baltimore at noon February 23 on his way to his inauguration. Ferrandini's plot failed because Lincoln, forewarned by Detective Allan Pinkerton and the War Department, changed his travel plans, arriving in Baltimore early in the morning on February 23, 1861, evading the assassins.[14]

In early April 1865, Confederate Torpedo Bureau expert Frank Harney, traveling with an escort from Mosby's Rangers, was captured and taken to the Old Capitol Prison. He had black powder and fuses in his baggage that was to be used to detonate some important target. In 1907, the purpose of Harney's mission came to light in the memoir of Col. Edward Ripley of the Ninth Vermont Infantry. His regiment liberated Richmond in April 1865. A soldier attached to the Torpedo Bureau, William H. Snyder, went to Ripley, surrendered, and unloaded his conscience: a detail of men from the Torpedo Bureau had been sent on a secret mission just before Richmond's fall. Snyder believed the mission was to blow up the White House and President Lincoln.[15]

The Harney plot had some potential for success. According to William A. Tidwell, James O. Hall, and David W. Gaddy, the Confederate high command had instructed Colonel Mosby to send a detachment of 150 men to act as Harney's escort to support the attempt.[16] Further, the long-hidden original statement of George Atzerodt given to the War Department after his apprehension indicated that Booth was aware of the explosives plot and of its failure.[17]

After Harney's capture, Booth changed the plan from kidnapping to assassination sometime before April 13. The only evidence on that point is Booth's remark to Lewis Powell on April 11 quoted above. The original group of kidnapping accomplices never met again. Booth reassembled a new group of accomplices from the old kidnap plot on April 13–14, 1865.[18] Booth had two meetings with Mary Surratt on April 14. Booth had learned that Mrs. Surratt planned to go out to Surrattsville to collect a debt owed to her by Mr. Nothey that afternoon when Louis Weichmann came to Booth's hotel room to borrow his buggy. Booth told Weichmann that he had sold his rig and gave Weichmann ten dollars to rent a buggy. He also entrusted a package that Mrs. Surratt would drop off for him at the Surrattsville tavern. Weichmann, an unwitting accomplice, rented a buggy and drove Mrs. Surratt to the Surrattsville tavern. She waited there for some response from Nothey after sending a note to him. She left the package, later identified as Booth's binoculars, with John Lloyd's sister since Lloyd was not at the tavern that afternoon. Before Mrs. Surratt and Louis Weichmann reembarked for Washington, Lloyd, very drunk, returned from the Charles County Court House. Mrs. Surratt had a brief conversation with Lloyd out of Weichmann's hearing, then inveigled Lloyd to help repair their buggy, which had a damaged leaf spring. Later that afternoon after Mrs. Surratt and Weichmann had returned from Surrattsville, Booth came to the Surratt boardinghouse and spoke with Mary Surratt in private. There is no record of what transpired between Booth and Mary Surratt, just hours before the assassination plot was to be executed.

Booth met with Atzerodt, Herold, and Powell in the Herndon House in Washington at 7:00 p.m. April 14, assigning 10:00 p.m. as the time to strike. Although the trial record and other documents are not clear, this meeting probably occurred after Booth had his private conversation with Mary Surratt. Booth would murder President Lincoln. Atzerodt was to kill Vice President Andrew Johnson, and Lewis Powell, accompanied by David Herold, would attack and kill Secretary of State Seward.[19]

BOOTH'S ALLEGED ACCOMPLICES ARRESTED

The secretary of war discovered the identity of some of Booth's possible accomplices after searching Booth's hotel room. A letter from Samuel Arnold to Booth talked about "go and see how it will be taken in R___d" (i.e., to see what the Confederate government thought about Booth's plan to capture the president).[20] Before the identity of the author of the "Sam" letter was known, Voltaire Randall, one of Baltimore provost marshal McPhail's detectives, informed McPhail that Sam Arnold and Michael O'Loughlen were boyhood friends of Booth and may have been part of the conspiracy to harm the president. McPhail telegraphed the War Department, not knowing of the "Sam" letter, that he intended to arrest Arnold and O'Loughlen.[21] O'Loughlen turned himself in after learning he was wanted, and Arnold was arrested at Fortress Monroe where he had found work as a clerk.[22]

On the morning of April 17, Edman Spangler, a stage carpenter and scene shifter at Ford's Theatre, was arrested as one of Booth's accomplices. On April 14, Booth had ridden up Baptist Alley behind Ford's Theatre on his mission to kill the president. Ned Spangler had worked on the Booth family home in Bel Air, Maryland, in the 1850s and was a friend of Booth. Spangler did small favors for Booth when he was in Washington.[23] Booth asked Spangler to hold his horse for a few minutes. Spangler told Booth that he had to be inside to move scenery but would have Joseph "Peanuts John" Burrows, a peanut vendor, hold Booth's horse.[24] According to the sworn testimony of Jacob Ritterspaugh, another stage carpenter, Spangler had told Ritterspaugh, who had recognized the fleeing assassin as John Wilkes Booth, to keep quiet about Booth's identity.[25] That statement was sufficient for the military to arrest Spangler.

John Surratt Jr. and his mother kept a safe house for Confederate agents, spies, and blockade runners at 604 H Street NW in Washington. John Surratt Jr. held meetings at the house attended by John Wilkes Booth, George Atzerodt, and Lewis Powell. Atzerodt and Powell rented rooms from Mrs. Surratt. Powell at that time used a cover story that he was "Mr. Wood," a Baptist minister.[26] Mrs. Surratt's permanent residents included Eliza and John Holohan, a bounty broker, and their two children who had an apartment on the third floor front. Mrs. Surratt shared her second-floor apartment with boarder Appolonia Dean. Mrs. Surratt's daughter Anna shared her room with Honora Fitzpatrick, a nineteen-year-old unmarried woman, daughter of a local banker. John Surratt Jr. shared his third-floor rear room with his friend Louis Weichmann, a former seminarian at St. Charles Seminary in Baltimore.[27] John Surratt Jr. and Weichmann had been fellow seminarians until 1862, when both men left the seminary. Surratt left to run the family's tavern at Surrattsville, Maryland, when his father died suddenly in the summer of 1862. Weichmann had tried his hand at teaching and then was hired as a clerk for the Commissary General of Prisoners, at substantially better pay than he received from teaching.[28]

Lewis Powell and Mary Surratt were arrested at the Surratt boardinghouse on H Street on the night of April 17. District of Columbia police detectives had visited the Surratt House early on the morning of April 15 and kept the place under surveillance until Susan Jackson, one of Mrs. Surratt's African American servants, told the police that John Surratt had come home on the sixteenth.[29] The War Department had also questioned Louis Weichmann and the other boarders at the Surratt House on the fifteenth and sixteenth. The two agencies did not share information. The War Department sent several officers commanded by Major H. W. Smith on the night of April 17 to arrest Mrs. Surratt, relying on Susan Jackson's statement.[30] Lewis Powell then showed up at the door with a pickax over his shoulder, claiming that Mrs. Surratt had hired him to dig a drain the next day and he was only there to find out what time to start work. Powell, unfamiliar with Washington's streets, had ridden from the Seward house on horseback and lost his way because David Herold, his accomplice, fled the scene before Powell emerged from the Seward house.[31] The detectives called in Mrs. Surratt and asked her if she had ever seen the ditchdigger before. She answered, "Before God, Sir, I do not know this man and have never seen him and I did not hire him to dig a gutter for me."[32] Mrs. Surratt later claimed she could not identify Powell, known to her as "Mr. Wood," because she had poor eyesight. The detectives arrested Powell along with Mrs. Surratt, her daughter, and several inhabitants of the Surratt boardinghouse.[33] The military called in William Bell, Secretary Seward's doorman, to General Augur's headquarters where Powell had been taken after his arrest. Bell recognized Powell as the man who had forced his way into Secretary Seward's house on the night of April 14.[34] Powell was taken away to the Washington navy yard and confined aboard the monitor USS *Montauk*, which would become the holding facility for the principal male alleged accomplices.

George Atzerodt, assigned to murder Vice President Andrew Johnson, had second thoughts about carrying out the assassination. After attempting to steady his nerves at the Kirkwood House bar, he decided to flee without carrying out his mission. Atzerodt mounted his horse, rode east to the Pennsylvania House past the commotion on Tenth Street around Ford's Theatre, took another drink, and returned his horse to Kelleher and Pywell's stable. He took a horse car to the Washington navy yard and tried to persuade an acquaintance to take him in for the night. When his request was turned down, he took the horse car back to the Pennsylvania House and checked in for a short sleep. By 6:00 a.m. on April 15, Atzerodt was fleeing Washington on foot. He threw away his knife and pawned his revolver in Georgetown. He had relatives in Montgomery County, and made his way to the house of his cousin, Harman Richter. He spent the night of April 15–16 at Kinder's Mill a few miles from the Richter farm. He was apprehended by a patrol of the First Delaware Cavalry under the command of Sgt. Zachariah Gemmill. Provost Marshal McPhail took custody of Atzerodt and took down Atzerodt's statement, which implicated other accomplices in the assassination affair.[35]

About 4:00 a.m. on the morning of April 15, 1865, the household of Dr. Samuel Mudd was awakened by someone pounding on the front door. Dr. Mudd answered the door. David Herold, who had joined up with John Wilkes Booth on Booth's flight from Washington around midnight April

14–15, had dismounted and rapped on Dr. Mudd's door. John Wilkes Booth remained on horseback. His leg had been injured, according to Herold, from a fall from his horse. According to Dr. Mudd's own statements, the man with the leg injury said his name was "Tyson" and the other man said he was "Henson." Mudd examined Booth, determined that the small bone in his leg was broken, and made up a splint to hold the small bone in place. Mudd helped Booth upstairs and put him in bed to rest. When the family arose a few hours later, the Mudds fed Herold breakfast, but Booth refused to eat. Dr. Mudd and Herold set out on horseback to locate a carriage that could be used to transport the injured Booth. Stopping at Dr. Mudd's father's house first, the two found that his carriage was not in running order. They then headed for Bryantown south of the Mudd farm to try to locate a carriage. Bryantown was swarming with Union cavalrymen searching for the assassins. Herold turned back before Mudd reached town and went back to the Mudd farm. Mudd continued on and learned that John Wilkes Booth had shot President Lincoln. He spurred his horse toward home to confront his houseguests and get them to leave the house at once. He was successful. Booth remounted his horse and rode off with Herold between 4:00 and 6:00 p.m., crossing Zekiah Swamp to their next destination, the home of Samuel Cox.[36]

Dr. Mudd went to church Easter Sunday, April 16, at St. Peters Church, his parish church. He encountered his cousin Dr. George Mudd, a strong Union man, and told him that two strange men had come to his house on the early morning of April 15, one suffering from a broken leg. Samuel Mudd asked his cousin to report the incident to the Union cavalry detachment in Bryantown. George Mudd saw nothing urgent about informing the authorities and waited until Monday the seventeenth to inform the local detachment commander, Lieutenant Dana. Dana in turn passed the information to Lieutenant Lovett of the provost marshal's office, who rode out to the Mudd farm with two civilian detectives to interrogate the doctor. Mudd told the detectives that he had been visited by two men whom he did not know on the early morning of the fifteenth, patched up the broken leg of the man who called himself "Tyson," kept the patient overnight, and allowed them to leave the next afternoon. Lovett and his detectives came back to the farm a second time to interrogate Dr. Mudd at length. His wife told the detectives that the man named "Tyson" had a false beard that slipped off his face as he came downstairs to leave on the fifteenth. She also obliged the detectives by producing the boot cut from the leg of "Tyson" in order to reduce his fracture. The detectives examined the boot and found "J. Wilkes" on the inside of the boot. Mudd was arrested and taken to the Old Capitol Prison.[37] The detectives later confirmed that the boot was specially made for John Wilkes Booth.

David Herold traveled with Booth through southern Maryland from the Mudd farm to a hiding place in the swamp awaiting transportation across the

Potomac arranged for by Thomas Jones, a Confederate agent. Booth and Herold landed on the Virginia side of the Potomac on April 25. They made contact with Confederate Signal Corps agent Thomas Harbin and his assistant and members of the Confederate underground Elizabeth Quesenberry and Dr. Stuart. The fugitives crossed the northern neck after spending the night in the home of a free person of color to Port Conway, Virginia, on the Rappahannock. Herold and Booth crossed the Rappahannock on a ferry accompanied by Absalom Bainbridge, Willie Jett, and Mortimer B. Ruggles, three members of Mosby's Rangers.[38] The Rangers led Booth and Herold to the farm of Richard Garrett about three miles south of the Rappahannock. Garrett agreed to put the men up for the night. Luther Baker and Everton Conger, two National Detective Police officers, and an escort from the Sixteenth New York Cavalry, following incorrect information from local sources, landed on the Potomac about ten hours after Booth and Herold crossed the Rappahannock. The detectives debriefed the ferry operator at Port Conway, who described Booth and Herold and the three Rangers to the officers as the men ferried across the Rappahannock the previous afternoon. Baker and Conger followed up on information from the ferry owner's wife that one of the Rangers, Willie Jett, was staying at his girlfriend's residence, a hotel in Bowling Green, Virginia. The detectives and the escort went to the hotel, found Jett in bed, dragged him out, and told him to take the detectives and escort to the place where Booth was staying. Booth and Herold were surrounded on the early morning of April 26, and Herold surrendered to the authorities. Booth was shot and mortally wounded by Sgt. Boston Corbett when he refused to surrender. Herold was taken into custody and transported to the USS *Montauk* by steamer from the Rappahannock while the wagon bearing Booth's corpse trundled along behind Herold's military captors.[39]

John Wilkes Booth was dead. Except for John Surratt, Booth's alleged accomplices were in custody. More than two hundred other men were arrested and confined in the Old Capitol Prison because the government believed that they had some knowledge of the conspiracy to kidnap President Lincoln, or they were believed to have aided and abetted the escape of Booth and Herold. Only Arnold, Atzerodt, Herold, Mudd, O'Loughlen, Powell, Mrs. Surratt, and Edman Spangler were tried for conspiracy, treason, and murder. Thomas Jones, Samuel Cox and his son, and other men who assisted Booth and Herold were held for a time and released by the government without preferring charges. John Surratt Jr. fled the United States and was aided by Catholic clergy in evading capture in Canada until Confederate agents arranged for his passage to England aboard an English vessel. He would be captured in Egypt in 1867 and returned to the United States for an orthodox criminal trial in federal court in the District of Columbia, which resulted in a hung jury.[40]

The secretary of war, Attorney General James Speed, and President Johnson were ready to start proceedings against the alleged accomplices. Secretary Stanton, relying on an oral opinion from Attorney General Speed, decided that the alleged accomplices would be tried by military commission for violations of the law of war, ignoring the provisions of the Habeas Corpus Act of 1863.

WHY WAS LINCOLN MURDERED?

Black Flag Warfare: The Kilpatrick-Dahlgren Raid of 1864

Professor William Hanchett detailed multiple motives for Lincoln's assassination in *The Lincoln Murder Conspiracies*. He assigned two motives to Lincoln's would-be assassins: retaliation and elimination of a tyrant.[41] Two scenarios provide the motive for the crimes committed by Booth and his accomplices. The first is retaliation.

On February 11, 1864, Union brigadier general Hugh Judson Kilpatrick received orders to report at once to the president in Washington. Kilpatrick was a cavalry division commander in the Union Army of the Potomac. On his return, Kilpatrick reported to acting Cavalry Corps commander David

Figure 1.1. Hooded Prisoners Transferred from Monitor to Shore for Trial.
***Source: Frank Leslie's Illustrated Newspaper*, May 27, 1865.**

McM. Gregg that he was sent by President Lincoln to see Secretary of War Stanton. Stanton ordered Kilpatrick to plan a raid on Richmond to free Union prisoners of war at Belle Isle and Castle Thunder.[42] Kilpatrick sent his plans to Army of the Potomac commander George G. Meade, who sent the plans to Cavalry Corps commanding general Alfred Pleasonton for review. Pleasonton pronounced Kilpatrick's plan unworkable.[43] Meade went ahead and approved Kilpatrick's plan over Pleasonton's objections. Colonel Ulric Dahlgren commanded a detachment of cavalry that was part of Kilpatrick's cavalry raid on Richmond. Kilpatrick divided his command into two groups. The largest group under his command was to remain on the north side of the James River and attack the lightly protected north side of Richmond from the direction of Mechanicsville. Dahlgren's smaller detachment was to cross the James to the south side at Goochland Court House, cross over the James at Richmond, and meet Kilpatrick's column within the city. Dahlgren, son of Admiral John Dahlgren, was killed in action and his address to his men and his special order to his detachment were recovered from his body and published in the *Richmond Sentinel* on March 5, 1864. The third paragraph of the address read as follows:

> We hope to release the prisoners from Belle Island first, and having seen them fairly started, we will cross the James River into Richmond, destroying the bridges after us and exhorting the released prisoners to destroy and burn the hateful city; and do not allow the rebel leader Davis and his traitorous crew to escape.[44]

Dahlgren's orders to his men were even more specific:

> We will try and secure the bridge to the city (one mile below Belle Isle) and release the prisoners at the same time. . . . The bridges once secured, and the prisoners loose, the bridges will be secured and the city destroyed. The men must keep together and well in hand, and once in the city it must be destroyed and Jeff. Davis and Cabinet killed.[45]

General Robert E. Lee had the Dahlgren address and orders photographed and sent a copy to General Meade, together with a scathing letter demanding to know if the order to capture or kill President Davis represented Union policy. Meade fired off a return stating he had no knowledge of any plot to harm President Davis. Meade said he had never authorized such an attempt and later confided to his wife that the Dahlgren order was probably genuine. Kilpatrick claimed that the orders to kill President Davis were a forgery added to Dahlgren's original orders.[46]

The Confederate States of America had a motive and could provide the opportunity to kidnap or assassinate Abraham Lincoln in retaliation for the bungled attempt to murder Jefferson Davis. Edward Steers devoted a chapter in *Blood on the Moon* to the Kilpatrick/Dahlgren raid that provoked the Confederate government to retaliate by concocting a devious plot carried out by Dr. Luke Blackburn. Blackburn was a pro-Confederate physician who collected the garments and bedclothes of yellow fever victims in the Bahamas. Blackburn intended to start a yellow fever epidemic in Union-held cities. Packages of clothing were shipped to New York City and to New Bern, North Carolina, by a merchant named Godfrey J. Hyams, who later became a witness for the prosecution in the Booth accomplices' trial. A carpetbag containing the clothing from a yellow fever victim was also intended to be delivered to President Lincoln.[47] Steers also detailed a plot to blow up the White House during a state reception that failed because Frank Harney, the Confederate explosives expert who had gunpowder, fuses, and other equipment for the mission, was captured by Union cavalry before he could reach his target.[48] Retaliation for the plot to kill President Jefferson Davis and his cabinet seemed to be the primary motive for both plots.

Lincoln's Tyranny

The second scenario relates to Lincoln's excessive use of presidential power on dissenters. According to Professor Hanchett, Abraham Lincoln was widely vilified in the Democratic press and in Southern newspapers that described his summary program to curb dissenters as a form of tyranny. Lincoln did suspend the writ of habeas corpus several times during the war. He allowed the War Department to try civilians by military commission in Missouri, Kentucky, and elsewhere for arson, guerilla activity, illegally buying and exporting Confederate cotton, and other criminal offenses. Lincoln's administration arrested between thirteen thousand and thirty thousand allegedly disloyal Northern civilians without probable cause, interning them for the duration of the war unless the detainees took a loyalty oath to the United States.[49]

In early April 1861, seven Southern states had passed secession ordinances and had declared themselves independent.[50] United States property had been seized by the secessionists; the secessionists had formed a new government in Montgomery, Alabama, with Jefferson Davis, a former U.S. senator, as head of state.[51] Half the officer corps of the army had resigned, leaving the army without competent leadership. In Washington, D.C., all telegraph communications with the North had gone dead. There were rumors that Maryland secessionists had destroyed the bridges on the Philadelphia, Wilmington & Baltimore Railroad (PW&B) to block the travel of militia troops to Washington to protect the capital from secessionist attack.[52]

On the fourteenth, secessionist artillery had opened fire on a United States military post, Fort Sumter. Lincoln issued a call for seventy-five thousand militia from the states that remained in the Union to put down the insurrection in South Carolina.[53] By the nineteenth, the post had surrendered to the secessionists. The United States capital was defenseless. Across the Potomac, Virginia had called a convention to vote on seceding from the Union. The District of Columbia was surrounded by slave states that threatened secession over the call-up of militia. The governor of Maryland seemed incapable of quelling pro-secessionist guerrilla activities, and to top that, his own legislature was scheduled to meet to consider a secession ordinance that would take Maryland out of the Union and make Lincoln and his government virtual prisoners in the District of Columbia.[54] Congress was not in session and no declaration of war could be passed until it returned to the city. Maryland militia colonel Isaac Trimble organized parties of pro-secessionist militia into bridge-burning parties that destroyed the PW&B bridge over Big Gunpowder Falls, cutting off rail access to Baltimore and Washington from Philadelphia.[55]

This was the worst crisis the United States government ever faced. The Japanese sneak attack on Pearl Harbor and the terrorist attack of September 11, 2001, pale in comparison to the 1861 crisis. Newly inaugurated president Abraham Lincoln, protected only by a handful of regular soldiers and by a corporal's guard of civilian volunteers led by his friend Maj. David Hunter,[56] sat in the White House with his cabinet, trying to save what was left of the United States. On the nineteenth, Lincoln asked his attorney general, Edward N. Bates, to look into the possibility of issuing a decree of martial law that would permit the United States to protect its lifeline with the North, the rail system from Washington through Annapolis Junction, Baltimore, and the Susquehanna Ferry to Wilmington and Philadelphia. Then Lincoln could put a strip of land either side of the railroad right of way under military rule and use newly arrived militia units from Northern states to protect key railroad bridges and control the civilian population.

The next day Attorney General Edward N. Bates's chief assistant, Titian J. Coffey, turned in a memorandum of legal authority drawn from international law treatises, defining "martial law" and warning the president that Congress alone could suspend the writ of habeas corpus and declare martial law. This was not what Lincoln wanted to hear.[57] General Winfield Scott, the commanding general of the U.S. Army, wanted to order Major General Benjamin F. Butler to arrest the secessionist Maryland politicians in Annapolis, but Lincoln at first told him not to do so.[58] That afternoon the Sixth Massachusetts Militia Regiment, on its way to defend Washington from Southern aggression, crossed Baltimore from the PW&B station to the Baltimore & Ohio station in columns of fours. An ugly crowd gathered: rocks were thrown, someone fired a shot from the crowd, and the Sixth Massachusetts let go a volley into the mob, killing several Baltimoreans. Seven members of the Sixth Massachusetts were the first Union fatalities of the war.[59] The Sixth Massachusetts troop train arrived at Washington National Depot on the nineteenth. They were dispatched to the Capitol and went in to camp in and around the building.

Union militia units continued to trickle into Washington to provide a defensive perimeter for the national capital. A Pennsylvania militia unit came in by train from Harrisburg on the nineteenth. Major General Benjamin F. Butler, a Massachusetts militia officer, managed to land two shiploads of Northern militia from his home state and New York at Annapolis, and put them aboard the functioning Baltimore & Ohio branch line railroad to Washington. The Eighth Massachusetts and Seventh New York joined the Sixth Massachusetts quartered in and around the Capitol. These regiments provided a defense force for the capital and relieved Major Hunter's corporal's guard at the White House.[60] Next day, General Scott warned the president that Washington was still under the danger of imminent attack by secessionists. Lincoln acted: on the twenty-seventh, he directed Secretary of State William H. Seward to issue an order to General Scott establishing martial law along the right of way of the Baltimore & Ohio and PW&B Railroads:

> The Commanding General of the Army of the United States:
>
> You are engaged in suppressing an insurrection against the laws of the United States. If at any point on or in the vicinity of any military line which is now or which shall be used between the City of Philadelphia, and the City of Washington you find resistance which renders it necessary to suspend the writ of *habeas corpus* for the public safety, you personally or through the officer in command at the point where resistance occurs, are authorized to suspend the writ.[61]

Article II § 9 of the Constitution did provide for emergency suspension of the writ of habeas corpus. "The privilege of the Writ of Habeas Corpus shall not be suspended, unless when in Cases of Rebellion or Invasion the public Safety may require it." The attorney general and most legal authorities such as former Supreme Court justice Joseph Story believed that the writ could be suspended only by act of Congress. But Congress was not in session and would not be recalled to Washington until July. Lincoln would act without waiting for congressional approval.

The writ of habeas corpus is an ancient legal means for testing the legality of confinement. In theory, the writ requires the custodian of a person alleged to be unlawfully detained to show cause why a court order should not be issued to free the detainee. The writ is initiated by filing a petition in a court having jurisdiction to hear such petitions, alleging that an individual is unlawfully confined, specifying the reasons, and identifying the person who by name is the custodian of the object of the writ. The presiding judge then sends notice of hearing to show cause to the custodian, permitting the custodian to be heard in open court as to why the confined person ought to remain confined. It was a writ often invoked in royal courts in the seventeenth and eighteenth century to free political prisoners.[62] "The great writ" was imported as part of the common law. It was provided for in the U.S. Judicial Code of 1789 and was widely used in the nineteenth century to test the legality of confinement of prisoners before trial and to test the legality of induction or enlistment into the army or militia on active duty. The power of the writ of habeas corpus to prevent the unlawful detention and seizure of United States citizens was a favorite Fourth of July speech topic. It was also a very practical legal tool that permitted the judicial branch of the U.S. government to review the conduct of the executive branch with respect to the detention of U.S. citizens.[63]

Secretary Seward's order also implicitly authorized General Scott and the department commander to invoke "martial law." In the mid-nineteenth century, "martial law" was widely thought to be some type of separate body of precedential law, although the great commentators such as Francis Lieber, who wrote General Order 100 for the Governance of the Army in the Field, correctly identified "martial law" as military rule for the sake of winning the conflict.[64]

General Andrew Jackson had suspended civil liberties in New Orleans for a period of time during the War of 1812 and had imprisoned a state judge for allegedly antiwar actions.[65] General Winfield Scott had issued a martial law proclamation in Mexico in 1848 after defeating the Mexican army and running Antonio Lopez de Santa Anna out of his capital, Mexico City.[66] There were no historical precedents for invoking martial law to protect a civilian rail system from saboteurs. In our time, the federal writ of habeas corpus is often used by criminal defense lawyers to test the legality of a state-imposed sentence for a crime, in an attempt to free a convicted felon. It has become something of a legal pariah. Congress has severely curtailed the use of the writ and the writ is seldom used in state criminal proceedings, since states have adopted mandatory postconviction relief statutes to channel postdecision review of convictions into a more conventional review.[67]

Rights of the Accused in 1865

Although the law of criminal procedure has changed a great deal from what it was in Lincoln's time, the basic constitutional rights of an accused date all the way back to the adoption of the Bill of Rights. A summary of the rights accorded by the Constitution and by the law of criminal procedure would have included the following guaranties.

Probable Cause to Arrest

Before a federal peace officer was entitled to arrest anyone, the peace officer needed probable cause, a legal justification normally established by applying for an arrest and search warrant to a federal magistrate who passed on the information the peace officer had obtained to show the accused may have committed a federal offense. The magistrate would then issue a warrant and require the peace officer to return the accused and any evidence seized to the magistrate for a hearing.[68] As an emergency alternative, a peace officer could arrest without a warrant if an offense was committed in his presence, or the peace officer had independent probable cause to believe the accused had committed a felony. However, a warrantless arrest was suspect, and the accused had to be produced before a magistrate within twenty-four hours for a hearing on whether there was probable cause to detain the accused.[69]

Notice and Hearing on Charges

The Sixth Amendment to the U.S. Constitution required that an accused in federal court was entitled to notice of the charges against him, the right to present a defense to those charges, and the right to legal counsel.[70] State constitutions contained similar provisions.[71] The way this was accomplished was by a hearing on probable cause and let to bail. If evidence was seized by the peace officer, the peace officer was required to show that the search that turned up the evidence was reasonable under the Fourth Amendment or the evidence would be returned to the accused. Although the federal justice system did not provide for free legal counsel, the magistrate permitted the accused to hire a lawyer to speak for him at the preliminary hearing and thereafter.

Habeas Corpus

If an accused believed he was wrongfully and unlawfully detained contrary to law, and he was not brought before a magistrate promptly, he could file a writ of habeas corpus in a U.S. District or Circuit Court. The court would order the United States to produce the prisoner in court to show cause why the prisoner should not be released. This was an evidentiary hearing on the merits of probable cause to confine the accused. It was available before trial and after trial. All states had similar provisions for issuing a writ of habeas corpus.[72]

Trial by Jury

The Sixth Amendment also guaranteed that the accused would be tried before a jury of his peers in open court.[73] Secret proceedings and nonjury trials were unconstitutional. State constitutions also guaranteed trial by jury to criminal defendants.[74]

Proof of Guilt beyond a Reasonable Doubt

Although not imported into the Fifth Amendment guaranty of a fair criminal trial until the mid-twentieth century, the requirement that the state prove guilt beyond a reasonable doubt originated in the 1780s.[75] Most states adopted the maxim that proof of guilt must be beyond a reasonable doubt, while fumbling with an attempt to define "reasonable doubt."[76]

Judicial Review of Conviction

If the jury found the accused was guilty and the trial judge issued a judgment of conviction, the conviction could be challenged by writ of error to the U.S. Circuit Court or to the U.S. Supreme Court.[77] Suing out a writ of habeas corpus after conviction was an alternative means of obtaining judicial review of a conviction. President Lincoln would ultimately suspend all these rights by the midpoint of the war throughout the nation for one class of citizens: those who opposed the draft and argued for a negotiated settlement with the Confederacy.

The Suspension of Civil Liberties under the Secretary of State

President Lincoln assigned the task of administering the suspension of civil liberties to Secretary of State Seward in April 1861. The suspension of habeas corpus along the Philadelphia to Washington railroad line was followed by suspension of habeas corpus in Key West, Florida.[78] The Florida order authorized the military commander of the Union department to set up military rule in Key West and suspend the writ of habeas corpus after deposing the civilian authorities. Key West happened to be the main naval base for the Gulf Blockade Squadron.

Ex parte Merryman

Seward's program of military arrest of civilians was tested by an irate Marylander, John Merryman, who was arrested May 25, 1861, by order of Major General William H. Keim, a Pennsylvania militia officer, and turned over to the tender care of Major General George Cadwalader, commandant at Baltimore's Fort McHenry. Merryman hired a lawyer who immediately filed a petition for habeas corpus in the Circuit Court of Maryland. The petition was presented to Chief Justice Roger B. Taney, the circuit justice, who ordered Cadwalader to bring Merryman to the courthouse in Baltimore and show cause why he was detained. Cadwalader refused to appear in court, citing the president's suspension of habeas corpus along the railroad corridor. This caused the elderly chief justice of the United States to write a scorching opinion chastising the president for illegal imposition of the suspension of the writ of habeas corpus.[79] Taney pointed out that the suspension of habeas corpus clause of the Constitution appeared in Article I that enumerated the powers of Congress.[80] He agreed with Joseph Story that only Congress could suspend the great writ.[81] Taney criticized the president and his minions in the following language:

> But the comments before me show, that the military authority in this case has gone far beyond the mere suspension of the privilege of the writ of habeas corpus. He has, by force of arms, thrust aside the judicial authorities and officers to whom the constitution has confided the power and duty of interpreting and administering the laws, and substituted a military government in its place, to be administered and executed by military officers.[82]

Taney's rebuke lacked any means of enforcing his opinion: the president and the executive department alone had the power to compel obedience to Taney's writ. The chief justice had nothing more potent to compel authority than the filing of his opinion for the benefit of history.

By the time Lincoln sent a special message to Congress on July 4, 1861, justifying his extreme measures during the crisis that spring, three executive orders had suspended the writ of

habeas corpus. This message contained a rationale for taking these steps: necessity. Lincoln asked Congress rhetorically:

> To state the question more directly, are all the laws but one to go unexecuted, and the government itself go to pieces, lest that one be violated? Even in such a case, would not the official oath be broken, if the government should be overthrown, when it was believed that disregarding the single law, would tend to preserve it?[83]

Congress then ratified Lincoln's suspension of civil liberties by an interim resolution.

In August 1861, following the defeat of Brig. Gen. Irvin McDowell's Army of Virginia at Manassas and its ignominious flight to the safety of the Washington defenses, President Lincoln and Secretary Seward became worried that the Maryland legislature might vote the state out of the Union. Early in September, Maj. Gen. George B. McClellan, the new commander of the Union Army of the Potomac, and Secretary of War Cameron were brought into the discussion of how to handle the Maryland legislature. Cameron issued an order to Maj. Gen. John A. Dix, department commander at Baltimore, to prevent the Maryland legislature from passing a secession ordinance. Dix sent a list of legislators to Cameron and McClellan identifying pro-secession legislators. Cameron told Dix to order the arrest of six Maryland legislators who were whisked off by steamer to incarceration in New York City. Modern writers believe that these arrests were ordered by General McClellan, a "War Democrat," without first obtaining approval from the

White House. Modern commentators also believe that neither man consulted Secretary Seward before making the arrests.[84] The arrest of the legislators does not appear to have been part of Seward's plan for suspension of civil liberties.

Seward was responsible for suspension of civil liberties, including the arrest of disloyal U.S. citizens in the railroad corridor. Most of the early arrests of alleged disloyal civilians were made outside the rail corridor in such far-off venues as Missouri and Illinois. At best, Seward's detention of disloyal citizens was haphazard, partial, and incomplete. Frederick Bancroft, his biographer, believed that Seward had no intention of prosecuting any of the detainees for treason or other crimes; his aim was to take a few active, vociferous antigovernment activists temporarily out of circulation.[85]

Seward also made an attempt to censor newspapers friendly to the Democratic cause, ordering the arrest of the editor of the *Hagerstown Mail* for alleged disloyal publications. He was quickly released from custody by taking the loyalty oath, and Seward continued on his campaign of newspaper cleansing by ordering the New York postmaster not to accept five New York City newspapers for mailing.[86]

The Democratic left wing press hammered away at the theme that Lincoln was a tyrant who unilaterally destroyed civil liberties, imprisoned political opponents, and tried civilians by military commission without benefit of trial by jury. All this, unfortunately, was supported by substantial evidence. Even though Seward shut down several left wing newspapers, the public outcry from the left could not be silenced.

The Suppression of Civil Liberties by the Secretary of War

In February 1862, President Lincoln shifted the responsibility from Seward to the secretary of war. Simon Cameron, his initial appointee, had been a flawed man for the job. His inability to separate the nation's interest from his need to take care of political cronies from Pennsylvania led Lincoln to move him out of the War Department. Edwin M. Stanton, the new secretary, was a nationally famous trial lawyer with a justifiable reputation as a bulldog. He was exactly the kind of man to balance Lincoln's cabinet and clean up the corrupt War Department's allocation of choice defense contracts as political boodle. He was also the perfect man to run a comprehensive program of military rule wherever the president needed such rule.

The administration's plan for suspension of civil liberties matured under Stanton's guidance and expert management. The maturation process took more than a year. The first step was Lincoln's issuance of Executive Order No. One Relating to Political Prisoners. After bashing the federal judiciary for failure to support his use of suspension of civil liberties, he directed that all political prisoners who took an oath of allegiance to the United States be freed. However, the order excepted those suspected of spying for the Confederacy and any person whose release would be "incompatible with public safety."[87]

The Militia Act of 1862 authorized a limited form of national draft. Congress provided that the president could draft any member of the militia not previously called to active duty to serve for nine months' time. Secretary Stanton followed with a War Department order suspending the writ of habeas corpus for persons resisting the draft and engaged in disloyal practices.[88] On August 8, 1862, Stanton issued an order directing all U.S. marshals and other law enforcement officers to arrest "any person or persons who may be engaged, by act, speech, or writing to discourage volunteer enlistments" and directing that the offenders arrested on these charges be tried by a military commission.[89] President Lincoln issued a second order suspending the writ of habeas corpus after the Battle of Antietam on September 24, 1862. This order instituted nationwide suspension of the writ.[90]

Ex parte Vallandigham

Lincoln's and Stanton's program of arbitrary arrests and trial by military commission occasionally backfired and caused an adverse reaction. The case of Congressman Clement Vallandigham is the most egregious example of the program's shortcomings. Major General Ambrose E. Burnside had been the commanding general of the Army of the Potomac during the disastrous December 1862 Battle of Fredericksburg and the "mud march" of January 1863. As a reward for his unsuccessful turn at commanding the major Union field army in the country, he was exiled to the military district of a peaceful backwater of the war. In April, Burnside issued General Order 38 pertaining to disloyal persons, which promised that "declaring sympathies with the enemy will no longer be tolerated in this department. Persons committing such offenses will be at once arrested with a view to being tried [by military commission]."[91] The order was consistent with Secretary Stanton's crackdown on those who opposed the draft.

Unfortunately, the department was the home base of antiwar Dayton congressman Clement L. Vallandigham. Vallandigham made a fiery speech against the war in his home district in Ohio. Afraid of Vallandigham's influence on volunteer enlistments in Ohio, General Burnside ordered Vallandigham arrested on May 2, 1863:

> On Tuesday morning last I caused the arrest of the Hon. C. L. Vallandigham. He is now in this city, undergoing trial before a military commission for uttering sedition. Some trouble was caused in Dayton on account of his arrest, but all is now quiet. I hope to maintain perfect order in other portions of this department. There is necessarily much excitement among his friends. We are all hoping to hear of the glorious and final success of General Hooker.[92]

Vallandigham was a very cagey politician: he allowed his supporters to spread rumors that he would file a petition for writ of habeas corpus in the Circuit Court of Ohio before Justice Noah H. Swayne of the U.S. Supreme Court. Stanton then issued a general order suspending the writ of habeas corpus with respect to Vallandigham.[93] He left the order on Lincoln's desk, but the president did not sign the order. Vallandigham was tried before a military commission in Cincinnati. He was charged with uttering disloyal remarks at the Mount Vernon rally against the government and inciting the population to resist General Burnside's General Order 38.[94] Vallandigham disputed the jurisdiction of the commission. Nonetheless, the commission proceeded to try him for disloyal remarks, found him guilty, and sentenced Vallandigham to close confinement for the duration of the war. The incident proved to be a political embarrassment to the Lincoln administration. Lincoln changed the sentence of confinement to banishment: Vallandigham was escorted to Confederate lines in Tennessee and turned over to the Confederacy.[95] Banishing a native-born U.S. citizen was contrary to law and to the United States Constitution.[96] Vallandigham waged a campaign for Ohio's governorship in 1864 from Canada and later returned from exile before the war's end.

Vallandigham's lawyers filed a petition for writ of habeas corpus with the U.S. District Court for the Southern District of Ohio. When the district judge refused to issue the writ, Vallandigham petitioned the U.S. Supreme Court for certiorari to challenge the jurisdiction of the military commission that convicted Vallandigham. The certiorari petition was denied, even though trial of civilians by military commission was never authorized by Congress, let alone by the U.S. Constitution. Vallandigham did not raise the banishment issue. Justice Swayne dodged the implications of Vallandigham's petition: that the Lincoln administration had instituted an unconstitutional system of military courts for civilian trials. There are ways in which lawyers and judges can avoid committing political suicide: Swayne chose one such way. He examined the difference between the power of the English courts to issue writs of habeas corpus to free people unlawfully detained and the power to issue such writs granted by Article III of the U.S. Constitution and concluded that the U.S. Supreme Court had no power to issue a writ of habeas corpus to free a civilian held unlawfully by military authorities.[97]

After the Vallandigham episode was concluded, Secretary Stanton set out to develop a systematic plan for dealing with the antiwar dissenters in the loyal Northern states. This was, he believed, necessary because the antiwar protesters would likely interfere with the direct draft of men from the states.

Suppressing the Copperheads[98]

The Republican and Democratic Parties established paramilitary organizations to support their political agendas. During the 1860 election, the Republican Party had organized marching societies called the "Wideawakes" to parade in support of Republican candidates throughout the North. These marching societies were hardly military in organization or in character. The Midwest, however, was another case. Partisan political violence characterized the 1862 congressional elections. Gangs of toughs broke up rival political meetings, and there were gun battles in Indiana and Illinois between Democrats and Republicans.[99] However, after the 1862 midterm congressional elections changed the political balance of power in the Illinois and Indiana state legislatures in favor of peace-at-any-price Democrats, Governor Yates of Illinois and Governor Oliver P. Morton of Indiana were moved to take action against Democratic acts of violence directed at Republicans. Since armed companies of Democrats were drilling and marching in order to protect the Democrats from pro-Republican armed gangs, the two governors, with the cooperation of the federal military commanders for the districts of Illinois and Indiana, began arming members of the Union League from state and federal arsenals to repel assaults by armed Democrats.[100]

The Democratic Party had two wings: war and antiwar. Antiwar Democrats were the dominant group in Ohio, Indiana, and Illinois because these states had originally been settled by Southerners, and midwestern farmers had used the Ohio and Mississippi Rivers to ship their grain and hogs to market for thirty years before the war. The antiwar Democrats had been involved in the formation of secret societies, variously known as the Knights of the Golden Circle, Order of American Knights, and Sons of Liberty. These secret societies had been investigated by a state grand jury in Indiana and were said to have at least fifteen thousand members in the fall of 1862.[101]

The Republican governors of Illinois and Indiana perceived these secret societies as threats to national security and to Republican control of the electoral process. Some action had to be taken to stop the growth of these groups. Prompt action was required because the United States was about to conduct a direct draft of men for the first time in U.S. history. Congress, acting on dubious constitutional grounds, passed the Enrollment Act of 1863.[102] The statute established a nationwide military police presence; every congressional district had one or more provost marshals whose duty it was to supervise the draft.[103] The provost marshal was specifically enjoined to arrest deserters and enemy spies. Section 24 of the Enrollment Act was directed toward anyone who should "procure or entice, or attempt to procure or entice a solider in the service of the United States to desert."[104] Section 25 also made a felony out of anyone who resisted the draft or counseled any drafted man not to appear for induction.[105] In both instances, the provost marshal was instructed to deliver these miscreants to the civil authorities for criminal prosecution.

Section 38 of the act opened up the prosecution of civilians by military authorities before military tribunals. It mandated that any person, during time of war, who "shall be found lurking or acting as spies, in or about any of the fortifications, posts, quarters or encampments of the United States, or elsewhere, shall be triable by a general court martial or military commission, and shall, upon conviction, suffer death."[106]

Arbitrary Arrest of Suspected Disloyal Persons

Secretary Stanton promptly implemented this act by seeing to it that provost marshal generals with the rank of colonel were appointed for every state and provost marshals with the rank of captain were appointed for all congressional districts within the state. The provost marshals became responsible for keeping a list of deserters whose residences lay in their districts and thus put them in position to arrest the deserter and his family. The provost marshals' efforts were supplemented by detachments of soldiers who arrested suspected deserters and those who harbored them (i.e., their families). These arrests were made without recourse to the civil authorities for an arrest warrant.

Draft resistance stiffened in June 1863 as the first day for selecting inductees approached. In July 1863, the first draft selection sparked riots throughout the Northeast, the most spectacular being the weeklong rampage in New York City, put down only with the assistance of combat troops sent from the field of Gettysburg.[107] State judges complacently issued writs of habeas corpus to the provost marshal of the district demanding he bring newly inducted men before the state court to show cause why the man had been drafted.[108] President Lincoln would not put up with interference with the draft by state judges, although then-current legal authorities held that a state judge could issue a writ of habeas corpus to a federal official.[109] After a protracted discussion of the exact wording of the proclamation with his divided cabinet, President Lincoln issued a proclamation on September 15, 1863, suspending the writ of habeas corpus with respect to everyone serving in the military, and all "prisoners of war, spies, and aiders or abettors" in U.S. custody.[110]

The loyal states were afflicted with military arrests of civilians without warrant, without preferring charges, much as the border states of Kentucky and Missouri had experienced it since 1861.[111] Civilians would be tried before military commissions rather than the U.S. District Court for whatever criminal acts the military thought were best punished by the military. Prior to mid-1863, offenders that were tried by military commission were limited to civilians engaged in guerilla activities, dishonest military contractors, and civilians employed by the army.[112] Draft resisters, draft evaders, those who counseled resistance to the draft, and disloyal persons were added to the groups that would be prosecuted by military commissions.

The best-known military trials of draft resisters occurred in Harrisburg, Pennsylvania, as a result of the "Fishing Creek Confederacy Conspiracy." Twenty-four eastern Pennsylvanians from Columbia County were tried by military commission for draft resistance. Fifteen were acquitted, and only three of the eight men convicted were sentenced to prison.[113]

Thousands of alleged disloyal citizens were arrested and confined for the duration of the war without any formal charges being preferred against them. At war's end, they were freed without any explanation for their detention. The number of people arrested and detained is unclear. *The American Annual Encyclopaedia and Register of Important Events of the Year 1865* cited the provost marshal general's records to support a figure of thirty-eight thousand military arrests during the war.[114] John A. Marshall's *American Bastille* estimated the number at "from ten to twenty thousand" in the original 1869 edition, according to Mark Neely, and raised the figure to "thirty thousand" in the 1885 revised edition.[115] The most commonly accepted figure is 13,535, which was quoted by James G. Randall from a private War Department search made for him in the 1930s.[116]

President Lincoln had suspended the power of U.S. judges to issue writs of habeas corpus to challenge the arrest. Any disloyal person whom the provost marshal believed was in fact guilty of disloyal activities would be tried before a military commission consisting of commissioned officers of the department. Trial by jury was not permitted. The verdict, judgment, and sentence of the military commission was reached according to the law of war (not according to U.S. criminal law and procedure), and punishment prescribed by the commission was not subject to judicial review by an independent judge. The president personally reserved the right to review all death sentences.

The Lincoln administration justified its policies as a matter of military necessity, particularly after the institution of the military draft. Democratic opponents accused the administration of using the suppression of civil liberties as a means of stifling opposition to the Lincoln administration, pointing to the high-profile cases of arbitrary arrest of Congressman Vallandigham, and newspaper editors of antiadministration newspapers, and the Camp Douglas conspirators, claiming these men were simply antiwar Democrats who spoke out in mass meetings and in print about the evil of suppressing civil liberties.

Secretary Stanton also established a nationwide secret police, the National Detective Police, headed by Col. Lafayette Baker. Baker's men had nationwide authority to arrest and confine disloyal persons in Old Capitol Prison without charges for the duration of the war. Baker was the principal agent behind the arrest and confinement in April–May 1865 of more than two hundred men and women believed to be implicated in the assassination of Lincoln. The left wing of the Democratic Party and the families of men who were swept up in Stanton's dragnet had motive and opportunity to assassinate Lincoln, whom they believed was a tyrant.

Ex parte Milligan

In August 1864, the provost marshal for the Military District of Indiana arrested Lambdin Milligan, William Bowles, and four other men suspected of conspiring to free Confederate prisoners at Camp Douglas in Chicago. The conspiracy involved arms shipped in from Canada destined to arm eight thousand Confederate prisoners of war in Camp Douglas, who would be freed by the Sons of Liberty during the Democratic National Convention. The plot was engineered by the Confederate Secret Service consisting of Clement C. Clay of Alabama, Jacob Thompson of Mississippi, and his aide Capt. Thomas Hines, a former member of Morgan's cavalry.[117] The Confederates enlisted Clement Vallandigham, the congressman-in-exile, who was living in Windsor, Ontario, and scheming to get back to Ohio to run for governor. Vallandigham contacted the state commanders of the Sons of Liberty from Illinois, Indiana, Ohio, Missouri, and New York who spent time with him in June 1864. The general plan was to create a Northwestern Confederacy of states that was neutral and would remain out of the fight. The state commanders were to organize armed bands to carry out the revolution against the central government. Vallandigham quickly bowed out as leader of the conspiracy, allowing the state commanders and the Confederate Secret Service to arrange the uprising.[118]

Harrison H. Dodd of Indianapolis emerged as the strongest personality among the state commanders. The insurrection was originally planned to coincide with the Democratic National Convention in Chicago set for August 16, 1864. Confederate cavalry was positioned in western Kentucky to cooperate with the Sons of Liberty and to attempt to free Confederate prisoners of war.[119] The Confederate Secret Service supplied Dodd and his fellow state commanders with $75,000 to carry out the plan, which in its final phase was reduced to engineering a breakout of Confederate prisoners at Camp Douglas.[120]

Dodd enlisted other Hoosiers in the plan from the beginning. One of his most active helpers was Dr. William Bowles, proprietor of the French Lick Health Spa in southern Indiana. Bowles was apparently involved in large-scale arms purchases made by the conspirators resulting in crates of weapons being shipped to Dodd's office in Indianapolis. The August 29, 1864, deadline for the general uprising and prisoner freeing passed without a revolution. Confederate saboteurs started incendiary fires in Cairo, Illinois, and roamed about western Indiana probing for local support for the uprising. September waned, and in early October, U.S. authorities apprehended Andrew Humphrey in Sullivan County, Indiana. Swift military arrests brought in Dodd, Dr. Bowles, Lambdin Milligan, a Montgomery County lawyer, and many others. The U.S. military commander appointed a military commission to try Dr. Bowles, Milligan, Stephen Horsey, Humphreys, Horace Heffren, and J. J. Bingham in a seven-week-long state trial covered by the national newspapers and given top billing in the papers. The details of the conspiracy, the identification of its alleged membership, and the aid and comfort of the Confederacy to the conspirators came out from former Sons of Liberty who turned state's evidence to save their lives. Predictably, the military commission sentenced all the convicted conspirators (there was no doubt that the commission would convict them all) to die.

The Copperheads, particularly those active in conspiracies to free Confederate prisoners of war, had motive and opportunity to assassinate Abraham Lincoln. The Copperheads received funds from Confederate agents in Canada and were incited to stir up trouble for the Union.

THE TRIAL OF BOOTH'S ALLEGED ACCOMPLICES

President Andrew Johnson issued an order on May 1, 1865, that the alleged accomplices of John Wilkes Booth would be tried by military commission. President Johnson received advice from Secretary Stanton and Attorney General Speed on the lawfulness of trial by military commission.[121] Speed did not issue a written opinion until July 1865, after four of the defendants were found guilty and were executed. There is no record of the oral advice Speed gave to President Johnson and Secretary Stanton. Speed's predecessor Judge Edward Bates and Navy Secretary Gideon Welles opposed trial by military commission.[122] The cabinet was convened to ponder the impact of trying the accused accomplices by military commission on May 9, 1865. Secretary Stanton and Attorney General Speed argued in favor of a secret trial by military commission, but no formal vote was taken.[123] The reaction of the press to trial by military commission was generally favorable, although the *New York Times* editorialized against a secret trial.[124] The accomplices of John Wilkes Booth would be tried by a military commission consisting of very loyal, high-ranking Union officers on the third floor of the Washington Arsenal Penitentiary.[125]

NOTES

1. Edward Steers Jr., *Blood on the Moon: The Assassination of Abraham Lincoln* (Lexington: University Press of Kentucky, 2001), 91.
2. Thomas Nelson Conrad, *The Rebel Scout. A Thrilling History of Scouting Life in the Southern Army* (Washington, D.C.: National, 1904), 117–28. See also William A. Tidwell,

James O. Hall, and David W. Gaddy, *Come Retribution: The Confederate Secret Service and the Assassination of Lincoln* (Oxford: University of Mississippi Press, 1988), 281–86, implicating Confederate secretary of state Judah P. Benjamin in Conrad's plot.

3. Tidwell, Hall, and Gaddy, *Come Retribution*, 253–65.

4. Samuel Bland Arnold, *Memoirs of a Lincoln Conspirator*, ed. Michael W. Kauffman (Bowie, Md.: Heritage Books, 1995), 22–23; Steers, *Blood on the Moon*, 62–63.

5. Michael W. Kauffman, *American Brutus: John Wilkes Booth and the Lincoln Conspiracies* (New York: Random House, 2004), 138–40; Steers, *Blood on the Moon*, 71–74. Charles Martin agreed to ship Booth's theatrical wardrobe trunks via one of his blockade runner schooners. Martin's ship was shipwrecked in the St. Lawrence River, and Booth's trunk was recovered and sold at auction.

6. Steers, *Blood on the Moon*, 82.

7. Steers, *Blood on the Moon*, 145–50.

8. Steers, *Blood on the Moon*, 77.

9. Steers, *Blood on the Moon*, 77–78, 283.

10. Steers, *Blood on the Moon*, 85–86.

11. The 140th Indiana was part of General Sherman's army when a detail from the command went to Washington for presentation of new regimental colors. See more on the history of the 140th Indiana Infantry in Frederick H. Dyer, *A Compendium of the War of the Rebellion* (Des Moines, Iowa: By the author, 1908), 1157 (hereafter Dyer's *Compendium*); also available at https://archive.org/details/08697590.3359.emory.edu .

12. See Lincoln's speech to the 140th Indiana dated March 17, 1865, in Don E. Fehrenbacher, ed., *The Speeches of Abraham Lincoln* (New York: Library of America, 1999), 690–91.

13. Steers, *Blood on the Moon*, 86–89. Booth played in a benefit performance at Ford's Theatre on March 18, portraying Beccaria in *The Apostate*.

14. Michael J. Kline, *The Baltimore Plot: The First Conspiracy to Assassinate Abraham Lincoln* (Yardley, Pa.: Westholme, 2008), 160–61. This account is also based on Daniel Stashower, *The Hour of Peril: The Secret Plot to Murder Lincoln before the Civil War* (New York: Minotaur, 2013).

15. H. Donald Winkler, *Lincoln and Booth* (Nashville: Cumberland House, 2003), 63.

16. Tidwell, Hall, and Gaddy, *Come Retribution*, 27–28.

17. Atzerodt said: "Booth said he had met a party in N. York who would get the Prest. certain. They were going to mine the end of the pres. House, near the War Dept. They knew an entrance to accomplish it through. Spoke about getting friends of the Presdt. to get up an entertainment & they would mix it in, have a serenade & thus get at the Presdt. & party." George Atzerodt's confession—which was not admitted as evidence at the trial of the conspirators—is available at Douglas Linder, ed., Famous Trials Project, University of Missouri, Kansas City, http://law2.umkc.edu/faculty/projects/ftrials/lincolnconspiracy/atzerodtconf.html.

18. The precise date on which Booth dropped the kidnapping conspiracy and formed an assassination conspiracy is not revealed by any of the evidence at the trial of Booth's alleged accomplices. Booth and Powell had traveled to New York City on March 25, returning early in April. Atzerodt did not come to Washington until April 13. Herold's whereabouts from March 17 to April 14 are a mystery. John Surratt had left for Richmond, returned, and was on his way to Canada to carry out a mission for Confederate general Edwin Lee: to survey the Elmira, New York, prisoner of war compound, noting possible ways to invade the compound, drive off the Union guards, and free the prisoners. See John Surratt, lecture delivered on December 6, 1870, Rockville, Md., available at http://rogerjnorton.com/Lincoln55.html.

19. Steers, *Blood on the Moon*, 112.

20. The "Sam" letter is printed in full in James Swanson, *Manhunt: The Twelve-Day Chase for Lincoln's Killer* (New York: Harper Perennial, 2007), 133–35.

21. Voltaire Randall, one of Provost Marshal McPhail's detectives, knew that Sam Arnold was a friend of Booth and suggested that Arnold should be arrested before the identity of the writer of the "Sam" letter was disclosed to McPhail. Steers, *Blood on the Moon*, 171.

22. Arnold, *Memoir of a Lincoln Conspirator*, 51–52.

23. Kauffman, *American Brutus*, 44. Spangler fed Booth's horses at the livery stable where the horses were boarded.

24. Kauffman, *American Brutus*, 44.

25. A summary of the testimony of Jacob Ritterspaugh can be found in Benn Pitman, ed., *The Assassination of President Lincoln and the Trial of Conspirators: David E. Herold, Mary E. Surratt, Lewis Payne, George A. Atzerodt, Edward Spangler, Samuel A. Mudd, Samuel Arnold, Michael O'Laughlin* (Cincinnati: Moore, Wilstach & Baldwin, 1865), 2:97; Kauffman, *American Brutus*, 44. Ritterspaugh claimed that Spangler slapped him across the face and told him "'Don't say which way he went.' I asked him what he meant by slapping me in the mouth, and he said, 'For God's sake, shut up;' and that was the last he said."

26. Kaufmann, *American Brutus*, 171–72.

27. Kate Clifford Larson, *The Assassin's Accomplice* (New York: Basic Books, 2008), 41.

28. Kaufmann, *American Brutus*, 155.

29. Steers, *Blood on the Moon*, 177.

30. Larson, *Assassin's Accomplice*, 100.

31. Steers, *Blood on the Moon*, 175–76, quoting the *Baltimore Clipper*, April 20, 1865.

32. Testimony of Maj. H. W. Smith in Pitman, *Assassination of President Lincoln,* 122–23.

33. Steers, *Blood on the Moon*, 176–77; Larson, *Assassin's Accomplice*, 100.

34. Steers, *Blood on the Moon*, 177.

35. Steers, *Blood on the Moon*, 166–69.

36. Steers, *Blood on the Moon*, 144–46.

37. Steers, *Blood on the Moon*, 146–50.

38. Kaufmann, *American Brutus*, 305. Jett and Ruggles were not listed as members of the Forty-Third Virginia Bn., Mosby's Rangers. Bainbridge was carried on Mosby's rolls. See NARA microfilm 324-207-11 RG 94 (service records of members of 43rd VA Bn.).

39. Steers, *Blood on the Moon*, 192–206.

40. Steers, *Blood on the Moon*, 222–27.

41. William Hanchett, *The Lincoln Murder Conspiracies* (Urbana-Champaign: University of Illinois Press, 1989), 7–11, 33–34. See also Steers, *Blood on the Moon*, 43–46, on the Dahlgren raid.

42. The account of the Dahlgren raid is based on Steven Z. Starr, *The Union Cavalry in the Civil War* (Baton Rouge: Louisiana State University Press, 1981), 2:58–77.

43. Starr, *Union Cavalry in the Civil War*, 59.

44. The text of the Dahlgren address is available at http://www.mdgorman.com/Written_Accounts/Sentinel/1864/richmond_sentinel_351864.htm . See also Address of Ulric Dahlgren enclosed with letter of Gen. Robert E. Lee, in U.S. War Department, *The War of the Rebellion: A Compilation of the Official Records of the Union and Confederate Armies* [also known as *The Official Record of the War of the Rebellion*, hereafter "OR"], series 1, vol. 45 (Washington, D.C.: Government Printing Office, 1880–1901), 178–79.

45. Address of Ulric Dahlgren enclosed with letter of Gen. Robert E. Lee, OR series 2, vol. 45, 179–80.

46. Letter of Maj. Gen. Geo. G. Meade to H. Cram dated April 18, 1864, reproduced at http://clevelandcivilwarroundtable.com/articles/comment/meade.htm.

47. Steers, *Blood on the Moon*, 39–51.

48. Steers, *Blood on the Moon*, 58–59.

49. Mark Neely details Lincoln's program in a groundbreaking work that involved hundreds of hours of graduate student research at the National Archives in his *The Fate of Liberty*. See Mark E. Neely Jr., *The Fate of Liberty: Abraham Lincoln and Civil Liberties* (New York: Oxford University Press, 1992).

50. Alabama, Florida, Georgia, Louisiana, Mississippi, South Carolina, and Texas formed the original Confederate States of America at Montgomery in March 1861. Arkansas, Tennessee, North Carolina, and Virginia seceded after April 15, 1861. Although Missouri and Kentucky did not leave the Union, each state maintained a shadow government in exile that sent senators and representatives to the Confederate government.

51. "Confederate States of America," available at http://www.history.com/topics/american-civil-war/confederate-states-of-america . See also "Confederate States of America," *Encyclopedia Britannica Online*, http://www.britannica.com/EBchecked/topic/131803/Confederate-States-of-America.

52. Margaret Leech, *Reveille in Washington 1860–1865* (New York: Harper & Bros., 1941; New York: Time, 1962). Citations refer to the Time edition.

53. William H. Rehnquist, *All the Laws but One: Civil Liberties in Wartime* (New York: Knopf, 1998), 17.

54. For background on Maryland's secession crisis, see Bradley T. Johnson, *Confederate Military History: Maryland*, in *Confederate Military History: A Library of Confederate States History, in Twelve Volumes, Written by Distinguished Men of the South, and Edited by Gen. Clement. A. Evans of Georgia*, ed. Clement A. Evans, 2:22–27 (Atlanta: Confederate, 1899; Secaucus, N.J.: Blue & Grey, 1981).

55. Johnson, *Confederate Military History: Maryland*, 23. Johnson asserts that Gov. Thomas Hicks ordered Trimble to destroy the bridges.

56. Edward A. Miller Jr., *Lincoln's Abolitionist General: The Biography of David Hunter* (Columbia: University of South Carolina Press, 1997), 54–57. See also Leech, *Reveille in Washington*, 71–73. Leech noted that Capt. Irvin McDowell also had a small detachment of regulars stationed at the Capitol Building, and D.C. militia had been mustered into service. Hunter's command consisted of the Frontier Battalion led by James G. Lane, an infamous Kansas jayhawker, and the Clay Battalion, led by Cassius M. Clay. The Frontier guards went to the White House and the Clay Battalion remained at Willard's Hotel.

57. Neely, *The Fate of Liberty*, 5.

58. Neely, *The Fate of Liberty*, 6–7.

59. Johnson, *Confederate Military History: Maryland*, 20–22. See also http://www.actonmemoriallibrary.org/civilwar/regiments/Mass/6mass.html.

60. Leech, *Reveille in Washington*, 82.

61. Rehnquist, *All the Laws but One*, 25. Mark Neely quotes another version published by Roy P. Basler, the editor of *The Collected Works of Abraham Lincoln*, that describes the railroad route as the makeshift route through Perryville, Annapolis Junction, to Washington that bypassed the destroyed PW&B bridges in Harford County, Maryland. This more limited version was superseded by Seward's authorized version.

62. Although the writ existed before 1679, the English Habeas Corpus Act of 1679 authorized royal courts to issue the writ to test the legality of confinement.

63. For a detailed examination of the writ of habeas corpus in times of emergency, see Brian Farrell, "Habeas Corpus in Time of Emergency: A Historical and Comparative View," *Pace International Law Review Online Companion*, April 2010, particularly 88–89 relating to President Lincoln's suspension of the writ.

64. Francis Lieber, *Instructions for the Government of Armies of the United States in the Field, Sect. I Art. 3 & 4. Originally promulgated as Gen. Order 100, 1863* (Washington, D.C.: Government Printing Office, 1898) (hereafter "Lieber Code").

65. Michael Warshauer, "Andrew Jackson and the Constitution," Gilder Lehrman Institute of American History, www.gilderlehrman.org.

66. Winfield Scott, *Memoirs of Lt. Gen. Winfield Scott Written by Himself*, 2 vols. (New York: Sheldon, 1864); see 1:285–98 for Scott's understanding of martial law and 2:538–51 for the imposition of martial law.

67. See Eric M. Freedman, *Habeas Corpus: Rethinking the Great Writ of Liberty* (New York: New York University Press, 2001), concerning the Antiterrorism and Effective Death Penalty Act of 1996 (Pub. L. 104-132, 104th Congress, 1st Sess. 110 Stat. 1214) (AEDPA). That statute, passed after the Oklahoma City bombing, provided that the authority of federal judges to grant habeas corpus is barred unless the state court's adjudication of the claim has resulted in a decision that (a) is contrary to, or has involved an unreasonable application of clearly established federal law as determined by the Supreme Court of the United States; or (b) has resulted in a decision that was based on an unreasonable determination of the facts in light of the evidence presented in the state court proceeding. See 28 U.S.C. §§ 2244, 2254.

AEDPA has sharply limited second or successive habeas petitions, with several exceptions. Petitioners who had already filed a federal habeas petition were required first to secure authorization from the appropriate United States Court of Appeals, to ensure that such an exception was at least facially made out.

68. Joel Bishop, *Criminal Procedure; or, Commentaries on the Pleading and Evidence in Criminal Practice*, 3rd rev. ed., book 3 §§ 155–163 (Boston: Little, Brown, 1880), 182.
69. Bishop, *Criminal Procedure*, book 3 § 214.
70. U.S. Const. amend. VI: "In all criminal prosecutions, the accused shall enjoy the right . . . to be informed of the nature and cause of the accusation."
71. See, e.g., Del. Const. art. I, § 7 (1837); Mass. Const. Declaration of Right, art. XII (1780); N.Y. Const. art. I, § 1 (1846); S.C. Const. art. IX, § 2 (1861); Tex. Const. art. I, § 16 (1845).
72. See, e.g., Ala. Const. art. I, § 17 (1861); Calif. Const. art. I, § 5 (1849); Conn. Const. art. 1, § 14 (1818); Fla. Const. art. I, § 11 (1861); Ill. Const. art. XIII, § 13 (1848).
73. U.S. Const. amend. VI: "In all criminal prosecutions, the accused shall enjoy the right to speedy and public trial, by an impartial jury of his peers."
74. See, e.g., R.I. Const. art. I, § 10 (1843); Tenn. Const. art. I, § 9 (1796); Va. Declaration of Rights, § 8 (1776); Wis. Const. art. I, § 7 (1848).
75. James Q. Whitman, *The Origins of Reasonable Doubt* (New Haven, Conn.: Yale University Press, 2008), quoting John H. Langbein, *The Origins of Adversary Criminal Trial* (New York: Oxford University Press, 2003), 33.
76. See, e.g., State v. King, 20 Ark. 166, 167 (1859); Giles v. State, 6 Ga. 276, 285 (1849); Commonwealth v. Webster, 5 Cush. (59 Mass.) 285, 320 (1850); Donnelly v. State, 26 N.J.L.601, 615 (1857). Simon Greenleaf, *A Treatise on the Law of Evidence*, 12th ed., ed. Isaac F. Redfield (Boston: Little, Brown, 1866; orig. pub. 1858), 1:16–17.
77. Judicial Code of 1789 §§ 13, 22 1 Stat. 73.
78. The executive order may be found in Neely, *The Fate of Liberty*, 9–10.
79. Ex parte Merryman, 17 Fed. Cas. 144 (C.Ct. Md. 1861).
80. Ex parte Merryman, 17 Fed. Cas. 148.
81. Ex parte Merryman, 17 Fed. Cas. 151–52.
82. Ex parte Merryman, 17 Fed. Cas. 152.
83. Abraham Lincoln, message to Congress, July 4, 1861, in Roy E. Basler, ed., *Collected Works of Abraham Lincoln* (Bloomington, Ind.: American Historical Review, 1953), 4:449 (hereafter *Collected Works of Abraham Lincoln*).
84. Neely, *The Fate of Liberty*, 15–17.
85. Frederick A. Bancroft, *The Life of William A. Seward* (New York: Harper & Bros., 1899), 2:276–77.
86. Neely, *The Fate of Liberty*, 45–47.
87. OR, series 2, vol. 2, part 115, 221–22 (February 14, 1862).
88. OR, series 2, vol. 4, part 117, 158–59 (August 8, 1862).
89. OR, series 2, vol. 4, part 117, 358 (August 8, 1862).
90. *Collected Works of Abraham Lincoln*, 5:436–37.
91. OR, series 1, vol. 23, part 2, 237 (April 14, 1863).
92. OR, series 1, vol. 13, part 2, 315–316 (Burnside to Stanton, May 7, 1863).
93. OR, series 3, vol. 1, part 587, Gen. Order 141 Adjutant Gen. Dept. (September 25, 1862) (individuals discouraging volunteer enlistment, resisting militia drafts, etc., liable to arrest and trial by military commission).
94. Ex parte Vallandigham, 68 U.S. 243 (1863) (preface by Wallace).
95. Rehnquist, *All the Laws but One*, 67.
96. In 1863, several states contained antibanishment clauses in their bill of rights. See, e.g., Ala. Const. art. I, § 27 (1861); Ill. Const. art. XIII, § 18 (1848); Kans. Const. Bill of Rights, § 12 (1857); Miss. Const. art. I, § 27 (1861); N.C. Const. Declaration of Rights, § 12 (1776); Ohio Const. art. I, § 12 (1851). The constitutionality of denationalization and potential banishment was finally settled by the Supreme Court in Trop v. Dulles, 356 U.S. 86, 102 (1958), ruling that a Civil War–era statute imposing loss of citizenship for desertion in time of war was barred by the Eighth Amendment because it was cruel and unusual punishment. The Supreme Court has never ruled that states and cities were barred from excluding convicted people from areas of the state or city. For background on the return of banishment from downtown Seattle under the rubric of exclusionary protective practices as punishment, see Katherine Beckett and

Steve Herbert, "Penal Boundaries: Banishment and the Expansion of Punishment," *Law & Social Inquiry* 35, no. 1 (2010).

97. Ex parte Vallandigham, 68 U.S. 248–51. Justice Swayne said that Congress had granted appellate power to the U.S. Supreme Court, and Congress made no provision for the U.S. Supreme Court to review the action of a military commission because such a body was not a court. Swayne acknowledged that Congress had given the court extraordinary writ power by section 14 of the Judiciary Act of 1789, but he denied that such writs could be issued against a military commission because it was not a court. By such specious reasoning, the face of the court was saved.

98. "Copperhead" was the name given by Republicans and the press for anti-war Democrats who often wore the copper indian head penny as an emblem.

99. Gilbert M. Tredway, *Democratic Opposition to the Lincoln Administration* (Indianapolis: Indiana Historical Bureau, 1973), 71–80.

100. Tredway, *Democratic Opposition to the Lincoln Administration*, 122–24.

101. Tredway, *Democratic Opposition to the Lincoln Administration*, 115–17. The grand jury report lumped the Democratic Mutual Protection Societies with the alleged disloyal Order of American Knights.

102. 12 Stat. Ch. 74 (1863).

103. 12 Stat. Ch. 74, § 6 (1863).

104. 12 Stat. Ch. 74, § 24 (1863).

105. 12 Stat. Ch. 74, § 25 (1863).

106. 12 Stat. Ch. 74, § 38 (1863).

107. *New York Times*, July 14, 1863, 1; July 15, 1863, 1; July 16, 1863, 1. See also Leslie M. Harris, *In the Shadow of Slavery: African-Americans in New York City 1626–1863* (Chicago: University of Chicago Press, 2003), 279–88, for a brief description of the New York City draft riot.

108. See, e.g., Griffin v. Wilcox, 21 Ind. 370 (1863) (held: Congress cannot suspend state's right to issue habeas corpus); In re Kemp, 16 Wis. 359 (1863) (state issued habeas corpus holding Congress cannot suspend state's power to issue writ; General Order 141 cited in opposition to holding).

109. Griffin v. Wilcox, 21 Ind. 370.

110. *Collected Works of Abraham Lincoln*, 6:451–52.

111. The story of Missouri during the early war is well told by Mark E. Neely Jr. Briefly, the U.S. government declared martial law in Missouri after the duly elected governor of the state declared for the Confederacy. Civilians who sabotaged railroad bridges and staged guerilla raids on loyal Union forces were tried before military commissions and in some instances condemned and shot to death. Brig. Gen. Thomas Ewing issued General Order 11 clearing all civilians out of several border counties that were hotbeds of pro-secession sympathy. Although the civilian courts remained open for business, the military had instituted military rule that lasted to the end of hostilities in 1865. See Neely, *The Fate of Liberty*, 32–50.

112. Neely, *The Fate of Liberty*, 162–68.

113. Neely, *The Fate of Liberty*, 174.

114. *The American Annual Encyclopaedia and Register of Important Events of the Year 1865* (New York. D. Appleton, 1866), 5:414, cited in Neely, *The Fate of Liberty*, 113.

115. Neely, *The Fate of Liberty*, 114.

116. Neely, *The Fate of Liberty*, 115–16.

117. Tredway, *Democratic Opposition to the Lincoln Administration*, 177–79.

118. Tredway, *Democratic Opposition to the Lincoln Administration*, 179.

119. Tredway, *Democratic Opposition to the Lincoln Administration*, 183.

120. Tredway, *Democratic Opposition to the Lincoln Administration*, 187–88.

121. See Douglas Linder, ed., "Chronology of Lincoln Assassination Conspirators Trial," available at Famous Trials Project, University of Missouri, Kansas City, http://law2.umkc.edu/faculty/projects/ftrials/lincolnconspiracy/lincolnchronology.html.

122. See Edward Bates, *The Diary of Edward Bates 1859–1866*, ed. Howard K. Beale (Washington, D.C.: Government Printing Office, 1933), 483 (for diary entry for May 25, 1865) and 498–503 (for Bates's analysis of the Speed opinion); Gideon Welles, entry for May 9,

1865, in *Diary of Gideon Welles, Secretary of the Navy under Lincoln and Johnson* (Boston: Houghton Mifflin, 1911), 2:203–4.

123. *Diary of Gideon Welles*, 2:304.

124. See editorial, *New York Times*, May 15, 1865, 4; August 1, 1865, 2, quoting the *London Times*, July 17, 1865 (highly favorable to military commission).

125. See Barry Cauchon, "The Washington, D.C. Arsenal Penitentiary (Part 1 of 3)," *A Little Touch of History* (blog), July 2, 2009, https://awesometalks.wordpress.com/2009/08/02/the-washington-d-c-arsenal-penitentiary-part-1-of-3/. The building remains standing today as Fort Lesley McNair's Building 20.

Chapter Two

The Hunter Commission

> The Commission was organized to convict. The state of the public mind was such that the desire for revenge had taken the place of justice, and, for a time, a reign of terror prevailed.—John W. Clampitt, "The Trial of Mrs. Surratt"

On May 1, 1865, President Andrew Johnson directed the judge advocate general of the army to establish a military commission to try the "the persons implicated in the murder of the late President, Abraham Lincoln, and the attempted assassination of the Hon. William H. Seward, Secretary of State, and in an alleged conspiracy to assassinate other officers of the Federal Government at Washington City, and their aiders and abettors."[1]

Four days later, the War Department appointed a military commission to try the men and woman charged with conspiring to assassinate the president. The timing of the convening order for the military commission deserves comment.[2] Maj. Gen. David Hunter, Brig. Gen. James A. Ekin and Brig. Gen. Albion Howe, three of the senior officers appointed to the commission, had been assigned as honor guards for President Lincoln, while he lay in state in Washington. General Hunter was also one of the burial party that escorted President Lincoln's remains to Springfield, Illinois. He was returning to Washington following the May 4, 1865, interment of President Lincoln's body when Special Order 211 was issued on May 5.

The original panel included Brig. Gen. Cyrus Comstock and Col. Horace Porter. These officers were excused from the panel by the Adjutant General's Office on May 10 and Brig. Gen. James A. Ekin of the Quartermaster Corps and Col. Charles H. Tompkins were added to the panel to replace them. The nine members of the military commission were Maj. Gen. David M. Hunter, Maj. Gen. Lewis Wallace, Maj. Gen. August V. Kautz, Brig. Gen. Albion Howe, Brig. Gen. James A. Ekin, Brig. Gen. Robert S. Foster, Brig. Gen. Thomas M. Harris, Col. C. H. Tompkins, and Lt. Col. David R. Clendenin.[3]

PROFILES OF THE HUNTER COMMISSION MEMBERS

Secretary Stanton and Judge Advocate General Holt selected the commission members with considerable care. The officers selected were either career army officers or officers with strong Republican Party affiliation. Generals Hunter, Howe, and Kautz were West Point graduates. General Ekin, Colonel Tompkins, and Lieutenant Colonel Clendenin were career soldiers who did not attend West Point. Generals Wallace and Foster were Indiana Republican politicians. General Harris was a physician and a West Virginia Republican politician. Wallace, the only lawyer on the panel, had practiced law in Crawfordsville, Indiana, before the war. The panel would try the accused accomplices according to the law of war. Neither the Articles of War that governed military discipline in the army nor the penal laws of the District of Columbia would be employed for the trial. The commission would make up ad hoc rules of procedure guided by Judge Advocate General Joseph Holt and his staff. The commission may have adopted General Order 100, the Lieber Code, as substantive criminal law.[4]

Maj. Gen. David M. Hunter, President of the Commission

David M. Hunter, president of the commission, the person who would rule on all legal issues at trial, was the son of Rev. Andrew Hunter, a Presbyterian

Figure 2.1. The Hunter Commission. Left to Right: Lt. Col. David Clendenin, Col. Charles Tompkins, Brig. Gen. Thomas M. Harris, Brig. Gen. Albion Howe, Brig. Gen James A. Ekin, Maj. Gen. Lewis Wallace, Maj. Gen. David M. Hunter, Maj. Gen. August V. Kautz, Brig. Gen. Robert S. Foster, John A. Bingham, Col. Henry L. Burnett, Joseph Holt. *Source:* Library of Congress.

minister who was chaplain of the Third New Jersey Infantry of the Continental Line during the American Revolution. Reverend Hunter was a brigade chaplain at Newburg, New York, and General Washington occasionally attended his services. Andrew Hunter married his second wife Mary Stockton, daughter of Richard Stockton, signer of the Declaration of Independence, on October 13, 1794. David was their fourth child, born July 21, 1802.[5] David Hunter was appointed to the U.S. Military Academy in 1818 and graduated in the middle of the class in 1822.[6] He was commissioned second lieutenant of infantry and was posted to Fort Snelling on the fringe of settlement in the Northwest Territory.[7] Hunter challenged his commanding officer Col. Josiah Snelling to a duel in 1826, which Colonel Snelling declined. Instead, he preferred charges against Lieutenant Hunter, and a general court-martial was appointed to try Hunter. The trial never took place and the court martial was indefinitely adjourned.[8] In 1827, the court-martial was reappointed and tried Hunter for challenging his commanding officer to a duel. He was convicted and sentenced to be cashiered. Hunter presented a lengthy written memorandum detailing Snelling's invitation to his subordinates to challenge Snelling to a duel. President John Quincy Adams reduced his sentence and saved his career.[9] Lieutenant Hunter had tours of duty at garrisons in the old Northwest, including Fort Dearborn, Chicago, Illinois, from 1828 to 1831.[10] Lieutenant Hunter married Maria Kinsey, daughter of the founder of Chicago, in 1831. He also took title to eighty acres of land along the lakeshore.[11] Hunter resigned from the army in 1836 and became a land speculator and minor Whig politician. Hunter was a protégé of the "Long Nine" Whig representatives in the Illinois General Assembly. Hunter met Abraham Lincoln in 1841 when both men were delegates to the Illinois State Whig Convention. In 1842, Hunter was reappointed major and paymaster and assigned to dole out payrolls on the western frontier. He did not see service in the Mexican War and remained a major and paymaster in the fall of 1860, when he sent President-Elect Lincoln a series of letters warning him of a plot to prevent him from being inaugurated president. Hunter and Col E. V. Sumner were chosen to escort Lincoln to Washington. Hunter was appointed colonel of the Sixth U.S. Cavalry shortly after arriving in Washington and saw service as a division commander at the Battle of First Manassas July 21, 1861. Hunter received a serious wound at First Manassas, but was well enough to be posted as a newly minted brigadier general to Missouri in the fall of 1861 to relieve Maj. Gen. John C. Fremont, who had issued a premature emancipation proclamation freeing Missouri's slaves. In 1862, Hunter was appointed major general and reassigned to command the District of the South. Hunter successfully completed the siege of Fort Pulaski, Georgia, and issued an order enlisting African Americans in the First South Carolina (African American) Regiment without authorization from the War Department. He accompanied this with a proclamation freeing South Carolina's slaves. The

Lincoln administration disapproved of this act and issued a proclamation repealing emancipation, even though Lincoln would publish his own Emancipation Proclamation over strenuous objection in September 1862.

Hunter presided at the court-martial of Maj. Gen. Fitz John Porter in 1863. In 1864, he was made commanding general of the Army of the Shenandoah, winning a major victory over Confederate forces at Piedmont, Virginia, in June 1864. Hunter followed up on his victory by occupying Staunton and Lexington, Virginia, burning Virginia Military Institute (VMI) and the home of Governor Letcher, while on his way to capture and destroy the Confederate supply depot at Lynchburg, Virginia. Hunter failed to capture Lynchburg then retreated across the Alleghenies, opening the Shenandoah Valley to Lt. Gen. Jubal A. Early's raid on Washington. Hunter stepped down as army commander in August 1864 and was "awaiting orders" when President Lincoln was assassinated. He was commander of Lincoln's honor guard at his funeral and accompanied Lincoln's body home to Springfield in April–May 1865.[12] General Hunter retired in 1866 because he was beyond the age for retention on active duty. He made Washington his home and from time to time would talk to others about his role in the trial of the Lincoln assassination accomplices. He died February 2, 1886, after returning from a walk from his home to downtown Washington. He was buried in Princeton Cemetery, Princeton, New Jersey.[13]

Maj. Gen. Lewis Wallace, Commission Member

Lewis "Lew" Wallace, son of Indiana governor David Wallace, was born April 10, 1827, in Brookville, Indiana. Governor Wallace, an 1821 graduate of the U.S. Military Academy, served as congressman for his district and lieutenant governor and governor of Indiana.[14] Lew Wallace grew up in Indianapolis, Indiana, while his father served as lieutenant governor and governor. He attended grammar school in Covington and was briefly enrolled in Wabash College in Crawfordsville.[15] Wallace was a very indifferent student. He was sent to several other institutions during his youth by his father, but never completed his formal education.[16] Wallace volunteered for service in the First Indiana Volunteers in the Mexican War and served as a lieutenant in Company H.[17] The First Indiana arrived at the Rio Grande in the fall of 1846 and saw no action for several months, being detailed to guard stores at the mouth of the river. In the late fall of 1846, most of the regiment was sent to Matamoros on the Gulf Coast of Mexico.[18] The First Indiana took no part in General Taylor's engagement with Santa Anna at Buena Vista and returned home in the late spring of 1847. Wallace developed an interest in military matters, and he eventually became an officer in the Indiana militia. Wallace read for the law after returning from Mexico and was admitted to the bar in 1849, opening his law office in Covington, Indiana.[19] Wallace met

Susan Elston at a party given by his Mexican War commanding officer Col. Henry Lane. They were married in 1852. The Wallaces moved to Crawfordsville when Wallace was elected prosecuting attorney for his county.[20] In 1856, he was elected to the Indiana General Assembly from Crawfordsville, Indiana. Governor Oliver P. Morton appointed Wallace adjutant general of Indiana in April 1861; then he was appointed colonel of the Eleventh Indiana Infantry, seeing action in McClellan's West Virginia campaign.[21] Commissioned brigadier general of volunteers,[22] he joined Ulysses Grant's army before Fort Donelson and was promoted major general of volunteers on March 21, 1862.[23] Wallace, a division commander at the Battle of Shiloh, was five miles from the battlefield when General Grant gave him orders to advance immediately and form the right of the Union line. Wallace's division followed a circuitous route to the battlefield and arrived too late to influence the outcome on the first day of the battle.[24] Grant never forgave Wallace for arriving too late. Within months after Shiloh, Wallace was relieved of command.[25] Governor Morton drafted Wallace to take command of a green Indiana regiment in the fall of 1862 and to take the unit to Kentucky to oppose Gen. Braxton Bragg's invasion.[26] General Jeremiah Boyle appointed Wallace commander of all Union forces in Lexington, Kentucky. That order was superseded by Maj. Gen. Don Carlos Buell, who put Brig. Gen. William Nelson in command.[27] Wallace briefly commanded local defense forces at Cincinnati in October 1862 before returning to Crawfordsville to "await orders."[28] He was put in command of the commission of inquiry to review Maj. Gen. Don Carlos Buell's handling of the Battle of Perryville that occupied him into the late spring of 1863.[29] Later that summer, Governor Morton put Wallace in charge of Indiana militia opposing Confederate brigadier general John H. Morgan's invasion of Indiana.[30] In March 1864 Wallace was appointed commanding general of the Eighth Corps headquartered in Baltimore.[31] In July 1864, he commanded Union forces at the Battle of Monocacy, in which he and his much smaller command were defeated by General Early's Corps Army of Northern Virginia. Wallace bought time by delaying Early's advance on lightly defended Washington, D.C., at the cost of several hundred casualties and the rout of his small force, hardly larger than one infantry division.[32]

Wallace would go on to be president of the military commission that condemned Capt. Henry Wirz to death for mistreatment of Union prisoners at Andersonville,[33] and to be appointed territorial governor of New Mexico by President Hayes. Wallace suppressed the Lincoln County War, including capturing William Bonney (Billy the Kid) and obtaining his conviction for murder.[34] Wallace started writing *Ben Hur* in the early 1870s, finishing the novel in Santa Fe during his governorship. *Ben Hur* was published in 1885 and was atop the best seller list for more than fifty years, the most successful thing that Wallace did in his lifetime. It was made into feature-length movies in 1925 and 1959.[35] After Wallace left the New Mexico governorship, he returned to Crawfordsville to spend the last years of his life. Wallace died February 15, 1905. He devoted a single short chapter in his autobiography to the Lincoln assassination trial. Wallace recounts how he overcame boredom during the trial by sketching the panel, the prisoners and the lawyers, later making a composite portrait of the commission at work from his sketches.[36]

Maj. Gen. August V. Kautz, Commission Member

August Valentine Kautz was born in Baden, Germany, on January 5, 1828. The Kautz family emigrated from Germany to the United States before the Mexican War, settling in Brown County, Ohio. The Kautz family lived in the same town as the Jesse Grant family. August attended a local grammar school with Ulysses Grant.[37] August enlisted in the First Ohio Volunteers at the outbreak of the Mexican War. His regiment participated in General Taylor's campaign against Monterrey and took part in the Battle of Buena Vista.[38] Following war's end, Kautz was appointed to the U.S. Military Academy, graduating thirty-fifth out of forty-three in the class of 1852.[39] Commissioned a second lieutenant in the Fourth Infantry, Kautz saw action and was wounded in the Rogue River War of 1852–1853 and at Puget Sound in 1856.[40] Kautz had two wives and six legitimate children and a Native American companion by whom he had two children.[41] Kautz was promoted to first lieutenant in 1855, and captain in the Sixth U.S. Cavalry in April 1861. He took leave from the regular army to accept appointment as colonel of the Second Ohio Cavalry in 1862. The Second Ohio saw action in Missouri and Kentucky in 1862.[42] He commanded the Camp Chase remount depot in Columbus, Ohio, until April 1863, when he became commanding officer of a cavalry brigade. Kautz's brigade participated in the chase after Confederate brigadier general John Hunt Morgan's raiders, cornering the command in eastern Ohio and capturing half of the officers and men of Morgan's brigade. [43] Kautz was appointed chief of cavalry, Army of the James and was promoted to brevet brigadier general in 1864. Eventually, General Kautz became a division commander in the Twenty-Fifth Corps consisting of U.S. Colored Troops that secured Richmond after the flight of the Confederate government in early April 1865. [44] General Kautz was promoted to major general shortly before the Lincoln conspiracy trial began. He was a regular officer who served in Arizona and in the Pacific Northwest and was eventually promoted to brigadier general, U.S. Army in 1891. He retired in 1892. [45] General Kautz died September 4, 1895.[46]

Brig. Gen. Albion Howe, Commission Member

Albion Howe, a native of Standish, Maine, born March 3, 1818, was appointed to the U.S. Military Academy in 1837, graduating eighth in his class in 1841. Howe was commissioned a lieutenant of artillery and saw action in the Mexican War, receiving a promotion to brevet captain. After 1848, he was assigned to garrison duty until 1859, when he was a battery commander at Harpers Ferry after John Brown's raid. Captain Howe served as a battery commander in western Virginia early in the war and was then commissioned as colonel of volunteers, then brigadier general, taking command of the Third Brigade First Division, Fourth Corps Army of the Potomac during the Seven Days' Battle of June–July 1862. Howe served as a Sixth Corps division commander, Army of the Potomac at South Mountain, Antietam, Fredericksburg, and at Salem Church on May 3, 1863. Howe's division, the Sixth Corps, suffered heavy casualties at Salem Church but was in reserve at Gettysburg. Howe's division participated in the pursuit of Gen. Robert E. Lee's Army of Northern Virginia after Gettysburg. Howe made an enemy of Maj. Gen. John Sedgwick, his corps commander, and General Meade, the Army of the Potomac commander, by implying that Sedgwick and Meade lost the Battle of Chancellorsville through ineptitude in his testimony before the Joint Committee on the Conduct of the War. Following the unsuccessful Mine Run campaign in November 1863, Howe was assigned to command the Artillery Depot in Washington. He was replaced by Brig. Gen. George W. Getty as division commander. He was one of the officers detailed as guard of honor for President Lincoln's remains during the funerary trip from Washington to Springfield. At the time of the Hunter Commission trial, Howe was artillery depot commander. Howe retired from the army in 1882 as colonel of the Fourth U.S. Artillery. [47] He died January 25, 1897, in Cambridge, Massachusetts. [48]

Brig. Gen. James Ekin, Commission Member

James Ekin was a Pittsburgh native born August 31, 1819, who built steamboats for use on the Ohio River and its tributaries. He married Diana Craighead Walker in 1842. Ekin had five children, three of whom were minors when war was initiated. At the outbreak of war in 1861, Ekin was commissioned first lieutenant in a ninety-day regiment, the Twelfth Pennsylvania, in April 1861. After the mustering out of his regiment, Ekin became a captain in the Quartermaster's Department, promoted to colonel, and commissioned brevet brigadier general in March 1863. Ekin then became a career army officer, holding the commission of lieutenant colonel of the Quartermaster Corps from 1865 to 1882 when he was commissioned as a colonel. Ekin retired the next year. He died March 27, 1891, in Louisville, Kentucky, and is buried in Cave Hill National Cemetery. [49]

Brig. Gen. Robert S. Foster, Commission Member

Robert S. Foster, a native of Vernon, Indiana, born January 27, 1834, was a tinsmith living in Indianapolis when war broke out in 1861. [50] He was commissioned captain of the Eleventh Indiana, a ninety-day regiment commanded by Col. Lewis Wallace. Foster then accepted a commission in the Thirteenth Indiana, steadily being promoted to major and colonel of the regiment. The Thirteenth Indiana was part of Brig. Gen. James Shields's division for the spring of 1862. [51] Foster commanded the Thirteenth Indiana at the first Battle of Kernstown in March 1862. [52] The Thirteenth Indiana was on the field at the battle of Port Republic during Stonewall Jackson's famous Valley campaign of 1862. [53] Foster's Thirteenth Indiana was later transferred to the Fourth Corps stationed on the Virginia Peninsula. The Thirteenth Indiana was part of Ferry's Second Brigade, Second Division, Fourth Army Corps, Army of the Potomac, from July 1862 through September 1862. Ferry's brigade was transferred to the Seventh Corps stationed at Suffolk, Virginia. Foster, by this time a colonel of volunteers, commanded this brigade at times during the winter and spring of 1863. Lieutenant General James Longstreet's Confederate Corps besieged the Suffolk garrison from early April through May 4, 1863. Foster's brigade manned the Union trench line's southwestern flank during the siege.[54] In July, Foster's brigade was transferred to the Department of the South and put under the command of Brig. Gen. Israel Vogdes stationed at Folly Island, South Carolina.[55]

Foster was commissioned brigadier general of volunteers and sent to the Department of the South to take command of a brigade in the Tenth Corps during the siege of Charleston in the summer of 1863.[56] Foster served as chief of staff to Tenth Corps commander Quincy A. Gillmore in the spring of 1864. When the Tenth Corps was included in Maj. Gen. Benjamin F. Butler's Army of the James in 1864, Foster became a division commander in the Tenth Corps.[57] His division then became part of the Twenty-Fourth Corps Division during the siege of Petersburg. Foster's division took part in the second Richmond offensive in the fall of 1864.[58] Foster's Twenty-Fourth Corps Division was the lead division in the Union assault on Confederate Fort Gregg in the Petersburg trench line on April 2, 1865, that led to the Confederate withdrawal from Petersburg.[59] Foster's division was in the vanguard of the Army of the Potomac's pursuit of the Confederate Army of Northern Virginia, helping to corner General Lee's army at Appomattox Court House.[60] Foster, by then a brevet major general, resigned his commission after serving on the Hunter Commission. He returned to Indianapolis where he was city treasurer and later U.S. marshal for the Southern District of Indiana.[61] Foster died March 3, 1903, in Indianapolis and is buried in Crown Hill Cemetery.

Brig. Gen. Thomas M. Harris, Commission Member

Thomas M. Harris was born June 17, 1817, in Harrisville, Wood County, Virginia (now West Virginia) in the northern panhandle of the state. Harris's uncle Thomas Harris had founded the town forty years earlier.[62] Harris attended Marietta College for a short while then started his career as a common schoolteacher. He married Sophia T. Hall October 4, 1841, in Wood County. They were on the staff of the Parkersburg Seminary.[63] Harris took in some medical lectures at Louisville Medical College then was apprenticed to a local physician and left teaching for medicine in 1843, first in Richie County, then in Gilmer County, West Virginia, after 1856.[64] Dr. Harris was instrumental in raising the Tenth (West) Virginia Regiment in April 1862, and was commissioned lieutenant colonel of the regiment in May 1862.[65] Harris served in Maj. Gen. John C. Fremont's corps in western Virginia in the spring of 1862, primarily assigned to hunting down Confederate irregulars preying on Union families in the Alleghenies. The Tenth West Virginia did not see action against Stonewall Jackson's Confederate forces at McDowell in May 1862, nor was it on the field at Cross Keys in June 1862. Fremont's corps was defeated in both battles.[66] Harris's regiment was integrated into Brig. Gen. Robert Milroy's Eighth Corps, forming part of the Second Brigade, Second Division commanded by Brigadier General Cluseret.[67] The Tenth West Virginia was transferred to Brig. Gen. William W. Averell's Fourth Independent Brigade, Eighth Army Corps in the Kanawha Valley in March 1863 and remained part of that brigade through the next year and a half. Harris's regiment was in the thick of the fight at Droop Mountain in the fall of 1863.[68] Harris's regiment was attached to the Reserve Division until it became part of Third Brigade, First Division, Army of the Shenandoah in June 1864. Harris's brigade, commanded by Colonel Mulligan, remained in the vicinity of Leetown, Virginia. In mid-June 1864 Lt. Gen. Jubal A. Early's corps, Army of Northern Virginia, moved north down the Shenandoah Valley to put pressure on Washington, D.C. Harris's outpost at Leetown was attacked July 3, 1864, by Confederate cavalry. Mulligan withdrew his forces after repelling the first Confederate attack to Maryland Heights, overlooking Harpers Ferry.[69] Colonel Harris replaced Mulligan as brigade commander in time to see the Tenth West Virginia make a futile attempt to force a crossing of the river at Snickers Gap on July 18, 1864.[70] Colonel Harris commanded an Eighth Corps Division at the Battles of Fisher's Hill and Cedar Creek and was brevetted brigadier general in November 1864. Following the successful conclusion of Sheridan's Valley campaign in the late fall of 1864, General Harris's division was transferred to the Twenty-Fourth Corps, Army of the

James, in the siege lines at Petersburg. General Harris was appointed full brigadier general in March 1865.[71]

Harris was offered a colonel's commission in the U.S. Regular Army after his service on the Hunter Commission. Harris declined on account of his age and returned to his Harrisville home to practice medicine. General Harris was elected to the West Virginia House of Delegates in 1867, and was appointed West Virginia adjutant general in 1869. From 1871 to 1873, he was the U.S. pension agent for Wheeling, West Virginia. Harris continued to practice medicine during this period and up to 1882 when he retired. Ten years later, Harris wrote the *History of the Great Conspiracy*, his summary version of the Hunter Commission trial and of the lives of Booth's alleged accomplices. Harris was the only Hunter Commission member to publish a full-length account of the trial.[72] Harris followed up this book with a second book blaming the Lincoln assassination on the Roman Catholic church.[73] General Harris died September 30, 1906, in Harrisville. His remains were buried in the Odd Fellows Cemetery in Harrisville, Virginia.[74]

Col. Charles H. Tompkins, Commission Member

Charles H. Tompkins, son of an army officer, was born in Fort Monroe, Virginia, September 12, 1830. He was appointed a cadet at West Point from Brooklyn, New York, in 1847 but resigned in 1849, two years short of graduation. He enlisted in the First U.S. Dragoons in 1856 for five years' time. Tompkins's regiment fought with indigenous Native Americans in Utah and Nevada, including a major action near Pyramid Lake, Nevada. Sergeant Tompkins was discharged in December 1860. Tompkins was commissioned second lieutenant in the Second U.S. Cavalry in March 1861. Tompkins's regiment fought in a skirmish at Fairfax Court House, Virginia, in 1861. Lieutenant Tompkins charged through the Confederate cavalry that opposed his company. Seizing a carbine from an enlisted man, he killed the captain commanding the Confederate cavalry. He was awarded the Medal of Honor for this act of individual heroism in 1893.[75]

Following the Fairfax Court House fight, Lieutenant Tompkins was appointed regimental quartermaster. He commanded the First Vermont Cavalry from April through September 1862 and was then reassigned to the Quartermaster Corps. Tompkins found time to marry Augusta Root Hobbie December 17, 1862, just days after the Battle of Fredericksburg.[76] Although Tompkins never held another command billet, he was appointed brevet brigadier general on December 12, 1864, confirmed by the Senate on February 12, 1865.[77] Postwar Tompkins was a career army officer, serving in the Quartermaster Corps. Tompkins retired with the rank of colonel, U.S. Army in 1894. He fell and fractured his leg at Atlantic City, New Jersey, in 1914. The fracture became infected and Colonel Tompkins died January 15, 1915, in Washington, D.C., from this injury.[78]

Lt. Col. David R. Clendenin, Commission Member

David R. Clendenin was born June 24, 1830, in Little Britain Township, Lancaster County, Pennsylvania.[79] His parents moved to Whiteside County, Illinois, on the Mississippi River prior to 1850.[80] He married Sophia Ford in Galesburg, Illinois, on February 15, 1855.[81] In 1860 he was living in Whiteside and teaching school.[82] In April 1861, he enlisted in the Washington Clay Guards of the District of Columbia Infantry. By September 1861, he was a captain in the Eighth Illinois Cavalry Regiment. The Eighth Illinois Cavalry, originally commanded by Col. John F. Farnsworth, was part of the Harpers Ferry garrison in September 1862 that escaped capture by fording the Potomac River and escaping detection while marching around the base of Maryland Heights. Farnsworth was made a brigadier general and Lt. Col. William Gamble became colonel and regimental commander. Clendenin was commissioned lieutenant colonel of the regiment in December 1862. When Col. William Gamble became brigade commander, Lieutenant Colonel Clendenin became commanding officer of the regiment for the duration of the war. In February 1865, he was made a brevet colonel. On July 11, 1865, Clendenin was appointed brevet brigadier general, U.S. Volunteers.[83] After his service on the Hunter Commission, Clendenin remained in the Regular Army, retiring in 1891 as a full colonel. Colonel Clendenin died March 5, 1895, in Oneida, Knox County, Illinois.

The Hunter Commission members were not chosen by Secretary of War Stanton and Judge Advocate General Holt because they were fair and impartial. Generals Hunter and Howe would have been excused for potential bias in favor of the government if they had been called as jurors in a civilian criminal trial because each officer was personally involved with the funeral of Abraham Lincoln. General Hunter was also a friend of President Lincoln and his bodyguard early in the war. General Harris's anti-Catholicism would have prevented his sitting as a juror in a civilian criminal prosecution, since John Surratt, Mary Surratt, and Dr. Samuel Mudd were active, practicing Catholics. Generals Wallace and Foster were prewar Republican office holders. Counsel for the defendants had no opportunity to challenge members of the Hunter Commission for cause, because the commission's rules of procedure did not provide for challenging any member.

Defense counsel did not invoke Article 71 of the Articles of War, which permitted the accused in a general court-martial to challenge members of the court-martial panel for cause,[84] assuming that the Articles of War supplied any guideline for the trial of the accomplices. Since Judge Advocate General Holt and his assistant prosecutors were formulating the rules of procedure for the Hunter Commission ad hoc, defense counsel had no opportunity to object to any of the commission members for cause. Secretary Stanton and Judge Advocate General Holt took no chances with the commission members. They were never officially instructed to find the defendants guilty, but each soldier understood his duty to hear the evidence and to convict the defendants.[85]

NOTES

1. Presidential Special Order dated May 1, 1865, reprinted in Benjamin Perley Poore, ed., *The Conspiracy Trial for the Murder of the President, and the Attempt to Overthrow the Government by the Assassination of Its Principal Officers, Edited with an Introduction by Ben. Perley Poore* (Boston: J. E. Tilton, 1865), 1:5.
2. The text of Adjutant General's Special Orders 211 and 216 are not included in the OR (U.S. War Department, *The War of the Rebellion: A Compilation of the Official Records of the Union and Confederate Armies* [also known as *The Official Record of the War of the Rebellion*, hereafter "OR"] [Washington, D.C.: Government Printing Office, 1880–1901]). Benn Pitman noted both orders in his official summary transcript of trial. See Benn Pitman, ed., *The Assassination of President Lincoln and the Trial of Conspirators David E. Herold, Mary E. Surratt, Lewis Payne, George A. Atzerodt, Edward Spangler, Samuel A. Mudd, Samuel Arnold, Michael O'Loughlin* (New York: Moore, Wilstach & Baldwin, 1865), 17. See also Gen. Ct. Martial Orders 356 citing Special Order 216, OR, series 2, vol. 8, 696.
3. Edward A. Miller, Jr., *Lincoln's Abolitionist General* (Columbia: University of South Carolina Press, 1997), 248.
4. See Pitman, *Assassination of President Lincoln*, 17 (Special Order 216), 21, for the rules first adopted by the commission. See appendix, 410–19, for General Order 100 apparently adopted by the commission as substantive criminal law for purposes of the trial.
5. Miller, *Lincoln's Abolitionist General*, 2–3. Andrew Hunter taught briefly at Princeton, then resigned to be appointed chaplain of the Washington Navy Yard. He died February 24, 1823, and is buried in the Congressional Cemetery in Washington, D.C. See Congressional Cemetery interments available at http://www.congressionalcemetery.org/search-interment-records.asp.
6. Miller, *Lincoln's Abolitionist General*, 2–3.
7. Miller, *Lincoln's Abolitionist General*, 4. Hunter was assigned to Company A, Fifth U.S. Infantry.
8. Miller, *Lincoln's Abolitionist General*, 6–7.
9. Miller, *Lincoln's Abolitionist General*, 8.
10. Miller, *Lincoln's Abolitionist General*, 9.
11. Map of Chicago 1830 in Weston A. Goodspeed and Daniel D. Healy, eds., *Cook County, Illinois: Being a General Survey of Cook County Including a Condensed History of Chicago and Special Accounts of Districts Outside the City Limits; From the Earliest Settlement to the Present* (Chicago: Goodspeed Historical Association, 1909), 1:92.
12. Ezra Warner, *Generals in Blue* (Baton Rouge: Louisiana State University Press, 1964), 243; Thomas J. Reed, "Black Davey: The Life of Maj. Gen. David Hunter" (unpublished manuscript, 1997).
13. See Warner, *Generals in Blue*, 244.
14. Biography of David Wallace, Biographical Directory of the United States Congress, http://bioguide.congress.gov/scripts/biodisplay.pl?index=W000076. Wallace was admitted to the bar in 1824, moved from Brookville to Covington, Indiana, then to Indianapolis. Wallace, a Whig, was lieutenant governor of Indiana in 1831–1837 and governor in 1837–1840, presiding over the collapse of the state's finances and its overambitious internal improvement program for canals and railroads. After leaving the governorship, Wallace settled in Indianapolis and continued the practice of law. He was elected as a Whig to the Twenty-Seventh Congress

March 4, 1841–March 3, 1843 and failed to win reelection. Late in life he was elected judge of the Marion County Common Pleas Court, a position he held until his death in 1859.

15. Obituary, *New York Times*, February 16, 1905.

16. Beth Swift, "Lew Wallace and the Elstons," *Dear Old Wabash* (blog), December 6, 2010, http://blogs.wabash.edu/dear-old-wabash/2010/12/06/lew-wallace-and-the-elstons/.

17. See Oran Perry, *Indiana in the Mexican War* (Indianapolis: Office of the Adjutant General, 1908), for the record of the First Indiana Volunteers; available at http://www.ingenweb.org/mexican/1STSTAFF.HTM.

18. See Perry, *Indiana in the Mexican War*, 100, 108, 123 (excerpts from newspapers). See also letter from Lt. Lew Wallace dated December 19, 1846, at 127–28. Wallace said in his autobiography that he made his way with another officer to a hacienda south of Monterey surrounded by Mexicans who faded away in the morning, allowing Wallace and his friend to proceed to Buena Vista the day after the battle. That was as close as Wallace came to participating in battle. Lewis Wallace, *Lew Wallace: An Autobiography* (New York: Harper & Bros., 1906), 1:161–63 (hereafter *Autobiography*).

19. Joanne Spragg, "Lewis Wallace (1827–1905)," http://www.thelatinlibrary.com/chron/civilwarnotes/wallace.html.

20. Spragg, "Lewis Wallace."

21. See Wallace, *Autobiography*, 1:263–72, 288–315.

22. Wallace, *Autobiography*, 1:342.

23. Warner, *Generals in Blue*, 356.

24. See Ulysses S. Grant, "The Battle of Shiloh," in *Battles and Leaders of the Civil War*, vol. 1, ed. Robert Underwood Johnson and Clarence Clough Buel (New York: Century, 1888; T. Y. Yoseloff, 1956), 476–77, and Lew Wallace, "The March of Lew Wallace's Division to Shiloh," in *Battles and Leaders of the Civil War*, vol. 1, ed. Robert Underwood Johnson and Clarence Clough Buel (New York: Century, 1888; T. Y. Yoseloff, 1956), 607–10.

25. Wallace, *Autobiography*, 2:589–90. Wallace received a telegram telling him to report to Governor Morton. Morton told Wallace to make speeches to aid recruiting. Morton produced Secretary Stanton's telegram relieving Wallace.

26. Wallace, *Autobiography*, 2:591–93. Wallace assumed command of the Sixty-Sixth Indiana and crossed the Ohio before the Battle of Richmond.

27. Wallace, *Autobiography*, 2:594–600.

28. Wallace, *Autobiography*, 2:604.

29. Wallace, *Autobiography*, 2:643.

30. Wallace, *Autobiography*, 2:657–59.

31. Wallace, *Autobiography*, 2:668.

32. See Wallace, *Autobiography*, 2:698–798, for Wallace's version of the events of the Battle of Monocacy. For a thorough account of the Battle of Monocacy and Wallace's role in delaying Early, see Benjamin Franklin Cooling, *Monocacy: The Battle That Saved Washington* (Shippensburg, Pa.: White Mane, 1997).

33. Wallace, *Autobiography*, 2:852–61. See also Douglas Linder, ed., "Biography of Lewis Wallace," Famous Trials Project, University of Missouri, Kansas City, http://law2.umkc.edu/faculty/projects/ftrials/Wirz/BIO3.HTM.

34. Wallace, *Autobiography*, 2:911–25.

35. See Amy Liston, "Ben Hur," *Humanities* 30, no. 6 (2009), http://www.neh.gov/humanities/2009/novemberdecember/feature/ben-hur.

36. Wallace, *Autobiography*, 2:847–51.

37. Lawrence G. Kautz, *August Valentine Kautz, USA: Biography of a Civil War General* (Jefferson, N.C.: McFarland, 2008), 6–7. Dr. Lawrence G. Kautz had access to the journal of August V. Kautz, currently in private hands and unavailable to researchers.

38. Kautz, *August Valentine Kautz*, 9–14.

39. Kautz, *August Valentine Kautz*, 17–18.

40. Kautz, *August Valentine Kautz*, 23–27.

41. See Kautz, *August Valentine Kautz*, 51–52. Dr. Kautz gives the name of August's Native American companion as Tenas Puss (later anglicized to Kitty Etta). She bore two children fathered by Kautz (*August Valentine Kautz*, 51–53). Tenas Puss and her children remained on

the Nisqually Indian Reservation when Kautz left the West Coast at the beginning of the Civil War.

42. The Second Ohio Cavalry Regiment was organized at Cleveland and Camp Dennison, Ohio, August to October 1861. The regiment served in Missouri and Kansas from January to December 1862, then went to Camp Chase to be remounted. Frederick H. Dyer, *A Compendium of the War of the Rebellion Compiled and Arranged from Official Records of the Federal and Confederate Armies Reports of the Adjutant Generals of the Several States, the Army Registers and Other Reliable Documents and Sources* (Des Moines, Iowa: By the author, 1908), 1473–74; republished by Internet Archives, https://archive.org/details/08697590.3359.emory.edu.

43. Kautz, *August Valentine Kautz*, 85–104.

44. Warner, *Generals in Blue* , 258.

45. Warner, *Generals in Blue* , 258.

46. Kautz, *August Valentine Kautz*, 251–56.

47. Warner, *Generals in Blue* , 239–40.

48. See Warner, *Generals in Blue*, 240.

49. Biography of James A. Ekin, New Albany, Indiana, Public Library, http://nafclibrary.org/wp-content/uploads/2013/08/Ekin-James-Adams.pdf .

50. Charles W. Smith, *The Life and Military Service of Brevet Major General Robert S. Foster* (Indianapolis: Indiana Historical Society, 1915) (hereafter *Life of Foster*), preface.

51. Smith, *Life of Foster* , 525.

52. Smith, *Life of Foster* , 526.

53. History of the 13th Indiana Infantry, http://www.nps.gov/civilwar/search-battle-units-detail.htm?battleUnitCode=UIN0013RI ; Dyer, *Compendium*, 1123.

54. OR, series 1, vol. 18, 274–80, Report of Maj. Gen. John J. Peck (Foster commended for gallantry at 279); 288–90, Report of Brig. Gen. Michael Corcoran (Foster commended); Smith, *Life of Foster* , 528.

55. History of the 13th Indiana Infantry, http://www.nps.gov/civilwar/search-battle-units-detail.htm?battleUnitCode=UIN0013RI.

56. *New York Times*, April 2, 1864, 3 (Senate confirmed promotion to rank from June 12, 1863); Warner, *Generals in Blue*, 158–59.

57. Warner, *Generals in Blue*, 158–59.

58. Smith, *Life of Foster* , 528.

59. Smith, *Life of Foster* , 529–30.

60. Smith, *Life of Foster* , 34–35. Foster was offered a commission as lieutenant colonel in the Regular Army by General Grant, later following up with a commission and appointment in 1866, which Foster refused to accept.

61. Warner, *Generals in Blue*, 158–59.

62. "Obit. Dr. Thomas Maley Harris," *West Virginia Medical Journal* 1 (1907): 237–38.

63. "Obit. Dr. Thomas Maley Harris," 237.

64. "Obit. Dr. Thomas Maley Harris," 237.

65. Theodore F. Lang, *Loyal West Virginia from 1861 to 1865 with an Introductory Chapter on the Status of Virginia for Thirty Years Prior to the War* (Baltimore: Deutsch, 1895); republished by Internet Archive, http://www.archive.org/stream/loyalwestvirgin00langgoog/loyalwestvirgin00langgoog_djvu.txt.

66. H. E. Matheny, *Major General Thomas Maley Harris: A Member of the Military Commission That Tried the President Abraham Lincoln Assassination Conspirators* (Parsons, W.V.: McClain, 1963).

67. Matheny, *Major General Thomas Maley Harris*, 54. The brigade was at first under the command of Brig. Gen. Benjamin S. Roberts, a West Point graduate who had been the New York state geologist before the war. Roberts did not remain in command long. See Warner, *Generals in Blue*, 405–6. He was replaced by Brig. Gen. William W. Averell in May 1863 (Dyer, *Compendium*, 343).

68. Matheny, *Major General Thomas Maley Harris*, 69–74.

69. Matheny, *Major General Thomas Maley Harris*, 88–89.

70. Matheny, *Major General Thomas Maley Harris*, 94–95.

71. Warner, *Generals in Blue*, 209–10.

72. Thomas M. Harris, *Assassination of Lincoln: A History of the Great Conspiracy; Trial of the Conspirators by a Military Commission and a Review of the Trial of John H. Surratt* (Boston: American Citizen, 1892).

73. See Thomas M. Harris, *Rome's Responsibility for the Assassination of Abraham Lincoln* (Pittsburgh: Williams, 1897).

74. Warner, *Generals in Blue*, 210.

75. "Tompkins, Charles H.," Congressional Medal of Honor Society, http://www.cmohs.org/recipient-detail/1385/tompkins-charles-h.php.

76. "Tompkins," Congressional Medal of Honor Society.

77. John H. Eicher and David J. Eicher, *Civil War High Commands* (Palo Alto, Calif.: Stanford University Press, 2001), 532.

78. Eicher and Eicher, *Civil War High Commands*, 532.

79. Obit. David Clendenin, *Galesburg Republican-Register*, March 1895; republished in *Rich Hanson's Civil War Stories* (blog), August 31, 2013, http://monmouthrlhcw.blogspot.com/2013/08/general-david-ramsey-clendenin.html.

80. U.S. Census 1850, Whiteside, Cook Co., Ill., HH 64 FAM 64.

81. Illinois Marriage License David Clendenin to Sophia Ford, Knox County Court Record, Film #1404972, 1411909–1411921, and 1412045–1412060.

82. U.S. Census 1860, Lyndon, Whiteside, Cook Co., Ill., p. 874 HH 1821 FAM 1799.

83. "Obit. David Ramsey Clendenin," in *Memorials of Deceased Companions of the Commandery of the State of Illinois Military Order of the Loyal Legion of the United States from July 1, 1901 to December 31, 1911*, vol. 2 (Chicago: Military Order of the Loyal Legion of the United States, 1912), 224–27.

84. Article 71 reads as follows: "When a member shall be challenged by a prisoner, he must state his cause of challenge, of which the court shall, after due deliberation, determine the relevancy or validity, and decide accordingly; and no challenge to more than one member at a time, shall be received by the court." *Articles of War, Military Laws and Regulations for the Army of the United States* (Washington, D.C.: U.S. Adjutant General's Office, 1817), 19.

85. General Thomas M. Harris, the only Hunter Commission member to write extensively about the commission, stated what the War Department and the president feared: a civilian trial with a verdict of not guilty or a hung jury. According to Harris, "The first question that presented itself to the government in regard to these prisoners was, as to what kind of a trial should be given them, whether civil or military? The civil courts were open in the District of Columbia at the time, and had been all through the war. There was no question that a form of trial could be had in the civil courts; but there was at the same time as little question that, under existing circumstances, such a trial would only result in a miscarriage of justice. The great crime had been committed during the existence of a state of war, and the courts were only able to carry on their functions under the protection of the arms of the government." (Harris, *Assassination of Lincoln*, 82.)

Chapter Three

The Lawyers

> Because our Chief, so venerated and beloved (and no one venerated and love him more than I), has fallen by the hand of a ruthless assassin, it ought not to follow that the Constitution and law should be violated in punishing men suspected of having compassed his death, or that men not legally found guilty should be sacrificed in vengeance as victims generally because of the crime. There may be a lurking feeling among men which tends to this harshness of retribution, regardless of the innocence of those on whom vengeance may fall.—Plea to the Jurisdiction by Gen. Thomas Ewing, June 23, 1865

The three government prosecutors were accomplished lawyers and radicals. Brigadier General Joseph Holt, the U.S. judge advocate general, was a long-time public servant and gifted lawyer who had been President Buchanan's patent commissioner and attorney general. Colonel John A. Bingham, a long-time member of Congress, reelected to Congress for his district in Ohio in the fall of 1864, would be one of the leaders in drafting the Fourteenth Amendment to the Constitution. Lieutenant Colonel Henry L. Burnett, who graduated from Ohio State University Law School just before the war, would become a highly successful New York attorney after the Hunter Commission trial. Burnett was the lead prosecutor of the Northwest Conspiracy defendants tried by military commission in Indianapolis earlier in 1865, all of whom were sentenced to death.[1]

Individual defense counsel for the alleged accomplices were also highly qualified and with two exceptions, experienced trial lawyers. William E. Doster, representing George Atzerodt and Lewis Powell, was a Pennsylvania lawyer who had been the provost marshal for the District of Columbia in the latter part of the war. Brigadier General Thomas M. Ewing and Frederick Stone were cocounsel for Dr. Mudd. Thomas Ewing was one of the three Ewing brothers who were Maj. Gen. William T. Sherman's brothers-in-law.

Prior to the war he had been the first chief justice of the Kansas Supreme Court. He would have a postwar career as a major lawyer in Ohio and New York. Both were experienced trial lawyers. General Ewing also represented Edman Spangler. Stone also represented David Herold. Stone would be elected to Congress and would finish his career as a judge on the Maryland Court of Appeals. Walter S. Cox, counsel for Samuel Arnold and Michael O'Loughlen, was a longtime Washington trial lawyer who would be appointed a U.S. District Court judge and would preside at the trial of Charles J. Guiteau for the assassination of President James Garfield. Cox would later serve as founding dean of George Washington Law School. The lead counsel for Mrs. Surratt, Senator Reverdy Johnson, was a former U.S. attorney general and Maryland state judge. Johnson had a reputation for outstanding courtroom conduct, but he left the trial work to his inexperienced subordinates Frederick Aiken and John W. Clampitt after his loyalty to the Union was challenged by commission member Brig. Gen. Thomas Harris. The legend of the incompetence of defense counsel must be reevaluated.

THE PROSECUTORS

Brig. Gen. Joseph Holt, Judge Advocate General, U.S. Army

Joseph Holt was a native of Breckinridge County, Kentucky, born January 6, 1807.[2] His family were well-off planters and could afford to send Holt to Saint Joseph's College, Bardstown, Kentucky, and Centre College, Danville, Kentucky.[3] Holt was admitted to the Kentucky bar in 1829 and started his law practice in Elizabethtown. In 1832, Holt moved to Louisville and married Mary Harrison on April 24, 1839, in Bardstown, Kentucky.[4] Holt was commonwealth's attorney from 1833 to 1835 and also acted as assistant editor of the *Louisville Advertiser*.[5] Holt decided to move to Mississippi, setting up a law practice in Port Gibson, riding circuit to include Natchez and Vicksburg. Holt and his wife contracted tuberculosis: Holt recovered, but his wife died from the disease in 1846.[6] He left Mississippi for Kentucky to recuperate.[7] Holt married Margaret Wickliffe in March 1850 in Kentucky. In 1857, Holt was appointed commissioner of patents by President Buchanan, and served until 1859 when he was appointed postmaster general.[8] The postmaster general had enormous power relating to the appointment of postmasters in thousands of post offices throughout the United States. Holt's accomplishments as postmaster general included the firing of corrupt Philadelphia postmaster Gideon Westcott. Holt's regime was marked by fairness and impartiality in a cabinet post usually considered to be a political plum for the party in power.[9] While serving as postmaster general, Holt's second wife fell into a chronic illness that took her life.[10] He did not remarry. In January

1861, Holt was appointed secretary of war for the two remaining months of Buchanan's presidency.[11]

Holt was commissioned colonel and judge advocate general of the army in 1862[12] and in 1864 was appointed judge advocate general of the army with rank of brigadier general. Holt was the lead prosecutor in the court-martial of Maj. Gen. Fitz John Porter for failure to obey a lawful order during the Second Battle of Manassas.[13] Holt declined President Lincoln's offer of a cabinet appointment to the secretaryship of the Department of the Interior and to attorney general in 1865. Following the trial of the Lincoln assassination accomplices, Holt was a behind-the-scenes presence in the 1867 trial of John Surratt in district court in Washington. Holt still believed in the truth of evidence given by perjurer Sanford Conover and his colleagues who gave testimony implicating the Confederate president and secretary of war, as well as Confederate commissioners Jacob Thompson and Clement Clay in the Lincoln murder plot.[14] Holt served as judge advocate general until he retired on December 1, 1875. He had a quiet retirement and died in Washington on August 1, 1894. He is buried in the Holt Family Cemetery in Stephensport, Kentucky.[15]

Hon. John A. Bingham, Esq., Special Assistant

John Armor Bingham was born in Mercer, Pennsylvania, January 21, 1815. He had a grammar school education in Pennsylvania. His family moved to Cadiz, Ohio, in 1827.[16] John Bingham was an apprentice printer for two years before enrolling in Franklin College and entering the profession of law in 1840.[17] Bingham set up his practice in Cadiz and later in New Philadelphia, Ohio, and also was elected prosecuting attorney for Tuscarawas County.[18] He married his first cousin Amanda Bingham in 1844.[19] Bingham was elected to Congress for the Twenty-First District of Ohio in 1854 as a Whig and after 1856 as a Republican. He served continuously until 1861 when he lost his bid for a fourth term. The president appointed him judge advocate of the army with rank of major in 1862. He was also appointed solicitor of the U.S. Court of Claims. Bingham was elected again in a new district, the Sixteenth, in 1864, taking his seat in January 1865.[20] He served until 1873. Bingham was asked to become one of the prosecutors in May 1865.

In 1866, Congressman Bingham was a member of the Joint Committee on Reconstruction considering ways and means to deal with the four million newly freed African Americans. Bingham went to work on a constitutional amendment that would guarantee that no state would disenfranchise African Americans and relegate them to the status of slaves again. His final draft of the Fourteenth Amendment passed both houses and became law after ratification by two-thirds of the states.[21] Bingham's amendment made a radical change in the organic law of the United States. All U.S. citizens became citizens of the United States first and state citizens second. The amendment included an enforcement provision allowing Congress to pass legislation to prevent any state from making or enforcing "any law which shall abridge the privileges or immunities of citizens of the United States; nor shall any State deprive any person of life, liberty, or property without due process of law, nor deny to any person within its jurisdiction the equal protection of the laws."[22] After producing the Fourteenth Amendment, Congressman Bingham served as chair of the Committee on Claims. Bingham and Thaddeus Stevens managed the impeachment of President Andrew Johnson for high crimes and misdemeanors in office, for example, violating the Tenure of Office Act by attempting to fire Secretary of War Edwin M. Stanton. Bingham was not reelected in 1872. President Grant appointed Bingham U.S. ambassador to Japan, a post he held until 1885. Bingham died March 19, 1900, in Cadiz, Ohio. He was interred in Union Cemetery in Cadiz.[23]

Colonel Henry L. Burnett, Assistant Judge Advocate

Henry L. Burnett was born in Youngstown, Ohio, December 26, 1838. He was a lineal descendant of William Burnett, an eighteenth-century royal governor of New York and New Jersey. Burnett's grandfather was one of the financiers of the American Revolution. He was also an Ohio pioneer settling in the Western Reserve prior to 1800.[24] Henry Burnett left home at age fifteen to acquire an education on his own, despite his father's opposition. Burnett enrolled in Chester Academy and worked his way through the academy by doing odd jobs on campus. Burnett moved on to Hiram Institute and Ohio State University Law School, graduating in 1859.[25] Two years later, Burnett was commissioned lieutenant in the Second Ohio Cavalry.[26] Burnett saw action in the western theater and was promoted to major when a horse trampled him and injured him severely. After recovering, he was transferred to the judge advocate general's Corps of the Department of the Ohio.[27] Burnett was lead prosecutor in the trial of the Northwest Conspirators in Indianapolis in early 1865, obtaining convictions and death sentences for Lambdin Milligan and his coconspirators.[28] Secretary Stanton called Burnett to Washington to form part of the prosecutorial team for the trial of Booth's alleged accomplices.

Postwar Burnett moved to Buffalo, New York, serving as counsel to the Buffalo & Erie Railroad.[29] Burnett's first wife, Kitty, died shortly after the Hunter Commission trial. He then married Sarah Lansing in 1869.[30] She died in 1877. Burnett then moved to New York City, leaving his children with the Lansing family. Burnett married Agnes Suffren Tailer in 1881. In 1898, President McKinley appointed Burnett U.S. attorney for the Southern District of New York. President Theodore Roosevelt reappointed Burnett in 1903.

Burnett established a harness racing farm in Goshen, New York, after his term as U.S. attorney expired. He died in Goshen on January 4, 1916. He is buried in Slate Hill Cemetery, Goshen, New York.[31]

DEFENSE COUNSEL

Samuel Arnold, Michael O'Loughlen and Mary Surratt had engaged counsel before the trial started. Their attorneys had no opportunity to prepare, find witnesses, and sort out statements. In 1865 defendants had no right to discover exculpatory evidence held by the United States.

Senator Reverdy Johnson, Defense Counsel for Mary Surratt

Reverdy Johnson was born May 21, 1796, in Annapolis, Maryland.[32] John Johnson, his father, was an attorney who served in both houses of the Maryland General Assembly, was attorney general of Maryland from 1806 to 1811, a judge of the Maryland Court of Appeals from 1811 to 1821, and Maryland's chancellor from 1821 to 1824.[33] Reverdy Johnson graduated from St. John's College, Annapolis, in 1812, read for the law in his father's office, and was admitted to the bar in 1815. He began law practice in Upper Marlborough, Prince George's County.[34] Johnson joined the Baltimore law firm of Luther Martin in 1817. William Pinkney and Roger Brooke Taney were also associated with Martin's law firm. Johnson married Mary Mackall Bowie in 1819.[35] Reverdy Johnson coedited the reporter for the Maryland Court of Appeals from 1820 to 1827. Johnson ran for and was elected state senator in 1820 and on completing his term returned to private practice in 1829.[36] Johnson and Thomas Harris produced seven volumes containing the opinions of the Maryland Court of Appeals from 1800 through 1826 as official reporters for the court.[37] An 1842 accident in which Johnson lost vision in his left eye from a pistol shot ricochet left him with impaired vision for the rest of his life.[38] Johnson, a Whig, was elected to the U.S. Senate in 1844.[39] In March 1849, President Zachary Taylor nominated him for attorney general of the United States and he served for a little more than a year as the nation's premier lawyer.[40] Johnson returned to private practice in 1850 in time to be counsel to one of the parties in the Wheeling Bridge case, opposing Edwin Stanton.[41] Johnson and Stanton clashed again in the McCormick Reaper patent case in 1856. Stanton had Abraham Lincoln as cocounsel in this matter.[42] When the Whig Party collapsed, Johnson became a Democrat, supporting Stephen A. Douglas for the 1860 presidential nomination.[43]

In 1862, President Lincoln asked Johnson to revise the decisions made by Maj. Gen. Benjamin F. Butler during his occupation of New Orleans with respect to foreign governments.[44] While serving the president, Johnson was reelected to the U.S. Senate, taking his seat in March 1863.[45] Senator Johnson was a member of the Rules Committee during the impeachment trial of President Andrew Johnson. Johnson voted against impeachment and also produced a pamphlet supporting the president's innocence on all charges of high crimes and misdemeanors.[46] President Andrew Johnson appointed Senator Johnson U.S. ambassador to Great Britain in 1869. He negotiated a treaty with the Crown that provided a mechanism for the settlement of Anglo-American disputes arising out of the Civil War. The Senate refused to ratify the treaty. When Ulysses S. Grant took office in March 1869, Johnson resigned his ambassadorship and returned to private law practice in Baltimore. The United States retained Johnson as special prosecutor in the Ku Klux Klan cases. Senator Johnson died February 10, 1876, at his home in Annapolis.[47]

Frederick A. Aiken, Associate Defense Counsel for Mary Surratt[48]

Frederick Augustus Aiken was born in Shrewsbury, Massachusetts, September 20, 1837.[49] His family moved to Hardwick, Vermont, when he was a small child. Aiken attended Middlebury College but did not graduate. He took the editorship of the *Burlington (Vermont) Sentinel* in 1857. On June 1, 1857, Aiken married Sarah Weston.[50] Aiken studied for the law and was admitted to the Vermont bar in 1859.[51]

Aiken took the position of secretary to the Democratic National Committee in 1859. A supporter of Vice President John C. Breckinridge's candidacy for president in 1860, Aiken offered his services to Confederate president Jefferson Davis as a war correspondent, but Davis never replied to Aiken's letters.[52] Aiken then sought a commission in the Union Army. In 1861, he was allegedly commissioned a captain in a New York cavalry regiment being raised by Col. James B. Swain.[53] Captain Aiken appears in two letters in the *Official Record of the War of the Rebellion* as a volunteer aid to Brig. Gen. William F. Smith. He was not carried on the rolls of any Union regiment and was back in Washington by 1863, working for the Democratic Party. Aiken's obituary claims that he was promoted to colonel and wounded in action, but there is no evidence to support these assertions.[54] Aiken gave up the practice of law in 1868 and returned to journalism, taking a position as editor of the *Washington Sunday Gazette* in 1869. Two years later he was the city editor of the *Washington Chronicle*, followed by a position as news and dramatic editor of the *Washington National Republican*. In 1877, recovering from a serious illness, he took over as city editor of the newly founded *Washington Post*. Aiken died in 1878, allegedly from the effects of his war wounds.[55]

John W. Clampitt, Associate Defense Counsel for Mary Surratt[56]

John Clampitt, a native of the District of Columbia, was born in April 1839. He attended Columbian College, Washington, D.C., for at least two years before the Civil War.[57] He enlisted in Company A, Fourth District of Columbia Infantry, a ninety-day regiment, in 1861.[58] His battalion saw no action and was discharged in August 1861. In 1865, he was an attorney, living at home in Washington.[59] Postwar Clampitt went to work for the U.S. Postal Service and spent considerable time in Utah. He published a book called *Echoes from the Rocky Mountains* in 1889 based on his experiences in the Old West.[60] Clampitt lived in Deerfield, Lake County, Illinois, from 1880 through 1900.[61] He was a special examiner for Civil War pension applications and had a law office in downtown Chicago.[62] Clampitt published an article in 1880 in the *North American Review* later issued in book form titled "The Trial of Mary Surratt" in which he condemned the Hunter Commission as an unconstitutionally constituted judicial body. His account of the assassination and the trial contains a number of factual errors. Clampitt died in 1906 in Indianapolis, Marion County, Indiana.[63]

William E. Doster, Defense Counsel for George Atzerodt and Lewis Powell[64]

William E. Doster was a native of Bethlehem, Pennsylvania, born January 8, 1838. Doster's father owned the Moravian Woolen Mills at Bethlehem. William Doster attended Yale College then switched to Harvard Law School, graduating in 1859. Doster studied briefly at Heidelberg before returning to Northampton County. He was apprenticed to ex-governor Andrew Reeder then moved to Philadelphia. Doster recruited a cavalry company that eventually became infantry. He then raised a second cavalry company and was elected captain; Doster's unit became part of the Fourth Pennsylvania Cavalry. Doster was quickly promoted to major and served as the provost marshal for the military government of the District of Columbia until the spring of 1863, when he rejoined the Fourth Cavalry in time to fight in the Battles of Chancellorsville and Gettysburg. A bad case of malaria forced Doster out of active duty with his regiment in 1864, and he went to Washington as provost marshal until the end of the war in 1865. Doster had significant legal experience and a good legal education when he was appointed to defend George Atzerodt and Lewis Powell. He raised the issue of Powell's mental state at the time of his attack on Secretary Seward, suggesting that Powell had diminished mental capacity. Postwar, Doster came back to Northampton County, opened a law practice, and accepted appointment as a register in bankruptcy under the wartime Bankruptcy Act. Doster died July 2, 1919, the last surviving member of the Booth accomplices' legal defense group.[65]

Brig. Gen. Thomas Ewing, Defense Counsel for Dr. Samuel Mudd and Edman Spangler

Thomas Ewing, born August 7, 1829, was one of Maj. Gen. William T. Sherman's three brothers-in-law. Sherman was raised by the Ewings after his father's death. The Ewings were Roman Catholics. Tom Ewing grew up in Lancaster, Ohio.[66] He attended Brown College in Providence, Rhode Island, but left before graduation to accept appointment as President Zachary Taylor's private secretary.[67] After President Taylor's death, Ewing read for the law and was admitted to the bar in 1852. Ewing opened a law office in Cincinnati but, shortly after marrying Ellen Cox in 1856, left Ohio for Leavenworth, Kansas.[68] Ewing formed a law partnership with his brother Hugh Boyle Ewing and brother-in-law William T. Sherman. Thomas Ewing was a delegate to the 1858 Leavenworth Constitutional Convention and to the 1860 Peace Convention. In 1861, he was elected chief justice of Kansas.[69] Chief Justice Ewing resigned in 1862 to become colonel of the Eleventh Kansas Volunteers.[70] The Eleventh Kansas saw action at Fort Wayne, Cane Hill, and Prairie Grove in 1862–1863. In March 1863, he became the second member of his family to receive a brigadier general's commission. His older brother Hugh Ewing was commissioned brigadier general of volunteers in November 1862.[71]

In August 1863 General Ewing, department commander, issued General Order 11, clearing all residents from three Missouri counties bordering Kansas in order to suppress Confederate guerilla attacks on Kansans.[72] Western artist George Caleb Bingham painted the exodus in a famous painting, *Martial Law General Order 11*, that hangs in the Missouri State Historical Society.[73] General Ewing delayed Maj. Gen. Sterling Price's September 1864 invasion of Missouri by holding Fort Davidson, Pilot Knob, Missouri, outnumbered five to one by Price's army. General Ewing brought off his one thousand Union soldiers from Pilot Knob without being detected.[74] He was brevetted major general of volunteers in 1865 for wartime services. General Ewing resumed law practice in Washington, D.C., from 1865 to 1871, then returned to Lancaster, Ohio, opening a law office in his hometown. General Ewing, a Greenback Democrat, was elected to two terms in the U.S. House of Representatives but lost the 1878 governor's election to Democrat Richard Bishop. General Ewing relocated to New York City after finishing his second term in Congress. He continued to practice law until his death in January 1896.[75]

Frederick Stone, Counsel for David Herold and Associate Counsel for Dr. Samuel Mudd

Frederick Stone, born February 7, 1820, in Charles County, Maryland, was an 1839 graduate of St. John's College, Annapolis, Maryland.[76] Stone read for the law and was admitted to the bar in 1841. Stone's great-grandfather Thomas Stone was a Maryland Continental congressman and a signer of the Declaration of Independence. He married Maria Louisa Stonestreet in 1852 and lived on a plantation in Charles County, Maryland, near Port Tobacco.[77] By 1865 he had more than twenty years' experience as an attorney and had the reputation of being the most able attorney in Charles County.[78] Stone had been appointed commissioner to revise Maryland's rules of pleading and practice in 1852. In 1864, he was elected to the Maryland House of Delegates representing Charles County. Stone agreed to represent David Herold after Herold's mother and sisters begged him to take the case. Stone also assisted Thomas Ewing with the defense of Samuel Mudd. Stone served two terms in the U.S. House of Representatives from 1867 to 1871. Ten years later Stone was appointed to the Maryland Court of Appeals, serving until 1891. Frederick Stone died October 17, 1899, in La Plata, Charles County, Maryland.[79]

Walter S. Cox, Counsel for Michael O'Loughlen and Samuel Arnold[80]

Walter S. Cox, born October 26, 1826, in Georgetown, Washington, D.C., graduated from Georgetown College in 1843. He received his master of arts from Georgetown in 1844. Cox then attended Harvard Law School, receiving an LL.B. from Harvard in 1847. Cox had his own Washington law office from 1848 to 1879. He held a variety of public offices during this time: recorder for the City of Georgetown, alderman for Georgetown, and auditor for the District of Columbia Supreme Court. Samuel Arnold and Michael O'Loughlen retained him as counsel shortly before the first day of the Hunter Commission trial. Cox was highly qualified to present the best case for both men. Cox became a part-time law professor for Columbia University Law School, the ancestor of George Washington University Law School in 1874. In 1879, President Hayes appointed Cox to the federal bench. Judge Cox presided at the trial of Charles J. Guiteau, the assassin who murdered President James Garfield in the Washington, D.C., railroad station in 1881. Cox served as U.S. district judge for the District of Columbia from 1879 to 1899. Following his retirement from the bench, Judge Cox became the first dean of George Washington University Law School.[81] Judge Cox died in 1902. He is buried in Oak Hill Cemetery, Washington, D.C.[82]

THE STRATEGIES AND TACTICS OF THE CONTESTING SIDES

The Prosecution's Theory of the Case

Joseph Holt, John A. Bingham, and Henry Burnett had a single unified strategy during the trial: establish that John Wilkes Booth and the defendants had carried out the attacks on Lincoln and Seward and attempts on the lives of Johnson and Ulysses S. Grant under orders from or with support from Confederate president Jefferson Davis and the Confederate commissioners in Canada, Clement C. Clay and Jacob Thompson and their agents. If the prosecution established that Booth's group was sponsored by the Confederate government, then the unindicted coconspirators—Davis, Clay, Thompson, et al.—would be morally and politically responsible for the death of President Lincoln and the attack on Secretary Seward. Public opinion in the North would be galvanized behind the most severe and repressive measures designed to destroy the power base for the Southern aristocrats who were deemed responsible for starting the war. The first two trial days were devoted to taking evidence in secret against Davis and the other Confederate high command members involved in organizing and funding Booth's conspiracy. The prosecution had three major witnesses, Sanford Conover, James B. Merritt, and Richard Montgomery, who told the Hunter Commission that they were witnesses to conversations between Booth, Clay, and Thompson in Montreal in the fall of 1864. One of those conversations included a statement from Thompson that Richmond approved of Booth's plan to assassinate President Lincoln.[83] Conover gave damaging testimony about Booth's meetings with Clay, Thompson, and their secretary William C. Cleary in Montreal. Merritt, a physician, also swore to statements from Clay and Thompson approving Booth's plot to murder President Lincoln in the fall of 1864.

Once the prosecution proved the general existence of a conspiracy involving high-ranking Confederate government officials, the cases again the individuals indicted for treason and conspiracy were relatively easy to make. Any act committed by any of the indicted conspirators would be attributed to all, making every member guilty of murder, attempted murder, and treason. The prosecution had to prove that each indicted individual was a member of the conspiracy. Since the prosecution did not have to establish guilt beyond a reasonable doubt and could convict and sentence each individual by two-thirds majority vote of the commissioners, conviction of the indicted individuals would be simple and straightforward.[84] Proving that Atzerodt, Herold, and Powell were Booth's accomplices was based on their own confessions. It would be more difficult to prove that Arnold and O'Loughlen were accomplices, but Arnold's letter to Booth and eyewitness testimony placing O'Loughlen in Washington on April 14 at a soirée at Secretary Stanton's feting General Grant the night before would suffice. The prosecution could show that Mrs. Surratt, Dr. Mudd, and Edman Spangler aided and abetted Booth's plot. The commission would have to make the inferential leap from aiding and abetting to conspiracy membership for these people. Proving that Mrs. Surratt knowingly aided and abetted would be very difficult and would be based almost entirely on circumstantial evidence from Mrs. Surratt's boarder Louis Weichmann and John Lloyd, the proprietor of the Surratt tavern. The evidence against Dr. Mudd was also tenuous, since it would depend on proof that he met with Booth several times before April 14, and sheltered Booth on April 15 knowing that he had murdered the president. The prosecution had no direct evidence that Mudd knew he was helping a felon on April 15. There was no proof that Edman Spangler had ever been part of the conspiracy, and the prosecution would have to be content with proving that Spangler aided and abetted Booth's escape by arranging for Joseph Burrows to hold his horse and his remark to Jake Ritterspaugh not to tell the authorities that the man who murdered Lincoln was John Wilkes Booth.

Defense Theories

There was no single defense strategy for the defense counsel to follow. David Herold had no credible affirmative defense to his involvement with Booth. George Atzerodt's counsel could argue that Atzerodt never made an attempt to kill Vice President Johnson, but his confession would show his knowing participation in the murder plot. Lewis Powell's strange behavior could raise the issue of moral insanity, for example, not guilty by reason of insanity, the plea that saved Congressman Daniel Sickles's life in 1859. William Doster could not find an expert who would testify that Powell was morally insane, but he had eyewitness evidence that Powell was indeed a very strange man. It was his only hope to mitigate a death sentence.

Samuel Arnold's counsel could argue that his client withdrew from the conspiracy before April 14 because he had taken a government job at Fortress Monroe before that date, even though the "Sam" letter seemed to indicate that Arnold had not broken off his relationship with Booth before April 14. O'Loughlen had an alibi of sorts: he could produce his friends who would swear that on the night of April 14, he was celebrating with them and not hunting down General Grant for Booth.

Counsel for Mrs. Surratt had a sound defense strategy: establish by favorable character witnesses that Mrs. Surratt was not the kind of person to join a murder conspiracy. Mrs. Surratt's lawyers would have to do their best to discredit Louis Weichmann and John Lloyd to offset their damaging evidence. Sentiment among male commissioners would favor a case showing that she may have been the unwitting tool of Booth who sent her to Surrattsville with his binoculars and a message to John Lloyd. Dr. Mudd's counsel had a solid defense line: Mudd never admitting knowing that Booth had murdered the president until the afternoon of April 15 when Booth and Herold were departing from his house for the passage across Zekiah Swamp. Since he was obliged to care for anyone who was injured, the fact that Mudd set Booth's fracture, splinted it, and kept him overnight to rest would not show that Mudd was part of Booth's conspiracy. Defense counsel would have to discredit prosecution witness Daniel Thomas, who testified to Mudd's alleged statements showing his knowledge of the plot to murder Lincoln made well before April 14. Thomas was mentally ill, and the defense could put on evidence showing that he was not worthy of belief. Defense counsel could also muster several defense character witnesses who would testify that Mudd was a person of general good moral character, one unlikely to be involved in a murder plot.

There was no credible evidence against Edman Spangler other than Ritterspaugh's relation of Spangler's hearsay remark and the admitted fact that Booth asked Spangler to hold his horse outside Ford's Theatre on the night of April 14. Since the commission was not bound by the reasonable doubt rule, it could convict on the theory it was possible that Spangler knowingly aided and abetted Booth's escape. His counsel did his best to argue the point that the case against Spangler was so weak that he would not have been indicted in a civilian court.[85]

One may ask why defense counsel had no unified strategy to offset the prosecution's case. None of the defense counsel left any letters, diaries, or other documents explaining their strategy for the defense raised for their clients. All defense counsel concurred in challenging the jurisdiction of the Hunter Commission. The challenges were presented by Senator Johnson and General Ewing and were adopted by the other defendants. The civilian courts in Washington, D.C., were open for business, and no credible threat of Confederate invasion existed to give any color to "necessity" as the basis for trying the accomplices by military commission. Senator Reverdy Johnson prepared a plea to the jurisdiction to be argued to the commission.[86] In the confusion and turmoil surrounding retention of counsel just before and during the commission sessions, Johnson did not argue that the Habeas Corpus Act of 1863 compelled the secretary of war to turn over the accomplices to the civilian courts for indictment and trial. Neither Johnson nor any of the very able defense lawyers considered filing a writ of habeas corpus to test the confinement of the accomplices by the military. Since President Lincoln had suspended the writ of habeas corpus for the District of Columbia in 1862, defense counsel may have thought the filing of that writ, or the rarely used writ of error coram nobis was a useless act. Senator Johnson's plea to the jurisdiction was similar to the arguments made on behalf of Northwest Conspiracy member Lambdin Milligan, whose habeas corpus petition was pending before the Circuit Court in Indianapolis at the time Johnson made his argument.

General Thomas Ewing also made an argument addressing the jurisdiction of the Hunter Commission. His argument tracked that of Senator Johnson.[87] Since the Hunter Commission was not likely to hold that it had no jurisdiction to try Booth's alleged accomplices, the pleas to the jurisdiction must have been intended to "make a record" that would support a writ of habeas corpus in the District Court for the District of Columbia. What is surprising is the failure on the part of defense counsel to follow up on the plea to the jurisdiction with a writ of habeas corpus to test the lawfulness of the confinement of the alleged accomplices and the jurisdiction of the Hunter Commission.

The prosecutors were a highly qualified team that was accustomed to work together, and throughout the trial all three prosecutors pursued the proof that Booth and his accomplices were part of a grand conspiracy engineered by Jefferson Davis and his Canadian henchmen to destabilize the Union. All three worked to present a coherent account of the grand conspiracy that allowed them to drag in irrelevant atrocity evidence arguably part of the grand conspiracy. Since the prosecutors also made up the ground rules for trial as the proceedings rambled on, they exerted tightfisted control over the admission of evidence, supported by the favorable rulings of General Hunter.

The defendants had no coordinated plan for defense. This was a weakness inherent in the last-minute call for defense counsel for Atzerodt, Spangler, and Powell, and in the potential defenses that could have been raised, for example, moral insanity for Powell. Individually, Reverdy Johnson, Thomas Ewing, and Walter Cox were as competent as the prosecutors. William E. Doster proved to be a very competent attorney as did Frederick Stone. Frederick Aiken and John W. Clampitt were inexperienced lawyers who had never tried a murder case. Counsel for each defendant concentrated on a defense for their client, ignoring any common defense strategy, other than Johnson's and Ewing's pleas to the jurisdiction. Fortunately, defense counsel did not engage in recrimination and finger-pointing accusations against the defendants whom counsel were not representing. Lack of a sound common strategy probably did not hurt the alleged accomplices' potential case for acquittal. The Hunter Commission members knew that they were expected to bring in a guilty verdict against all the defendants.[88]

NOTES

1. Much information from the trials, like the plea to the jurisdiction by Gen. Thomas Ewing, is taken from the transcript of proceedings prepared by Ben Perley Poore. See Ben Perley Poore, ed., *The Conspiracy Trial for the Murder of the President, and the Attempt to Overthrow the Government by the Assassination of Its Principal Officers, Edited with an Introduction by Ben. Perley Poore*, vol. 1 (Boston: J. E. Tilton, 1865); also available at http://www.surrattmuseum.org/ben-perley-poore-the-conspiracy-trial-tr. Poore, *Conspiracy Trial*, 1:6.

2. Elizabeth Leonard, *Lincoln's Forgotten Ally: Judge Advocate General Joseph Holt* (Chapel Hill: University of North Carolina Press, 2011), 7.
3. Leonard, *Lincoln's Forgotten Ally*, 9–11.
4. Leonard, *Lincoln's Forgotten Ally*, 9–11.
5. Ezra Warner, *Generals in Blue* (Baton Rouge: Louisiana State University Press, 1964), 232.
6. Warner, *Generals in Blue*, 232.
7. See Holt biography at http://www.mrlincolnswhitehouse.org/inside.asp?ID=135&subjectID=2.
8. Leonard, *Lincoln's Forgotten Ally*, 81–82, 94–97.
9. Leonard, *Lincoln's Forgotten Ally*, 94–95, 98–99.
10. Leonard, *Lincoln's Forgotten Ally*, 107.
11. Leonard, *Lincoln's Forgotten Ally*, 114–17.
12. Leonard, *Lincoln's Forgotten Ally*, 158.
13. Leonard, *Lincoln's Forgotten Ally*, 167–69. Major General David Hunter was president of the Porter court-martial. Holt's position was that of trial counsel and recorder, privileged to attend the deliberations of the panel after the close of the evidence.
14. Leonard, *Lincoln's Forgotten Ally*, 270–75. Holt was personally offended and shocked by the closing argument of Richard Merrick that painted Holt as the person who concealed the Hunter Commission's recommendation of mercy for Mary Surratt from President Johnson, and the manipulator of the witnesses for the prosecution.
15. Warner, *Generals in Blue*, 232.
16. Gerard N. Magliocca, *American Founding Son: John Bingham and the Invention of the Fourteenth Amendment* (New York: New York University Press, 2013), 6–8.
17. Magliocca, *American Founding Son*, 9–10 (print shop), 11–16 (Franklin College).
18. Magliocca, *American Founding Son*, 24–25.
19. Magliocca, *American Founding Son*, 25.
20. Magliocca, *American Founding Son*, 39–40 (first election campaign), 55–59 (Dred Scott and leader in the Kansas Crisis), 83–84 (lost reelection 1862 and appointment), 87–89 (comeback in 1864 election).
21. Magliocca, *American Founding Son*, 108–27.
22. U.S. Const. amend. XIV.
23. Congressional biography of Rep. John A. Bingham available at http://bioguide.congress.gov/scripts/biodisplay.pl?index=b000471.
24. J. Fletcher Brennan, ed., *Biographical Cyclopaedia and Portrait Gallery of Distinguished Men with a Historical Sketch of the State of Ohio* (Cincinnati: John C. Yorkston, 1880), 6:1354.
25. Brennan, *Biographical Cyclopaedia*, 6:1354.
26. Biography of Henry L. Burnett in *The National Cyclopedia of American Biography Being the History of the United States as Illustrated in the Lives of the Founders, Builders and Defenders of the Republic, and of the Men and Women Who Are Doing the Work and Moulding the Thoughts of the Present Time Edited by Distinguished Biographers from Each State Revised and Approved by the Most Eminent Historians, Scholars and Statesmen of the Day* (New York: James T. White, 1910), 14:272; republished in http://www.iment.com/maida/familytree/burnett/bioportrait.htm.
27. Biography of Henry L. Burnett, *National Cyclopedia*, 14:272.
28. Benn Pitman, ed., *The Trials for Treason at Indianapolis: Disclosing the Plans for Establishing a Northwest Confederacy* (Cincinnati: Moore, Wilstach & Baldwin, 1865), 9.
29. "Burnett, Henry L.," National Park Service, Civil War Soldiers and Sailors profile, http://www.nps.gov/civilwar/search-soldiers-detail.htm?soldierId=EDF03989-DC7A-DF11-BF36-B8AC6F5D926A.
30. Biography of Henry L. Burnett, *National Cyclopedia*, 14:273.
31. Brennan, *Biographical Cyclopaedia*, 6:1354; U.S. Census 1900, Manhattan, New York, ED, 103 p.6B, HH 49 FAM 83.
32. Edward Steers Jr., *Blood on the Moon: The Assassination of Abraham Lincoln* (Lexington: University Press of Kentucky, 2001), 218.

33. Bernard C. Steiner, *Life of Reverdy Johnson* (Baltimore: Norman Remington, 1914), 2–3.
34. Steiner, *Life of Reverdy Johnson*, 3.
35. Steiner, *Life of Reverdy Johnson*, 3.
36. Steiner, *Life of Reverdy Johnson*, 8–9.
37. Steiner, *Life of Reverdy Johnson*, 10.
38. Steiner, *Life of Reverdy Johnson*, 15. This may explain why Johnson was always photographed in profile.
39. Steiner, *Life of Reverdy Johnson*, 19–20.
40. Steiner, *Life of Reverdy Johnson*, 34.
41. Steiner, *Life of Reverdy Johnson*, 36. The Wheeling Bridge case involved the extent of the United States' jurisdiction over navigable waterways of the United States. The case eventually went to the U.S. Supreme Court on writ of error. See Pennsylvania v. Wheeling Belmont Bridge Co., 50 U.S. (9 How.) 649 (1850); later final opinion at 54 U.S. (13 How.) 518 (1852).
42. Pennsylvania v. Wheeling Belmont Bridge Co. See Seymour v. McCormick, 60 U.S. (19 How.) 96 (1857).
43. Steiner, *Life of Reverdy Johnson*, 43–45. See also "Biography of Sen. Reverdy Johnson," *Baltimore Barrister*, Summer 1979, 34; congressional biography of Reverdy Johnson available at http://bioguide.congress.gov/scripts/biodisplay.pl?index=j000169.
44. Steiner, *Life of Reverdy Johnson*, 58–59.
45. Steiner, *Life of Reverdy Johnson*, 61–74. Johnson voted against the Thirteenth Amendment on the ground that the United States had no power to emancipate slaves. He also voted against the Freedmen's Bureau. See Steiner, *Life of Reverdy Johnson*, 102–3.
46. Steiner, *Life of Reverdy Johnson*, 195–97.
47. "Biography of Sen. Reverdy Johnson," *Baltimore Barrister*, 34.
48. Steers, *Blood on the Moon*, 219.
49. Birth Certificate of Frederick A. Aiken, Town of Shrewsbury, Mass.
50. "Marriage Notice: Frederick A. Aiken to Sarah Olivia Weston, June 1, 1857," *Danville (Vt.) North Star*, June 2, 1857.
51. Obituary of Frederick A. Aiken, *Washington Post*, December 2, 1878, 2.
52. Obituary of Frederick A. Aiken.
53. Washington D.C., November 20, 1861: "We learn that Mr. Frederick A. Aiken, of this city, has accepted a captain's commission in Col. James B. Swain's regiment of cavalry, now being organized in New York. Mr. Aiken has been employed for some time past by the government in a confidential capacity, and the knowledge he has of the rebel leaders, and of the country about Washington, will, no doubt, be turned to good account in his new sphere." See Christine R. Christensen, "Finding Frederick," http://media.virbcdn.com/files/7a/70ad398a865a12f8-Aiken_05252012.pdf.
54. Christensen, "Finding Frederick."
55. Christensen, "Finding Frederick." The *Washington Post* ran an article in 2012 commemorating its first city editor, mentioning that Aiken and his wife had raised a small girl as their own, when the mother, alleged to be a prostitute, sued to recover her daughter. Aiken's widow survived him by more than thirty years. She never remarried. See John Kelly, "A Tip of the Hat to a Former *Post* Editor," *Washington Post*, June 13, 2012, B2.
56. Steers, *Blood on the Moon*, 219.
57. *Columbian College Catalog 1858–59* (Washington, D.C.: Thomas McGill, 1859), 8. Clampitt was a second-year student in the scientific curriculum.
58. "Clampitt, John W.," National Park Service, Civil War Soldiers and Sailors profile, http://www.nps.gov/civilwar/search-soldiers-detail.htm?soldierId=DE583A8D-DC7A-DF11-BF36-B8AC6F5D926A.
59. "Consolidated Enrollment Lists, Compiled 1863–1865," 620 vol., District of Columbia at 15 (National Archives Catalog ID: 4213514 / MLR Number NM-65 172).
60. John W. Clampitt, *Echoes from the Rocky Mountains: Reminiscences and Thrilling Incidents of the Romantic and Golden Age of the Great West, with a Graphic Account of Its Discovery, Settlement and Grand Development* (Chicago: Belford, Clarke, 1889).

61. U.S. Census 1880, Deerfield, Lake Co., Ill., p. 417D; see also U.S. Census 1880, Washington, D.C., p.245A, HH 185 FAM 228; U.S. Census 1900, Deerfield, Lake Co., Ill. ED 132, p.14B, HH 237 FAM 264.

62. Listing for "John W. Clampitt, Special Examiner of Pensions," in Reuben H. Donnelley, compiler, *Chicago City Directory 1887* (Chicago: Chicago Directory, 1887), 345.

63. "Death of John W. Clampitt," *Washington Post*, July 18, 1906, 2.

64. Steers, *Blood on the Moon*, 219.

65. Eric Wittenberg, "Bvt. Brig. Gen. William E. Doster," *Rantings of a Civil War Historian* (blog), March 6, 2008, http://civilwarcavalry.com/?p=704.

66. Ronald D. Smith, *Thomas Ewing, Jr.: Frontier Lawyer and Civil War General* (Columbia: University of Missouri Press, 2008), 4–7; Steers, *Blood on the Moon*, 219.

67. Smith, *Thomas Ewing, Jr.*, 14–16, 27.

68. Rossiter Johnson and John Howard Brown, eds., *The Twentieth Century Biographical Dictionary of Notable Americans* (Boston: Biographical Society, 1904), 4:25. See also "Thomas Ewing, Jr.," Missouri Civil War Sesquicentennial website, http://mocivilwar150.com/history/figure/295 . The Sherman & Ewing law firm also included Hugh Boyle Ewing, Thomas Ewing's brother, and Daniel McCook. All four men would become general officers during the Civil War.

69. Smith, *Thomas Ewing, Jr.*, 101–2.

70. Smith, *Thomas Ewing, Jr.*, 176–79.

71. Warner, *Generals in Blue*, 146.

72. Smith, *Thomas Ewing, Jr.*, 201–3. See General Order 11 summary available at http://www.civilwarmo.org/educators/resources/info-sheets/thomas-ewing-jrs-general-order-no-11.

73. See Fred R. Kline, "George Caleb Bingham: Artist of Missouri and the American Frontier," at George Caleb Bingham: Catalogue Raisonné Supplement of Paintings and Drawings website, http://www.georgecalebbingham.org/bio.htm.

74. Smith, *Thomas Ewing, Jr.*, 234–45.

75. See Johnson and Brown, *Twentieth Century Biographical Dictionary*, 4:25. The Ohio Bar Association also produced a biography of Ewing; see Michael Kauffman, "Biography of Thomas Ewing," in *Bench and Bar of Ohio*, ed. George Irving Reed, Emilius Oviatt Randall, and Charles Theodore Greve (Chicago: Century, 1897). See also "Thomas Ewing, Jr.," Missouri Civil War Sesquicentennial website.

76. Biography of Frederick Stone, Biographical Directory of the United States Congress, http://bioguide.congress.gov/scripts/biodisplay.pl?index=S000957.

77. U.S. Census 1860 Coomes, Charles Co., Md., p. 7, HH 52 FAM 52 (occupation lawyer: net worth $33,000 real property, $10,000 personal property).

78. Steers, *Blood on the Moon*, 219.

79. Biography of Frederick Stone, in Biographical Directory of the United States Congress.

80. Steers, *Blood on the Moon*, 219.

81. Federal Judicial Center, "Cox, Walter Smith," in Biographical Directory of Federal Judges, http://www.fjc.gov/servlet/nGetInfo?jid=525&cid=999&ctype=na&instate=na.

82. Interment record, Oak Hill Cemetery, http://www.oakhillcemeterydc.org/Burials/cowie.html .

83. Pitman, *Trials for Treason at Indianapolis*, 24 (testimony of Richard Montgomery).

84. The government's burden of proof is not mentioned in Alexander Macomb, *The Practice of Courts Martial* (New York: Harper & Bros., 1841), nor by Capt. S. V. Benet in *A Treatise on Military Law and the Practice of Courts-Martial* (New York: D. Van Nostrand, 1863), the standard references for trial by court-martial under the Articles of War. Both treatises mention the required majority vote for conviction.

85. Pitman, *Trials for Treason at Indianapolis*, 276–88. Ewing concluded that: "I have now presented to the Court every point in the evidence which seems to me may, by any possibility, be relied on as indicating guilty knowledge of or participation by Spangler in the conspiracy, or any of its crimes. From the natural partiality of a counsel to his client, I may not have noticed all that bears against him, or presented it in its true light, but I have earnestly sought, in this discussion, to show all that is of weight for or against him, extenuating nothing. I can see in the evidence no ground for such suspicion as would, in the civil courts, lead a grand jury to present

him for trial, and believe that, so far from his guilt being established beyond a reasonable doubt, a review of the evidence will leave, in few candid minds, a reasonable doubt of his innocence."

86. Pitman, *Trials for Treason at Indianapolis*, 251–62.

87. Pitman, *Trials for Treason at Indianapolis*, 264–67.

88. Thomas M. Harris, *Assassination of Lincoln: A History of the Great Conspiracy; Trial of the Conspirators by a Military Commission and a Review of the Trial of John H. Surratt* (Boston: American Citizen, 1892), 82–83.

Chapter Four

The Conduct of the Trial

> The fairness and equity characterizing the proceedings of a civil court had no sway in the decisions of a Military Commission that rejected or admitted just such testimony as its judge-advocate declared should be admitted or rejected. Under such a procedure nearly all evidence having weight for the defense was, on one pretext or another, rejected.—John W. Clampitt, "The Trial of Mrs. Surratt"

The trial began May 10, 1865, and ended on June 29, 1865. Three hundred sixty-six witnesses were called by all sides. Twenty-nine were African American Maryland and District of Columbia residents, previously barred from giving evidence against white people in federal courts.[1] Eighteen testified for the government, and eleven were witnesses for the defendants.[2]

THE ACCOMPLICES' INDICTMENTS

Booth's alleged accomplices were indicted by an information written by Judge Advocate General Holt in imitation of the charges and specifications for a general court-martial. Charge I alleged that prior to March 6, 1865, Booth's alleged accomplices named in Specification 1 conspired with:

> John H. Surratt, John Wilkes Booth, Jefferson Davis, George N. Saunders, Beverly Tucker, Jacob Thompson, William C. Cleary, Clement C. Clay, George Harper, George Young, and others unknown, to kill and murder . . . Abraham Lincoln . . . William Seward . . . [and] Andrew Johnson.[3]

Specification 1 contained the following language:

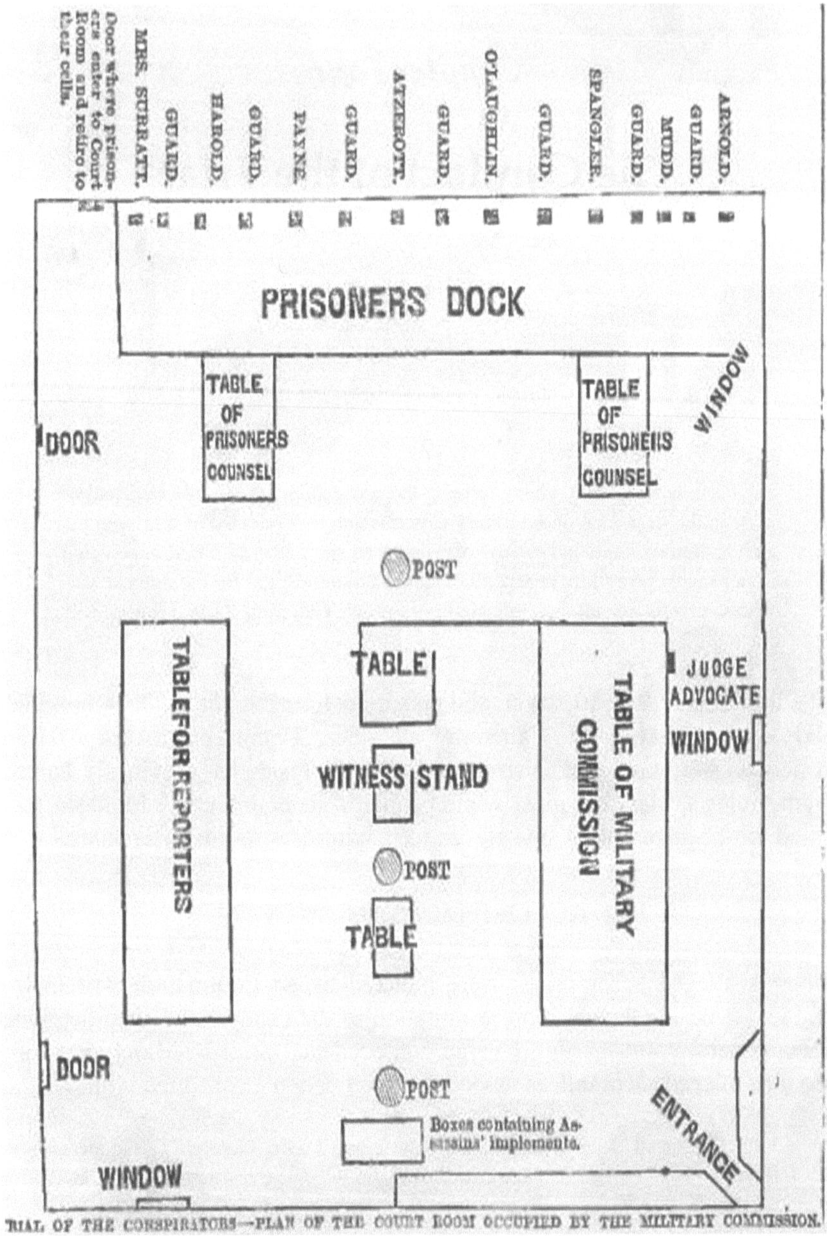

Figure 4.1. Courtroom Diagram. *Source: Frank Leslie's Illustrated Newspaper*, June 10, 1865.

> [The named conspirators and those unknown] unlawfully, and maliciously, and traitorously to kill and murder Abraham Lincoln, then President of the United States aforesaid, and Commander-in-Chief of the army and navy thereof; and unlawfully, maliciously, and traitorously to kill and murder Andrew Johnson, then Vice-President of the said United States, upon whom, on the death of said Abraham Lincoln, after the 4th day of March, A.D. 1865, the office of President of the said United States, and Commander-in-Chief of the army and navy thereof, would devolve; and to unlawfully, maliciously, and traitorously to kill and murder Ulysses S. Grant, then Lieutenant-General, and under the direction of the said Abraham Lincoln, in command of the armies of the United States aforesaid; and unlawfully, maliciously, and traitorously to kill and murder William H. Seward, then Secretary of State of the United States aforesaid, whose duty it was by law, upon the death of said President and Vice-President of the United States aforesaid, to cause an election to be held for electors of President of the United States, the conspirators aforesaid designing and intending by the killing and murder of the said Abraham Lincoln, Andrew Johnson, Ulysses S. Grant, and William H. Seward, as aforesaid, to deprive the army and navy of the said United States of a constitutional commander-in-chief, and to deprive the armies of the United States of their lawful commander, and to prevent a lawful election of President and Vice-President of the United States aforesaid, and by the means aforesaid to aid and comfort the insurgents engaged in armed rebellion against the said United States as aforesaid, and thereby to aid in the subversion and overthrow of the Constitution and laws of the said United States.[4]

The subspecifications charged Lewis Powell under his alias of Lewis Payne with "And in further prosecution of the said conspiracy and its traitorous and murderous designs," unlawfully and maliciously assaulting Secretary of State Seward with intent to kill him, and committing an assault upon Frederick W. Seward, Augustus H. Seward, Emrick W. Hansell, and George F. Robinson, with intent to kill each and every one of them.[5] George Atzerodt was charged with "And in further prosecution of the said conspiracy and its traitorous and murderous designs," lying in wait to murder Vice President Andrew Johnson.[6] David Herold's charge stated that, "And in further prosecution of said unlawful, murderous, and traitorous conspiracy," Herold aided, abetted, and assisted Booth's murder of President Lincoln, and further aided and abetted and assisted Booth's escape from the scene of the crime and concealing Booth from the authorities.[7]

Michael O'Loughlen was charged with "And in further prosecution of the conspiracy aforesaid, and of its murderous designs and treasonable purposes aforesaid," of lying in wait with intent to kill Lieutenant General Ulysses S. Grant, commander of the armies of the United States.[8] Samuel Arnold was charged with "unlawfully, and maliciously, and traitorously" aiding and abetting Booth and his associates and helping them to execute the conspiracy to kill President Lincoln, Secretary Seward, and Vice President Johnson.[9]

Mary Surratt was charged with "unlawfully, and maliciously, and traitorously" receiving, entertaining, and harboring Booth and the other named alleged accomplices save for Mudd and Spangler, knowing that Booth and his associates were planning to murder President Lincoln. She was also charged with aiding and abetting the escape of Booth and Herold.[10] Samuel Mudd was charged with "unlawfully, and maliciously, and traitorously" encouraging Booth and the other accomplices to murder President Lincoln and with aiding and abetting the escape of John Wilkes Booth and David Herold.[11] Edman Spangler was charged with "unlawfully, and maliciously, and traitorously" aiding and abetting John Wilkes Booth's entry to the presidential box at Ford's Theatre, and in barring and obstructing the door to the presidential box, and finally, aiding and abetting Booth's escape from Ford's Theatre.[12]

The indictment specified the elements of proof required to convict each defendant. Judge Advocate General Holt was presumed to know the federal law of treason. Article III section 3 of the U.S. Constitution stated that: "Treason against the United States, shall consist only in levying War against them, or in adhering to their Enemies, giving them Aid and Comfort. No Person shall be convicted of Treason unless on the Testimony of two Witnesses to the same overt Act, or on Confession in open Court." The Treason Act of 1790 tracked the constitutional provision.[13] Neither the Constitution nor the Treason Act said anything about trying U.S. citizens for treason before a military commission.

Secretary Stanton and Judge Advocate General Holt originally ordered that the trial be conducted in closed session, barring the general public. The ban was lifted after the first two days of trial, and the entire proceedings were reported by the press and by the official court reporter Benn Pitman. Pitman's transcript, which summarized testimony and omitted the lawyers' questions, was heavily edited by Henry L. Burnett. Ben Perley Poore produced a much better transcript for several newspapers, containing questions and answers and the president's rulings on points of law. The Poore transcript has been used extensively throughout this book because it is more reliable than the Pitman summary.

Throughout the trial, the judge advocate and his assistants advised the commission that the case was to be tried according to the law of war, that is, a body of international law principles commonly accepted at the time of the trial relating to the conduct of war. Book Three of Vattel's *Law of Nations*[14] was the most reliable source for this body of legal standards. The discussion of constitutional questions will refer to Attorney General Speed's opinion justifying trial of Booth's alleged accomplices by military commission and Vattel's authority for such treatment.

THE ATTORNEY GENERAL'S OPINION

Attorney General James Speed delivered an oral opinion to President Johnson, Secretary of War Stanton, and Judge Advocate General Holt prior to the president's order convening the Hunter Commission. After the trial was concluded and the death sentences for George Atzerodt, David Herold, Lewis Powell, and Mary Surratt were carried out, Speed issued a written opinion justifying the trial of the accomplices by military commission, even though the Habeas Corpus Act of 1863 directed that the alleged accomplices be turned over to the nearest civil authorities for indictment and trial in U.S. District Court. Attorney General Speed counseled President Johnson that Booth's alleged accomplices could be tried by military commission because they were enemy belligerents.

Speed also relied on the provisions of General Order 100 relating to trial of irregular combatants. Article 13 states that "cases which do not come within the Rules and Articles of War, or the jurisdiction conferred by statute on courts-martial, are tried by military commissions."[15] Article 82 states that irregulars who "commit hostilities, whether by fighting, or inroads for destruction or plunder, or by raids of any kind, without commission, without being part and portion of the organized hostile army," have divested themselves of the "appearance of soldiers . . . are not public enemies, and therefore, if captured, are not entitled to the privileges of prisoners of war, but shall be treated summarily as highway robbers or pirates."[16]

Speed stated the issue as "whether the persons charged with the offense of having assassinated the president can be tried before a military tribunal, or must they be tried before a civil court."[17] Speed asserted that:

> Martial law had been declared in the District of Columbia, but the civil Courts were open and held their regular sessions, and transacted business as in times of peace. Such being the facts, the question is one of great importance—important, because it involves the constitutional guarantees thrown about the rights of the citizen, and because the security of the army and the government in time of war is involved; important, as it involves a seeming conflict between the laws of peace and of war. Having given the question propounded the patient and earnest consideration its magnitude and importance require, I will proceed to give the reasons why I am of the opinion that the conspirators not only may but ought to be tried by a military tribunal.[18]

The attorney general conflated a declaration of martial law with the suspension of the writ of habeas corpus issued in September 1862 and in 1863 applying to any individual who was deemed to be a spy. Speed's interpretation of the law of war, in part follows Vattel. Speed states correctly that when a civil war becomes territorial, all the civilians on both sides of the war are enemies and according to the international law of war, enemy belligerents are entitled to the same treatment as enemy combatants in a war between internationally recognized sovereign nations. Speed opined that

> soldiers have a high sense of personal honor. The true soldier is proud to feel and know that his enemy possesses personal honor, and will conform and be obedient to the laws of war. In a spirit of justice, and with a wise appreciation of such feelings, the laws of war protect the character and honor of an open enemy. When by the fortunes of war one open enemy is thrown into the hands and power of another, and is charged with dishonorable conduct and a breach of the laws of war, he must be tried according to the usages of war. Justice and fairness say that an open enemy to whom dishonorable conduct is imputed, has a right to demand a trial. If such a demand can be rightfully made, surely it can not be rightfully refused. It is to be hoped that the military authorities of this country will never refuse such a demand, because there is no act of Congress that authorizes it. In time of war the law and usage of war authorize it, and they are a part of the law of the land.[19]

Speed's conclusion that the international law of war is part of the domestic law of the United States not requiring an act of Congress to authorize trial of belligerents by military commission is not supported by authority, nor is it consistent with Vattel and other international law treatises. Article I § 8 clause 17 of the Constitution lodges the power to prescribe tribunals and penalties for violating the law of nations in Congress alone.[20] Speed's opinion is noteworthy for its lack of citations to U.S. case law and to international treatises other than Wheaton's *Elements of International Law*.[21]

Attorney General Speed counseled President Johnson that Booth's alleged accomplices could be tried by military commission because they were enemy belligerents. Since the Supreme Court had carefully avoided classing the Confederate States of America as a belligerent nation state in *The Prize Cases*,[22] Speed was either undoing the careful opinion of the Supreme Court or ignoring it.

International law commentators had devoted some thought to civil war. According to Vattel, the combatants in a civil war, ostensibly citizens of the same sovereign state, should be treated as combatants in a war between sovereign states:

> Thenceforward constituting, at least for a time, two separate bodies, two distinct societies. Though one of the parties may have been to blame in breaking the unity of the state and resisting the lawful authority, they are not the less divided in fact. Besides, who shall judge them? who shall pronounce on which side the right or the wrong lies? On earth they have no common superior. They stand therefore in precisely the same predicament as two nations, who engage in a contest and, being unable to come to an agreement, have recourse to arms.[23]

This approach supported Speed's treatment of Booth's accomplices as agents of a foreign power. Vattel was silent on the appropriateness of trial by military commission for agents of the Confederate States. In order to justify trial by military commission, Speed also relied on articles 13 and 82 of General Order 100 relating to trial by military commission and of irregular combatants. General Order 100 required that irregulars engaged in hostile actions should be treated as civilian criminals, not as enemy soldiers with the protection of prisoner of war status.[24] It did not authorize the president or the secretary of war to try irregulars by military commission when civilian courts were open for business in the jurisdiction where the offense was committed. In May 1865, Washington, D.C., was not under any credible threat of invasion by Confederate troops. Although habeas corpus had been suspended for the District of Columbia in 1862, the Superior Court of the District of Columbia and the U.S. District Court were open for business. There was no justification by way of necessity to try any U.S. citizen by military commission. Speed also failed to address the specific requirements of the Habeas Corpus Act of 1863 that instructed military commanders who had arrested spies and traitors to turn over the list of those arrested to the relevant federal magistrate for the district for potential indictment by grand jury and a civil trial for indictable criminal acts.[25]

John Wilkes Booth's alleged accomplices were not enemy belligerents or Confederate irregular guerillas. The Booth accomplices were U.S. citizens involved in the commission of a series of crimes in the District of Columbia and in Maryland. If Speed had followed the Habeas Corpus Act of 1863, the alleged accomplices should have been indicted by grand jury, been informed of the charges against them, and should have been afforded a speedy public trial by a jury of twelve on those charges. The civilian rules of evidence and of criminal procedure should have been followed, in particular the criminal burden of proof beyond a reasonable doubt and the rule barring most forms of hearsay.

PLEAS TO THE JURISDICTION

Booth's alleged accomplices raised the issue of the Hunter Commission's jurisdiction to try the accomplices on two occasions. Senator Reverdy Johnson submitted a written plea to the jurisdiction of the Hunter Commission on June 16, 1865.[26] General Thomas Ewing also pled to the jurisdiction of the Hunter Commission nine days after Senator Johnson's plea was submitted.[27] Both pleas to the jurisdiction covered similar issues. Senator Johnson and General Ewing argued that the president of the United States had no power to convene a judicial tribunal that was not specifically authorized by Congress. They contended that the power to establish courts was exclusively that of

Congress, and President Johnson's order convening the military commission was ultra vires.[28] Both lawyers argued that the Lincoln assassination alleged accomplices were entitled to the benefit of the constitutional rights guaranteed by the Fifth Amendment, which both men argued was not available in a trial by military commission.[29] Senator Johnson also argued that trial by military commission deprived the defendants of the rights accorded to the accused under the Sixth Amendment.[30]

Johnson's and Ewing's arguments were parallel to those raised by Gen. James Garfield and David Dudley Field on behalf of the Northwest Conspirator Lambdin Milligan, an Indiana lawyer tried and found guilty of treason by an Indianapolis military commission. Milligan had filed a habeas corpus petition with the U.S. Circuit Court of Indiana on May 10, 1865. The circuit court had divided on the issuance of a show cause order and certified the same jurisdictional questions to the U.S. Supreme Court. The Supreme Court had not yet accepted jurisdiction over the case of Lambdin Milligan. The Milligan case would not appear on the Supreme Court's docket until December 1865, months after the end of the trial of Booth's alleged accomplices.[31]

Johnson also argued that President Johnson had no inherent power to convene a military tribunal. If Congress had not authorized such a trial, the president lacked authority to order the defendants tried by military commission.[32] Johnson pointed out that Congress had not authorized the president to try Booth's accomplices by military commission.[33] Senator Johnson noted that the alleged accomplices had been charged with treasonable actions in the charges and specifications issued by the Hunter Commission. He attacked the idea of "military treason" as some kind of treason not governed by the Treason Act of 1793 and by the Constitution, asserting that the offenses charged in the charges and specifications were committed in the District of Columbia and not in the field under control of a military commander.[34] He noted that a treason case cannot be tried by a military commission because the Treason Act required that the defendant charged with treason be indicted by grand jury within three years after the commission of the offense. The defendant was also to receive a list of witnesses against him prior to trial and had the right to challenge prospective jurors preemptorily. None of these rights were provided for in the order convening the Hunter Commission.[35] Finally, Senator Johnson warned the Hunter Commission that if it persisted in trying the alleged accomplices without jurisdiction, each of the commissioners could be criminally liable for the verdicts and judgments.[36]

General Ewing's plea to the jurisdiction was offered much later than Senator Johnson's plea. It was also much more concise. As noted above, General Ewing argued that the Hunter Commission had no jurisdiction over the defendants because it was convened by the president when the president had no authorization from Congress to try anyone by military commission.[37] Ewing argued that neither the president nor Congress could give the Hunter

Commission jurisdiction to try the Booth accomplices. Ewing noted that the power to overrule Congress and the Constitution was not granted to the executive branch of government.[38] Ewing also noted that if civilians could be tried by military commission for civilian offenses, the government should have descended into military despotism.[39]

The commission denied both pleas to the jurisdiction without issuing an elaborate opinion supporting its rejection of the jurisdictional arguments posed by Johnson and Ewing. In 1866, the majority opinion in *Ex parte Milligan* would conclude that military commissions such as the Hunter Commission could not be convened by the executive branch of government to try civilians when the place where the offenses were committed when the civilian courts were open and the jurisdiction was not under invasion.[40] The full court also concluded that the president could not send civilians to be tried by military commission if Congress did not first authorize the president to do so.[41]

The rules of criminal procedure and rules of evidence for the Hunter Commission were made up ad hoc as the trial moved along. General Hunter ruled on objections to admission of evidence during the trial. His rulings were not submitted to the whole panel for review. Judge Advocate General Holt was the official recorder for the commission, a position that allowed him to advise General Hunter how to rule on the objections raised by both the prosecutors and defense counsel. Holt and Bingham frequently interjected remarks during defense examinations of witnesses, scolding the witnesses who were about to repeat hearsay. The prosecution made eighty objections during the course of trial. Forty-two (52.5 percent) were sustained and only three were overruled. The commission sustained one of the twenty-eight objections raised by defense counsel. It overruled twenty-one (75 percent) of defense objections.[42]

Defense counsel failed to make any objection to the testimony of atrocity witnesses, including former Union prisoners of war incarcerated at Andersonville,[43] Belle Isle,[44] and Libby[45] prison camps. These witnesses gave evidence of atrocities committed by Confederate soldiers on Union prisoners of war. Other witnesses also related stories of the plot to rob banks and set fire to St. Albans, Vermont, in October 1864;[46] to start a conflagration in New York City on November 25, 1864;[47] and to infect soldiers and civilian populations in New York, Boston, and New Bern, North Carolina, with yellow fever in the summer of 1864.[48] Assuming without accepting the government's allegation that President Jefferson Davis, Secretary of State Benjamin, Confederate commissioners Clement Clay and Jacob Thompson, their secretary Cleary, and others were coconspirators with Booth and the defendants, inhumane treatment of prisoners of war by Captain Wirz, Dr. Blackburn's yellow fever plot, the New York City incendiary raid and the St. Albans bank robbery were other uncharged acts of misconduct not included in the charges and specifications against any of the eight defendants. By 1865, civilian courts had adopted the rule that criminal acts not alleged in the indictment could not be proved to show that the defendant was a person of bad moral character, although such evidence could be introduced to prove motive, criminal intent, guilty knowledge, criminal plan, or identity of the accused.[49]

The atrocity evidence, particularly mistreatment of Union prisoners of war, was unrelated to any of the charges and specifications. The prosecution did not offer any evidence that the conspiracy to assassinate President Lincoln was related to a larger conspiracy to mistreat prisoners, rob banks, burn buildings, or poison people with the clothing of yellow fever victims. The atrocity evidence prejudiced the commission against all the defendants and contributed to the ultimate verdict and punishment meted out to the defendants.

PERJURED TESTIMONY

The prosecution built its case for a conspiracy involving President Jefferson Davis, the Confederate commissioners, and other Confederate agents using Booth and his band of accomplices to destabilize the United States government at a time when the Confederate States had abandoned its capital and its field armies were surrendering to Union forces in Virginia and North Carolina. Defense counsel allowed the prosecution to introduce hearsay evidence from witnesses such as Sanford Conover, Richard Montgomery, and Dr. James B. Merritt[50] who repeated statements allegedly made in their presence by Clement Clay, Jacob Thompson, George N. Sanders, and their agents in Montreal and Toronto, who also had conversations with the Confederate agents in Canada that incriminated them, their superiors, and John Wilkes Booth. The conspiracy count was necessary to permit these witnesses to regale the commission with stories about letters received from Richmond that authorized Clay and Thompson to proceed with the Booth plot to murder President Lincoln. Civilian evidence law permitted the statements of conspirators made during the life of the conspiracy and in furtherance of the conspiracy to be admitted against every other identified conspirator.[51] At that time, it was not clear that the existence of a conspiracy could be proved from the words of the conspirators without corroborating evidence from other sources.[52]

The testimony from these three witnesses was the basis for linking Booth's conspiracy and his accomplices to the Confederate high command. It was compelling evidence, but there was one flaw: much of the evidence from these three individuals was perjured, casting doubt on any of the evidence from these three witnesses.

Sanford Conover

"Sanford Conover" was one of the alias used by Charles A. Dunham,[53] who was a lawyer and newspaper reporter who submitted letters for publication to the *New York Tribune*. According to his testimony before the Hunter Commission, Dunham had been drafted into the Confederate service and was assigned as a clerk to the War Department.[54] Dunham left the Confederacy sometime after 1862 and offered his services as a stringer to the *Tribune*, volunteering to go to Canada and get stories about the Confederate commissioners in Canada for the paper. He used the alias "James Watson Wallace" in Canada in the fall of 1864. Dunham made contact with Confederate agents, passing himself off as a loyal Confederate. He claimed to know the Confederate commissioners Clement C. Clay, Jacob Thompson, and their agents including George N. Sanders; Dr. Blackburn, the author of the yellow fever germ warfare attack; Beverly Tucker, William C. Cleary, and several other men.[55] Conover testified that he saw John Wilkes Booth in Montreal as early as October 1864[56] and also saw John Surratt in Montreal several times.[57] Conover said he saw John Surratt in Montreal in company with George Sanders and Jacob Thompson's company about a week before President Lincoln's assassination. Conover said he saw Surratt deliver dispatches from Secretary of State Benjamin to Thompson in Thompson's hotel room.[58] Conover said the meeting between Thompson and Surratt probably took place on April 7, 8, or 9, 1865.[59] Conover claimed that Jacob Thompson had invited him before that date to participate in the plot to assassinate President Lincoln.[60] The April 1865 meeting in Thompson's hotel room proceeded. Thompson read the dispatch from Secretary Benjamin and exclaimed, "That makes it all right," referring to the plot to kill President Lincoln and other high-ranking officials.[61]

Conover testified that he had his first meeting with Jacob Thompson in February 1865 in which Thompson told him that there was a plot to assassinate President Lincoln.[62] Thompson also showed Conover a blank commission in the Confederate army signed by Secretary of War Seddon used to protect agents and saboteurs who could claim military status. Thompson indicated a similar commission had been filled out for John Wilkes Booth.[63] Conover recalled conversations with William Cleary and George Sanders from February into April 1865 relating to the assassination of President Lincoln. Conover was tantalizingly vague about the dates of these conversations but did know that they took place at St. Lawrence Hall in Montreal.[64] Conover told the commission that he had sent a dispatch to the *Tribune* outlining the Lincoln conspiracy, but the *Tribune* refused to publish his story.[65] Conover insisted that his cover story was that he was a dedicated rebel willing to assist the conspirators. He said he used this strategy to gain access to the

Confederate commissioners and they never knew he was a newspaper correspondent.[66]

Under cross-examination, Conover reinforced his direct testimony. He recalled that John Wilkes Booth's commission in the Confederate army dated to December 1864 and told the commission that the commissions were cover for Confederate agents to avoid being treated as criminals.[67] Further examination rambled on into the St. Albans raid, the plot to poison Croton Reservoir, and the Northwest Conspiracy, all of which was extraneous to the plot to kill President Lincoln. The following day Conover regaled the commission with an account, largely accurate, of Dr. Blackburn's expedition to Bermuda to collect the clothing of dead yellow fever victims to be used to start epidemics in New York and Philadelphia.[68]

Richard Montgomery

Montgomery was called on May 12, at the beginning of the trial, during secret session.[69] He told the commission that in the summer of 1864 he had gone to the Canadian side of Niagara Falls where Confederate commissioners Clay and Thompson were awaiting some kind of response to their request for negotiations concerning the end of the war. Montgomery said he had known Thompson in Washington before the war.[70] Montgomery swore that he met with Thompson in January where the following exchange took place:

> A. He said a proposition had been made to him to rid the world of the tyrant Lincoln, Stanton, Grant, and some others; that he knew the men who had made the proposition were bold, daring men, and able to execute any thing that they would undertake, without regard to the cost; that he himself was in favor of the proposition, but had determined to defer his answer until he had consulted his Government at Richmond; and that he was then only awaiting their approval. He said that he thought it would be a blessing to the people, both North and South, to have these men killed.
>
> Q. This was in January?
>
> A. That was in January last.
>
> Q. What time in the month was it?
>
> A. It was about the middle of the month. I saw him a number of times. I could not give the exact day of that conversation.[71]

This testimony corroborated Conover's earlier story about the plot to kill President Lincoln and also pushes back the beginning date of the conspiracy to January 1865. Montgomery did not mention any kidnap plot. Although

Montgomery declared he never saw John Wilkes Booth in Canada, he repeated a statement made to him by W. C. Cleary, Thompson's private secretary, that Booth was one of the participants in the Lincoln assassination conspiracy.[72]

James Merritt

Holt's third witness was James Merritt. He claimed to be a physician who was a Canadian national and also a United States resident.[73] Dr. Merritt told the audience that he was in Canada practicing medicine except for a short visit to Detroit from May 1864 through the date of Lincoln's assassination.[74] Merritt lived in Lower Canada (Ontario) in 1864–1865 when he became involved with Confederate conspirators.[75] Later on, he encountered George N. Sanders in company with one of the agents he had met in Lower Canada, a Col. Steele. Sanders told Merritt that Lincoln would never serve a second term, implying that Lincoln would be killed before his inauguration.[76]

Dr. Merritt told the commission that in February 1865 he went to Montreal and met George Sanders who again repeated the threats on Lincoln's life to him.[77] According to Merritt, Sanders read a letter from President Jefferson Davis to him. Although Merritt could not remember the exact text of the letter, he did recall that President Davis authorized the assassination of Lincoln.[78] When pressed for a more exact date for this meeting, Merritt said it occurred in mid-February.[79] Merritt said that Sanders had mentioned John Wilkes Booth as a possible agent for assassinating Lincoln.[80]

Merritt also volunteered that he met John Wilkes Booth in Canada in October 1864, and also recalled meeting John Surratt.[81] Later he told the commission that he had seen Booth in Canada two or three times in company with George Sanders.[82] Merritt did not give dates and places for these encounters. Merritt then told the commission that he had seen David Herold in Canada and identified Herold from the witness stand.[83] According to Merritt, John Wilkes Booth was the cousin of Confederate captain John Y. Beall, who was tried and executed for treason as a result of the abortive plot to free the Confederate officer prisoners of war at Johnson's Island.[84] Merritt then recounted a meeting with Harper, Charles Caldwell, Randall, and a man named Ford in Canada. These men announced they were off to Washington for the purpose of "kicking up a row." Harper said to Merritt a little later that they were to assassinate Lincoln. Merritt assured the commission that Harper mentioned John Wilkes Booth by name and indicated that Booth would be in Washington when they arrived.[85] Merritt said he was then in Galt, Ontario, on April 10.[86] Ascertaining that Harper had started on his trip, Merritt went to a justice of the peace named Davidson to swear out a warrant against Harper and his accomplices. The justice refused to issue the writ, saying the whole scheme of Harper was preposterous.[87]

Merritt then told the commission that he had a meeting with Clement Clay and Jacob Thompson in February 1865 in Toronto to discuss the Jefferson Davis letter. According to Merritt, Clay understood and approved of Lincoln's assassination.[88] According to Merritt, Sanders mentioned to him and the other attendees that John Surratt was one of the men taking part in the assassination plot. The February meeting attendees included Colonel Steele and George Sanders, Captain Scott, and the assassination accomplices George Harper, Caldwell, Ford, Kirk, Benedict, George Young, and Byron Hill.[89]

Merritt also said that he knew in advance about the plot to burn New York City and to free the Confederate prisoners at Camp Douglas. He said he posed as a "good southern man" in order that his patients, primarily Confederates, would share information with him. Merritt said he communicated information about both plots to Colonel Hill, the provost marshal in Detroit.[90]

If these witnesses are to be believed, Jefferson Davis authorized Jacob Thompson and Clement C. Clay to engage Confederate sympathizers in Montreal, Toronto, and the United States to murder President Lincoln, Vice President Johnson, and Secretary Seward as early as February 1865. All three men identified John Wilkes Booth as a leading member of the assassination team. Merritt identified John Surratt as another key member of the assassination squad. Merritt identified David Herold as someone he saw in Montreal in the winter of early 1865. Montgomery identified Lewis Powell as a mysterious man he saw in a hotel in company with George Sanders and other Confederate agents. Sanford Conover also knew about Jefferson Davis's letter and Booth's connection with the assassination plot. He claimed to have informed the *Tribune* of the plot, thinking that Horace Greeley or one of his staff would inform the government in Washington of the assassination plot.

There was just one problem with the three men and their testimony before the commission in May 1865. They lied.[91] Merritt and Montgomery were paid informants hired by the Bureau of Military Justice and by Judge Advocate General Holt to insinuate themselves into the good grace of Confederate agents in Canada.[92] Conover's, Montgomery's, and Merritt's testimony was leaked to the press by court reporter Benn Pitman, and was published in Greeley's *New York Tribune* on June 7, followed the same day by publication in the *Toronto Globe*.[93] The alleged February meeting with Thompson and Clay and other Confederate agents could not have occurred because Clement Clay was not in Canada at all during the winter and early spring of 1865 and Jacob Thompson was away from his headquarters in Montreal in January, not returning to Montreal until mid-February.[94] Conover's testimony that Jacob Thompson solicited him to be one of the assassination team members in late January or early February 1865 was also false.[95]

Conover had told the commission that he testified in the trial of the St. Albans conspirators in February 1865. He did not tell the commission that he had stated in that hearing that he was a Virginia native with the rank of major in the Confederate army entitled to raise a regiment.[96] The glaring errors in the testimony of the three witnesses was published in the newspapers, and Conover took immediate evasive action. He prepared a spurious affidavit from "James Watson Wallace," the alias he used in Canada, saying that Sanford Conover was not one and the same person as Wallace, offering to come to Washington, D.C., and prove the falsity of the identification if the United States would cover his travel expenses. Conover would later say that he was forced at pistol point to make the affidavit by Confederate agents.[97] The Montreal newspapers published a story on June 10, 1865, while the Booth alleged accomplices' trial was still in session asserting that Wallace a.k.a. Conover had been jailed as a vagrant in Montreal. Judge Advocate General Holt and Maj. Gen. John A. Dix arranged to bail Conover out and bring him to Washington.[98] On June 28, before the trial had ended, Conover testified that he was forced to sign the "Wallace" affidavit but did not reiterate his claim to have met with Thompson, Clay, and Sanders in January 1865 in Montreal.[99]

On July 7, 1865, the *Toronto Globe* published a letter from Conover to Jacob Thompson dated March 20, 1865, introducing himself and offering to meet Thompson with whom he was not yet acquainted. This document shredded Conover's claim to have been an intimate of Thompson in January and February 1865.[100] July 7 happened to be the day when Atzerodt, Herold, Powell, and Mary Surratt were hanged in the yard of the Old Capitol Prison.

In August 1865, Judge Advocate General Holt and Secretary Stanton employed Conover as a special agent to uncover more evidence linking Jefferson Davis and Clement Clay to the conspiracy to murder President Lincoln. Conover produced affidavits from six men and two women relating to the acts of Clement Clay, Jacob Thompson, and other Confederate agents in Montreal pointing toward Davis's complicity in the murder plot. Conover hired these people and wrote out questions and answers for them so that when Judge Advocate General Holt questioned them, they would have the "right answers."[101] Holt interrogated these witnesses, John Nealy (a.k.a. John McGill), a New York City peddler; William A. Campbell (a.k.a. Joseph L. Hoare); and Joseph Snevel (a.k.a. William H. Roberts), a tavern keeper. Campbell and Snevel swore that they were present at a meeting in Richmond in late March 1865 with Jefferson Davis and John Surratt in which Davis approved of assassinating Lincoln and gave Surratt the letter referred to by Conover in his testimony before the Hunter Commission.[102]

Campbell and Snevel later admitted that they had never been in Richmond in their lives and told the judge advocate general's office that Conover had hired them to give false evidence against Davis.[103] Although the full scope of Conover's plot to fabricate evidence would not be exposed until Conover had appeared before a House Committee in November 1865 investigating Jefferson Davis's participation in the plot to kill President Lincoln, enough was known prior to the Hunter Commission's verdict and judgment handed out July 6, 1865, to cast grave doubt about the truthfulness of Conover's evidence. Dr. Merritt's claim to have sought a warrant to stop the assassins was a lie. Merritt admitted that Conover had solicited him to make up a story about the assassination that implicated the Confederate high command when testifying before Congress in 1866. Merritt was paid $6,000 for his lies.[104] Montgomery's testimony was also very doubtful. In the summer of 1865, he wrote Conover to tell him that Campbell was about to recant before the House Investigative Committee took his evidence under oath.[105] Dr. Merritt was subpoenaed by the committee and testified that his testimony before the Hunter Commission was perjured, that Conover had put him up to the false story about making a complaint to the justice of the peace.[106] Merritt also told the committee that Montgomery had been paid to deliver perjured testimony as well.[107]

Conover was indicted for perjury before the House Committee. Campbell and Snevel were the principal witnesses against Conover. He was convicted and sentenced to prison. In 1869, at the same time that President Johnson pardoned Samuel Mudd, Samuel Arnold, and Edman Spangler, he issued a pardon for Conover, who disappeared and was never heard from again.[108]

One may wonder if Conover's, Merritt's, and Montgomery's perjured evidence had any influence on the Hunter Commission's judgments of guilt against the alleged accomplices. Their evidence related to John Wilkes Booth's ties to the Confederate commissioners in Canada and their acting under orders from Richmond to approve Booth's assassination plot. Since the judge advocate general was pursuing a case showing that Booth was part of a grand conspiracy engineered by Jefferson Davis and the Canadian commissioners, the perjured testimony supported the grand conspiracy theory, linking every one of the defendants to a plot to murder Lincoln hatched in the fall of 1864. It allowed Holt and his associate prosecutors to introduce evidence relating to the plot to send clothing of yellow fever victims to cities under Union control to start an epidemic, and to tell the Hunter Commission that the conspirators were also responsible for the attempt to set fire to New York City. It covertly authorized the testimony of former Union prisoners of war about atrocities committed at Andersonville, all part of a concerted plan to destroy the Union.

Something was terribly wrong with the trial of Booth's alleged accomplices. Did Booth's alleged accomplices have a fair and impartial trial? The conduct of the trial by the Hunter Commission and Judge Advocate General Holt and his assistants raises fundamental questions relating to the right to a fair and impartial hearing that spills over into twenty-first-century treatment of the Guantanamo detainees. Chapter 7 will analyze the trial of the alleged accomplices from a constitutional law viewpoint and offer a commentary on the fundamental fairness of the trial.

NOTES

1. In Maryland and the District of Columbia, a slave was incompetent to testify against a white man. See United States v. Dow, 25 F. Cas. 901 (1 Taney 23) (Cir. Ct. D. Md. 1840). Held: Maryland rules of evidence apply to case: Act of 1717 bars free Negroes and slaves as witnesses against a white person; United States v. Beddo, 24 Fed. Cas. 1061 (4 Cranch Crim. Rep.664) (D.C. Cir. 1835), slave and free Negroes incompetent to testify against free Negro.
2. Edward Steers Jr., *Blood on the Moon: The Assassination of Abraham Lincoln* (Lexington: University Press of Kentucky, 2001), 216–17.
3. Ben Perley Poore, ed., *The Conspiracy Trial for the Murder of the President, and the Attempt to Overthrow the Government by the Assassination of Its Principal Officers, Edited with an Introduction by Ben. Perley Poore* (Boston: J. E. Tilton, 1865), 1:18–19; also available at http://www.surrattmuseum.org/ben-perley-poore-the-conspiracy-trial-tr.
4. Poore, *Conspiracy Trial*, 1:15–16.
5. Poore, *Conspiracy Trial*, 1:17–18.
6. Poore, *Conspiracy Trial*, 1:18.
7. Poore, *Conspiracy Trial*, 1:17.
8. Poore, *Conspiracy Trial*, 1:18.
9. Poore, *Conspiracy Trial*, 1:18.
10. Poore, *Conspiracy Trial*, 1:18.
11. Poore, *Conspiracy Trial*, 1:19.
12. Poore, *Conspiracy Trial*, 1:16–17.
13. 1 Stat. 112 (1790).
14. Emmerich de Vattel, *The Law of Nations or the Principles of Natural Law*, ed. Joseph Chitty (Philadelphia: T. & J. W. Johnson, 1853; repr. Lonang Institute, 2003; originally published in French, 1758).
15. Francis Lieber, Gen. Order 100 (1863), text from Yale Law School Avalon project, http://avalon.law.yale.edu/19th_century/lieber.asp.
16. Gen. Order 100 art. 82 (1863).
17. Opinion of Attorney General James Speed, July__ 1865, reported in Benn Pitman, ed., *The Trials for Treason at Indianapolis: Disclosing the Plans for Establishing a Northwest Confederacy* (Cincinnati: Moore, Wilstach & Baldwin, 1865), appendix 403 (hereafter "Speed opinion").
18. Speed opinion, 403.
19. Speed opinion, 403.
20. U.S. Const. art. I, § 8, clause 10 authorizes Congress "to define and punish Piracies and Felonies committed on the high seas, and Offenses against the Law of Nations." Congress never passed any statute that would authorize the president to convene a military commission to try civilians for felonies committed on dry land that were punishable by state law. Section 2 of the Articles of War provided "That in time of war, all persons not citizens of, or owing allegiance to, the United States of America, who shall be found lurking as spies in or about the fortification or encampments of the armies of the United States, or any of them, shall suffer death, according to the law and usage of nations, by sentence of a general courts-martial." It did not provide for the establishment of a military commission to try civilians for felonies.
21. Coleman Phillipson, ed., *Wheaton's Elements of International Law: Fifth English Edition Revised Throughout, Considerably Enlarged and Re-written by Coleman Phillipson, M.A., LL.D., Litt. D., of the Inner Temple, Barrister-at-Law with an Introduction by the Rt. Hon Sir. Frederick Pollock, Bt., D.C.L., LL. D.* (London: Stevens & Sons, 1916) (hereafter *Wheaton's Elements of International Law*). Speed's opinion anticipated the thinking of Attorney General John Ashcroft during the post–September 11 era, reinforced by a memo prepared by Professor

John Yoo. Yoo contended that President Bush had the inherent power to set up military commissions to try alleged terrorists under Art. II § 2: "The President shall be Commander in Chief . . ."—the same section of the U.S. Constitution relied on by Speed. See John Yoo, "Memorandum Opinion: The President's Constitutional Authority to Conduct Military Operations against Terrorists and Nations Supporting Them," U.S. Department Justice, Opinions of the Office of Legal Counsel, September 25, 2001, http://www.justice.gov/sites/default/files/olc/opinions/2001/09/31/op-olc-v025-p0188_0.pdf.

22. The federal executive and judicial branches struggled with the status of the Confederate States. If the courts and the president had recognized the Confederate States as a foreign power, then there would be a cloak of legitimacy for secession. Instead, the courts and the White House carefully avoided any express or implied acknowledgment of the Confederate States of America. In The Brig Amy Warwick; The Schooner Crenshaw, the Barque Hiawatha and the Schooner Brillitante (The Prize Cases) 67 U.S. 635 (1863), the U.S Supreme Court had allowed vessels seized by the U.S. Navy en route to and from Southern ports in the Confederacy to be sold as prizes of war without recognizing the Confederate States as a belligerent sovereign nation. It allowed the sale by analogy to the seizure of foreign belligerent shipping during blockade under international law. The Emancipation Proclamation issued by President Lincoln in January 1863 relied on the president's Article II § 2 power to wage war for its validity. The proclamation treated slaves in the Confederacy as if the Confederates were not a sovereign nation. Speed's argument with respect to the international law of war ignored the Lincoln administration's efforts to treat the Confederate States as a nonentity.

23. See Vattel, *Law of Nations*, 3:412–17 § 293.

24. Gen. Order 100 art. 82. This paragraph categorizes any person who commits hostilities without commission, without being part of an organized hostile army as people who "are not public enemies, and therefore, if captured, are not entitled to the privileges of prisoners of war, but shall be treated summarily as highway robbers or pirates."

25. See 12 Stats. 755 (Ch. 81 3 Mar. 1863).

26. See Benn Pitman, ed., *The Assassination of President Lincoln and the Trial of Conspirators David E. Herold, Mary E. Surratt, Lewis Payne, George A. Atzerodt, Edward Spangler, Samuel A. Mudd, Samuel Arnold, Michael O'Loughlin* (New York: Moore, Wilstach & Baldwin, 1865), 251. Senator Johnson's plea was abstracted from the Pitman trial transcript by the Surratt Society and is available at http://www.surrattmuseum.org/documents/Bplact14.pdf.

27. Pitman, *Assassination of President Lincoln*, 254. General Ewing's plea to the jurisdiction was also abstracted from the Pitman trial transcript by the Surratt Society and is available at http://www.surrattmuseum.org/documents/Bplact15.pdf.

28. Pitman, *Assassination of President Lincoln*, 251, 254 (Johnson plea and Ewing plea).

29. Pitman, *Assassination of President Lincoln*, 251, 254 (Johnson plea and Ewing plea).

30. Pitman, *Assassination of President Lincoln*, 251 (Johnson plea).

31. See Charles W. Fairman, *History of the Supreme Court of the United States: Reconstruction and Reunion, 1864–1888* (New York: Macmillan, 1971), 200.

32. Pitman, *Assassination of President Lincoln*, 251 (Johnson argument).

33. Pitman, *Assassination of President Lincoln*, 251 (Johnson argument).

34. Pitman, *Assassination of President Lincoln*, 251 (Johnson argument).

35. Pitman, *Assassination of President Lincoln*, 251 (Johnson argument).

36. Pitman, *Assassination of President Lincoln*, 251 (Johnson argument).

37. Pitman, *Assassination of President Lincoln*, 251 (Johnson argument).

38. Pitman, *Assassination of President Lincoln*, 251 (Johnson argument).

39. Pitman, *Assassination of President Lincoln*, 251 (Ewing argument).

40. Ex parte Milligan, 71 U.S. (4 Wallace) 2, 120–21 (1866).

41. Ex parte Milligan, 71 U.S. 120–121.

42. The author has audited the Poore transcript for all objections, finding 111 objections in all raised by all parties, excluding two objections made by commission members (objections to Senator Johnson and to Gen. Edward Johnson as incompetent). The prosecution made eighty, the defendants twenty-eight. Three objections were not ruled on. The prosecution waived thirty-five of its objections; defense counsel waived six. The Pitman transcript consists of

summaries of testimony, and many objections made by both sides do not appear in that transcript.

43. See, e.g., testimony of William Ball, in Poore, *Conspiracy Trial*, 2:130–32; Charles Sweenay, in Poore, *Conspiracy Trial*, 2:242–44; James Young, in Poore, *Conspiracy Trial*, 2:244–46.

44. See, e.g., testimony of surgeon Salome Masch, in Poore, *Conspiracy Trial*, 2:120–24; Benjamin Sweerer, in Poore, *Conspiracy Trial*, 2:128–30.

45. See, e.g., testimony of Frederick Memmert, in Poore, *Conspiracy Trial*, 2:124–28; Erastus Ross, in Poore, *Conspiracy Trial*, 2:136–38; John LaTouche, in Poore, *Conspiracy Trial*, 2:138–39.

46. See, e.g., testimony of George F. Edmonds, in Poore, *Conspiracy Trial*, 2:274–77.

47. See, e.g., testimony of John S. Young, in Poore, *Conspiracy Trial*, 2:247–50; Col. Martin Burke, in Poore, *Conspiracy Trial*, 2:402–3.

48. See, e.g., testimony of Godfrey Hyams, in Poore, *Conspiracy Trial*, 2:407–17. Hyams was Dr. Blackburn's accomplice, arranging for shipments of trunk loads of clothing from yellow fever victims to Boston, Philadelphia, Baltimore, and New Bern, North Carolina. See also testimony of W. L. Wall, commission merchant who took the trunks of clothing on consignment from Hyams, using the alias "Harris," in Poore, *Conspiracy Trial*, 2:417–18, and A. Brenner, in Poore, *Conspiracy Trial*, 2:418–20.

49. See, e.g., Francis Wharton, *The Criminal Law of the United States Comprising a Digest of the Penal Statutes of the General Government and of Massachusetts, New York, Pennsylvania, and Virginia with the Decisions on Cases Arising upon Those Statutes Together With the English and American Authorities upon Criminal Law in General* (Philadelphia: James Kay, Jun. and Brother, 1846), 491–92.

50. Poore, *Conspiracy Trial*, 3:109–35 (Conover); Poore, *Conspiracy Trial*, 3:79–89, 493 (Montgomery recalled); Poore, *Conspiracy Trial*, 3:90–108 (Merritt).

51. Wharton, *Criminal Law*, 491–92.

52. The "anti-bootstrapping rule" was not inserted into the federal law of evidence until 1944. That rule precluded the introduction of conspirators' statements until the prosecution offered sufficient evidence from independent sources showing the nature, extent, and membership of the conspiracy. See Glasser v. United States, 315 U.S. 60 (1944). The anti-bootstrapping rule was determined not to apply to federal prosecutions under the federal rules of evidence in Bourjaily v. United States, 483 U.S. 171 (1987). It is doubtful that any state had such a rule in 1865. Since the federal law of evidence followed the adjectival law of the state in which the court sat, in this case the District of Columbia, which borrowed adjectival law from Maryland, no District or Maryland cases as of 1865 prevented a conspiracy from being established from the utterances of the conspirators, uncorroborated by external evidence.

53. Seymour J. Frank, "The Conspiracy to Implicate the Confederate Leaders in Lincoln's Assassination," *Mississippi Valley Historical Review* 40 (1954): 629, 634.

54. Poore, *Conspiracy Trial*, 3:109.

55. Poore, *Conspiracy Trial*, 3:109.

56. Poore, *Conspiracy Trial*, 3:124.

57. Poore, *Conspiracy Trial*, 3:110.

58. Poore, *Conspiracy Trial*, 3:110.

59. Poore, *Conspiracy Trial*, 3:115.

60. Poore, *Conspiracy Trial*, 3:111.

61. Poore, *Conspiracy Trial*, 3:111. Conover remarked that Thompson had declared earlier that the assassination of Lincoln, Vice President Johnson, Secretaries Seward and Stanton, and Justice Chase would leave the U.S. government without a head. He also mentioned that General Grant was also targeted.

62. Poore, *Conspiracy Trial*, 3:112.

63. Poore, *Conspiracy Trial*, 3:113. Conover went on to say he had almost daily contact with Thompson in which Thompson continued to talk about the plot to murder Lincoln.

64. Poore, *Conspiracy Trial*, 3:114.

65. Poore, *Conspiracy Trial*, 3:115.

66. Poore, *Conspiracy Trial*, 3:117 (cross-examination by William E. Doster).

67. Poore, *Conspiracy Trial*, 3:123 (cross-examination by Frederick Stone).
68. Poore, *Conspiracy Trial*, 3:127–29.
69. Poore, *Conspiracy Trial*, 3:79.
70. Poore, *Conspiracy Trial*, 3:79–80. Montgomery said that he had frequent encounters with Thompson, Cleary, and other agents in St. Catharines and in Montreal up to the date of the assassination.
71. Poore, *Conspiracy Trial*, 3:81. Montgomery then told the commission about a conversation he had with Clement Clay in 1864 allegedly attended by Lewis Powell a.k.a. Lewis Payne.
72. Poore, *Conspiracy Trial*, 3:83. Cleary also allegedly told Montgomery that Booth had been to Canada in the summer of 1864 and in December 1864.
73. Poore, *Conspiracy Trial*, 3:90.
74. Poore, *Conspiracy Trial*, 3:100 (cross-examination by Mr. Aiken).
75. Poore, *Conspiracy Trial*, 3:90–91. Merritt identified three Confederate agents, one of whom discussed the assassination of Lincoln with him.
76. Poore, *Conspiracy Trial*, 3:91.
77. Poore, *Conspiracy Trial*, 3:91.
78. Poore, *Conspiracy Trial*, 3:92.
79. Poore, *Conspiracy Trial*, 3:93.
80. Poore, *Conspiracy Trial*, 3:93. Merritt volunteered the names of other men considered for the role of assassin: George Harper, Charles Caldwell, Randall, and Harrison.
81. Poore, *Conspiracy Trial*, 3:93.
82. Poore, *Conspiracy Trial*, 3:98.
83. Poore, *Conspiracy Trial*, 3:94.
84. Poore, *Conspiracy Trial*, 3:94.
85. Poore, *Conspiracy Trial*, 3:95–96.
86. Poore, *Conspiracy Trial*, 3:102. Merritt said he then went to a judge of the assizes who told him that the matter had to go to a grand jury.
87. Poore, *Conspiracy Trial*, 3:96.
88. Poore, *Conspiracy Trial*, 3:97.
89. Poore, *Conspiracy Trial*, 3:105.
90. Poore, *Conspiracy Trial*, 3:108.
91. William Tidwell reached the same conclusion. See William Tidwell, *April '65: Confederate Covert Operations in the American Civil War*, vol. 3 (Kent, Ohio: Kent State University Press, 1995).
92. Frank, "Conspiracy to Implicate the Confederate Leaders," 629, 631. Merritt's perjury was reported to Judge Advocate General Holt before the end of the trial. The secretary of state forwarded letters from Thomas Miller, the Galt County attorney, and Solicitor General Davidson. Miller was prosecuting people before Justice Davidson in April 1865. Miller said that Dr. Merritt had not appeared in court during the April sessions. Justice Davidson said that Merritt's story "was a miserable falsification." Letter of J. Davidson, J.P. to Thos. Miller dated June 17, 1865; letter of Thos. Miller to Frederick W. A. Bruce dated June 19, 1865; cover letter to W. Hunter dated June 27, 1865, reprinted in William C. Edwards and Edward Steers, Jr., eds., *The Lincoln Assassination: The Evidence* (Urbana-Champaign: University of Illinois Press, 2009), 891–92.
93. Frank, "Conspiracy to Implicate the Confederate Leaders," 634.
94. Frank, "Conspiracy to Implicate the Confederate Leaders," 634.
95. Frank, "Conspiracy to Implicate the Confederate Leaders," 635.
96. Frank, "Conspiracy to Implicate the Confederate Leaders," 636.
97. Frank, "Conspiracy to Implicate the Confederate Leaders," 637–38.
98. Frank, "Conspiracy to Implicate the Confederate Leaders," 637–38.
99. *New York Times*, June 28, 1865, 1.
100. Frank, "Conspiracy to Implicate the Confederate Leaders," 638. See also *Toronto Daily Globe*, July 7, 1865.
101. Frank, "Conspiracy to Implicate the Confederate Leaders," 642.

102. Frank, "Conspiracy to Implicate the Confederate Leaders," 642. Snevel was paid $375 by the judge advocate general, reinforced by $100 from Conover for fabricating the false affidavit. Frank, "Conspiracy to Implicate the Confederate Leaders," 648.

103. Frank, "Conspiracy to Implicate the Confederate Leaders," 642–43. Conover produced two other false witnesses: Farnum B. Wright (a.k.a. John Waters), a New York bricklayer who swore that he was a clerk for Confederate commissary general of prisoners Winder, who died in 1865. According to Wright, Winder revealed to him the assassination plot and identified Jefferson Davis as the moving party behind the plot. Conover's last perjured witness was Peter Stevens, a Nyack, New York, justice of the peace who swore that Wright's testimony was true.

104. Frank, "Conspiracy to Implicate the Confederate Leaders," 648.

105. Frank, "Conspiracy to Implicate the Confederate Leaders," 646. Montgomery, still an employee of the War Department, told Conover that Campbell had disclosed his supposed testimony to friends of Jefferson Davis and would be prompted to tell the committee that he had lied in his deposition.

106. Frank, "Conspiracy to Implicate the Confederate Leaders," 648. See H.R. Report 104 39th Cong. 1st Sess. 39 (1866).

107. Frank, "Conspiracy to Implicate the Confederate Leaders," 648.

108. Frank, "Conspiracy to Implicate the Confederate Leaders," 652. Conover collected letters from the judge advocate general and sent them to the *New York Tribune*, showing that Judge Advocate Holt had accepted his story in 1865 and had continued to support Conover legally and with funds through 1867.

Chapter Five

The Case against Mary Surratt

> Mr. Lloyd, I want you have those shooting-irons ready: there will be parties here to-night who will call for them. . . . Before God, sir, I do not know this man; and I have never seen him.—Ben Perley Poore, *The Conspiracy Trial for the Murder of the President, and the Attempt to Overthrow the Government by the Assassination of Its Principal Officers*

The case against Mary Surratt has occupied the thoughts of scholars, history buffs, true crime amateur sleuths, and the press since 1865. In order to understand the effect of President Johnson's and Secretary Stanton's orders to try Booth's alleged accomplices before a military commission, the evidence for and against Mrs. Surratt will be developed and analyzed.

Mary Surratt's conviction and execution was at first approved by the public, despite the Victorian conviction that women, the weaker sex, ought not pay with their lives for capital crimes. Later, public opinion began to shift in opposition to her execution. Fanned by a stout publicist, David DeWitt, late nineteenth-century opinion held that Mrs. Surratt was wrongfully executed because she was a hapless woman victim caught in the web of conspiracy spun by her son and John Wilkes Booth. Twentieth-century opinion came around to an appraisal of her actions and an assertion that she, like Dr. Samuel Mudd, was an innocent bystander arrested and prosecuted by a vindictive Secretary Stanton to make a point. Otto Eisenschiml was the propagator of this position in his two assassination books. Twenty-first-century opinion makers seem to be divided: Mrs. Surratt has her champion Elizabeth Steger Trindal, who believed that she was wrongfully convicted; Kate Clifford Larson argued persuasively that she was a knowing member of Booth's conspiracy, willingly aiding and abetting Booth's plot.

PROSECUTION WITNESSES

The government evidence against Mrs. Surratt boiled down to the testimony of Louis Weichmann, John Lloyd, and the police officers present at the Surratt boardinghouse when Lewis Powell turned up on Mrs. Surratt's doorstep on the seventeenth of April.

Figure 5.1. The Surratt Boardinghouse, H Street NW, Washington, D.C. *Source:* Library of Congress.

John Lloyd

John Lloyd, the proprietor of Surratt's tavern, testified early in the trial. He related the story of Mrs. Surratt driving out to Surrattsville in a rented buggy, and of the conversation that passed between the two.[1]

Lloyd said:

> The first thing she said to me was, Talk about the Devil, and his imps will appear, or something to that effect. I said, I was not aware that I was a devil before. Well said she, Mr. Lloyd, I want you have those shooting-irons ready: there will be parties here to-night who will call for them. At the same time, she gave me something wrapped up in a newspaper. I did not undo it until I got up stairs.

Q. Did you undo it immediately after you got up stairs?

A. As soon as I got up stairs and saw what it was.

Q. Did you lay it down, and leave the package anywhere before it was undone?

A. No, sir: I undid it when I laid it out of my hands.

Q. Are you positive again that Mrs. Surratt told you, at that time, that shooting-irons would be called for that night?

A. I am very positive.

Q. At what time in the evening did you state that you had this conversation with Mrs. Surratt?

A. I judge it was in the neighborhood of five o'clock. I have nothing to go by particularly, without going to the house. I took no particular pains to see. It might have been a little later than five o'clock.[2]

Lloyd then testified about the arrival of Booth and Herold at the tavern door on the night of April 14. Lloyd told the panel that he gave a Spencer carbine, a pair of field glasses, and whiskey to Herold.[3] Lloyd also gave the following testimony:

Q. Did they say any thing in regard to the assassination as they rode away?

A. Just as they were about leaving, the man who was with Herold [Booth] said, "I will tell you some news if you want to hear it" or something to that effect. I said, "I am not particular: use your own choice about telling news." "Well," said he, "I am pretty certain that we have assassinated the President and Secretary Seward." I think that was his language as well as I can recollect: "We have assassinated" or "killed the President and Secretary Seward."[4]

Lloyd's testimony at the 1867 trial of John Surratt in U.S. District Court varied from his 1865 story. He testified that John Surratt had left guns, a rope, and a monkey wrench with him for safekeeping sometime prior to April 14, 1865. Lloyd repeated his earlier evidence showing that he met with Mrs. Surratt and Louis Weichmann three or four days before the assassination. He asserted that Mrs. Surratt told him to have the shooting irons ready; they would be wanted in a few days. His earlier 1865 testimony put this conversation on the afternoon of April 14.[5]

Lloyd admitted he had been drinking heavily on April 14, and he also said he could not be certain of the conversation he had with Mrs. Surratt on that afternoon.

A. I staid in Marlboro' for some time after the trial was over, drinking and playing cards. I didn't leave there until pretty late; I suppose it was five or six o'clock, may-be later, when I got home. I do not remember distinctly, but it appears to me in the confused memory I have of it, that the sun was not more than half an hour high when I got home. It did not appear to me so.

Q. What persons did you find at home when you got there?

A. I found a good many gentlemen there—I suppose some ten or twelve. I saw there, among others, Mrs. Surratt and this man Weichman.

Q. State if you then had any conversation with Mrs. Surratt; and if so, on what part of your premises, and what that conversation was.

A. When I drove up in my buggy to the back yard, Mrs. Surratt came out to meet me. She handed me a package, and told me, as well as I remember, to get the guns, or those things—I really forget now which, though my impression is that "guns" was the expression she made use of—and a couple of bottles of whiskey, and give them to whoever should call for them that night.

Q. What did you say to her?

A. I do not know that I made any reply to her at all. I was in liquor at the time, and being so, I did not want to have any conversation with her.

Q. How long did she stay there after this?

A. I do not remember. I went into my back room and threw myself on the lounge, when I immediately turned sick from the effect of the liquor. As I was raising up she came in and told me that her buggy spring was broken, and that I must do something to mend it. I told her, as well as I remember, that I had nothing to do it with, only to tie it with some rope yarn that I had.

Q. Do you recollect what time that was?

A. That was late in the evening after I got home.

Q. Before dark?

A. Yes.[6]

George Cottingham

Deputy Marshal George Cottingham testified for the prosecution that he arrested John Lloyd at Surrattsville. He repeated Lloyd's testimony that Mrs. Surratt told him to have the firearms ready for someone that evening.[7] He

Figure 5.2. Surratt Tavern, Clinton, Md. ***Source:*** **Photograph by the author.**

also repeated Lloyd's statement that the firearms were brought to the tavern by John Surratt.[8] Mrs. Surratt's lawyers chose to recall Cottingham as a hostile witness. Cottingham described how he interrogated Lloyd for two days. At first, Lloyd denied any knowledge of the kidnap or assassination conspiracy. Cottingham threatened him with prosecution as an accomplice. Lloyd then broke down. He told Cottingham that "'O my God! If I should make a confession, they would murder me.' Said I, 'Who would murder you?'—'These parties that are in this conspiracy.'"[9] Lloyd then told Cottingham about the April 11 and April 14 conversations with Mrs. Surratt about the "shooting irons." Defense counsel Frederick Aiken was shocked by Cottingham's testimony. He recalled Cottingham after the testimony of several witnesses for Michael O'Loughlen.

> Mr. Aiken stated that he proposed to follow it up by asking the witness whether he had not made a different statement to him [Mr. Aiken] with reference to what Mr. Lloyd had said.

Assistant Judge Advocate Bingham. Ask him what he said to you.

Mr. Aiken [to the witness]. I ask you what I stated to you.

The Witness. If the Court will allow me, I should like to tell the whole conversation. I met Mr. Aiken at the Metropolitan Hotel on Saturday evening last, I think. He asked me to take a drink. I went up, and drank with him. He then said, "I am going to have you as a witness in this case." He asked me to sit down on a sofa, and have some conversation. I said no, it would not look well for me to be sitting there; but I would go outside and take a walk. When we went outside, the first question Mr. Aiken put to me was, whether I was a Catholic. I said I was not. We walked along; and he said, "Lloyd has made a confession to you." Said I, "Yes." He then said, "Will you not state that confession to me?" I declined to do it, but told he might ask any questions, and I would answer them. He put the question to me, if Lloyd had stated that Mrs. Surratt had come down there, and told him to have the fire-arms ready. I said not. I had an object in that answer. I am now on my oath; and when I have been put on oath I have spoken the truth, and I can have witnesses to prove what I say,—six cavalrymen, Mr. Lloyd's wife, and Mrs. Offutt. He wanted to pick out of me in the case. That is not my business. I am an officer, and I did not want to let him know any thing on either side: I wanted to come to the Court, and state every thing that I know. I told him distinctly that I would not give him that confession; that I had no right to do so.

Q. [By Mr. Aiken.] Did I ask you if Mr. Lloyd, in his confession, said any thing at all in reference to Mrs. Surratt?

A. You asked me first whether Lloyd had made a confession to me; and I said, "Yes." Said you, "What is that confession? I should like to know it." My answer to you was, "I decline giving you that confession; but, if you will ask a question, I will answer you." That question you put to me, and I answered, I said, "No."

Q. That Mr. Lloyd did not say so?

A. I did say so. I do not deny that.

Q. Then what did you tell me this afternoon with reference to it?

A. I told you the same thing over again in the court-room when you asked me, before I came upon the stand. It is a part of my business—I am a detective officer—to gain my object. I obtained the confession from Lloyd through strategy.

Q. Then you gave me to understand, and you are ready now to swear to it, that you told me a lie?

A. Undoubtedly I told you a lie there; for I thought you had no business to ask me.

Q. No business? As my witness, had I not a right to have the truth from you?

A. I told you you might call me into Court; and I state here that I did lie to you; but, when put on my oath, I told the truth.[10]

Kate Clifford Larson analyzed this exchange and concluded that Aiken was foolish in allowing Cottingham to continue his answer on direct examination.[11] Larson also asserted that Cottingham's admission that he lied to Aiken when Aiken interviewed him outside the courtroom humiliated Aiken and devastated Mary Surratt's case.[12] The exchange between Cottingham and Aiken also proved that Cottingham made a prior inconsistent statement to Aiken during his interview at odds with his repetition of Lloyd's story about the "shooting irons." Aiken damaged Cottingham's credibility as a witness.

Louis Weichmann

Louis Weichmann testified that he made John Surratt's acquaintance in 1859 when both men were in St. Charles Seminary studying for the priesthood.[13] Weichmann stated that he started boarding with Mary Surratt in November

1864. On January 15, 1865, Weichmann was introduced to John Wilkes Booth by John Surratt in the presence of Dr. Samuel Mudd.[14] Weichmann testified that John Wilkes Booth came to Mrs. Surratt's house ten to fifteen times between January 1865 and April 1865. He asserted that Booth often went up to John Surratt's room to have private conversations with Surratt. Weichmann stated that George Atzerodt also frequented the Surratt boardinghouse in early 1865.[15] Weichmann testified that Lewis Powell, a.k.a. Lewis Paine a.k.a. Mr. Wood, also stopped at the Surratt boardinghouse in the winter of 1865. At first, Powell represented himself as "Mr. Wood" having no specific occupation. He stayed overnight and took his evening meal in Weichmann's room. Several weeks later Powell returned to the Surratt House using the alias Lewis Paine, claiming to be a Baptist preacher.[16][17] Weichmann testified that the infamous blockade runner Sarah Slater stopped at the Surratt boardinghouse on her way to Richmond. John Surratt escorted her to Richmond.[18] Surratt returned from Richmond on April 3, 1865, carrying gold and U.S. greenbacks. Surratt announced that he was going to Montreal. Weichmann said that that was the last time he saw Surratt.[19]

On April 11, 1865, Weichmann was sent by Mrs. Surratt to rent a buggy. He said that on that date Mrs. Surratt asked him to borrow John Wilkes Booth's buggy for a trip to Surrattsville to see Mr. Nothey about a debt owed to her. Booth had sold his buggy, but he gave Weichmann ten dollars to rent a buggy for the trip.[20] Nothing was said about any conspiratorial activities on her first trip to see Nothey. On April 14, Weichmann drove Mrs. Surratt out to Surrattsville that afternoon. She received a package from John Wilkes Booth to deliver to John Lloyd, the proprietor of Surratt's tavern. There is no evidence that she knew what was in the package. She also had a letter from Mr. Calvert, one of her creditors, urging her to collect the payment for the land sold to Nothey.[21]

Weichmann told the commission that he was sent by Mrs. Surratt to see Booth and to ask Booth to come to the Surratt boardinghouse on April 2. Mrs. Surratt asked Weichmann to go to Booth on April 14 to ask him to come to her house a second time. Booth made visits to Mrs. Surratt on both dates.[22] Weichmann could not state what the subject of their conversations were on those two days.

On April 14, Weichmann drove Mrs. Surratt out to Surrattsville in an attempt to locate Mr. Nothey and collect the debt due her so that she could pay off Mr. Calvert. Weichmann observed Mrs. Surratt and John Lloyd having a conversation in low tones, none of which he was able to overhear.[23] Weichmann's evidence was circumstantial corroboration for Lloyd's assertion that Mrs. Surratt told him to have the shooting irons ready for the night of April 14–15 because he confirmed that Lloyd and Mrs. Surratt had a conversation in low tones on April 14. Weichmann's testimony demonstrated that John Wilkes Booth was a frequent visitor to the Surratt boardinghouse in the winter of 1865 where Booth met with known fellow accomplices. This circumstantial evidence showed that Mrs. Surratt knew that Booth, her son, and the other accomplices were planning to kidnap President Lincoln.

Booth's meeting with Mrs. Surratt in the early afternoon of April 14 just before she left for Surrattsville and Booth's entrusting her with a package for John Lloyd was inexplicable unless Booth had enlisted Mrs. Surratt as an accomplice in his plan to murder President Lincoln. Weichmann's evidence was circumstantial proof that Mrs. Surratt's "cover story" about going to Surrattsville to collect a debt from Mr. Nothey was untrue. It showed that the purpose of her April 14 trip to Surrattsville was to deliver a package for Booth and to have some sort of private conversation with John Lloyd. Although Weichmann steadfastly denied that his evidence implicated Mrs. Surratt as an accessory before the fact to murder, his testimony gave circumstantial support to the government's case against Mrs. Surratt.

The Detectives

R. C. Morgan, a detective in the War Department, testified that he was sent to the Surratt boardinghouse shortly before 11:00 p.m. on April 17, 1865, to conduct a search for papers and to arrest the residents. He met Major Smith and Captain Wermerskirk at the Surratt boardinghouse while these officers were arresting the residents. Lewis Powell turned up on the doorstep carrying a pickax. He asserted he was hired to dig a drain for Mrs. Surratt and came by for instructions.[24]

Major Smith, the lead detective, also testified to Powell's arrival at Mrs. Surratt's boardinghouse. Smith then turned to Mrs. Surratt and said:

> "Mrs. Surratt, will you step here a minute?" Mrs. Surratt stepped there. Said I, "Do you know this man?" She said, raising her right hand, "Before God, sir, I do not know this man; and I have never seen him." I then placed Payne under arrest, and told he was so suspicious a character, that I would send him to Colonel Wells's or General Augur's headquarters for further examination.[25]

Major Smith's evidence that Mrs. Surratt denied knowing Lewis Powell a.k.a. Paine appeared to be a deliberate lie. Her inability to identify Powell before the detectives was incredible when compared to Louis Weichmann's testimony about Paine's three overnight stays at the Surratt boardinghouse in the winter of 1865, and his assumed identity of Mr. Wood the Baptist minister.

Henry Von Steinacker

Mrs. Surratt's counsel thought that the evidence of Henry Von Steinacker, a Union deserter who joined the Confederate army and served as an engineer on the staff of Gen. Edward Johnson, was critical to the defense. Von Steinacker testified to an 1863 meeting between John Wilkes Booth and an accompanying trip by horseback. According to Von Steinacker, Booth told him that "Lincoln must go up the spout" (i.e., be killed) to aid the South's victory.[26] He also testified to a secret meeting between Booth and staff officers from General Johnson's division held three or four days after Von Steinacker's initial encounter with Booth. Von Steinacker was not invited to the meeting, but he did know what was discussed, a plot to kill President Lincoln involving Booth: "The purpose of the meeting was, as I was informed afterwards, to send certain officers on detached service to Canada and the borders, and to deliver prisoners, to lay Northern cities in ashes, and finally to get after the members of the cabinet, and to kill the President."[27]

It was unclear why Mrs. Surratt's defense counsel were so intent in discrediting this evidence that did not directly relate to their client. Defense counsel never objected to the introduction of any of the evidence regarding Confederate atrocities and covert actions in Canada.

DEFENSE WITNESSES

General Edward Johnson

Defense counsel called Maj. Gen. Edward Johnson, CSA for the purpose of rebutting the testimony of Henry Von Steinacker. General Harris, one of the members of the commission, objected to General Johnson giving evidence on the ground that he was incompetent having borne arms against the United States. Mr. Aiken reminded the panel that Willie Jett, a Confederate soldier who had not taken the oath of allegiance, had been allowed to give evidence for the prosecution. The objection was overruled.[28] General Johnson testified that Henry Von Steinacker was a private in the engineers on his staff. Johnson stated he had no knowledge of any meeting of officers in his division to discuss the assassination of President Lincoln.[29] Johnson stated that Von Steinacker was a Union deserter.[30] Oscar Heinrichs, an engineering officer on General Johnson's staff, was called for the defense. Heinrichs testified that he knew Von Steinacker, a private and draftsman on his staff. Heinrichs stated he did not know John Wilkes Booth and never heard any discussion of the assassination of President Lincoln among the officers of the division.[31]

Mrs. Surratt's defense counsel wasted time in attempting to discredit Von Steinacker's testimony. Defense counsel apparently did not make a concerted plan to discredit the prosecution's claim that Booth's plot was part of a much larger conspiracy to destabilize the United States government. No doubt the largely irrelevant evidence from several sources about Confederate covert activities in Canada and maltreatment of Union prisoners of war served to reinforce the notion that the Confederate high command had devised a plan to destabilize the United States in order to salvage a losing war.

Defense Character Witnesses

The defense called six character witnesses, five of whom were Rev. B. F. Wiget,[32] Rev. Francis Boyle,[33] Father N. D. Young,[34] Father Charles Stonestreet,[35] and Father Peter Lanihan.[36] All the priests testified that Mrs. Surratt's reputation was to the effect that she had a good Christian character. Two of the character witnesses had not had any contact with Mrs. Surratt for several years. Defense witness Z. G. Jenkins, Mary Surratt's brother, stated that Mrs. Surratt had a character trait of loyalty to the United States.[37] In a civilian court, defense character witnesses were permitted to testify as to the accused's good moral character. The trial judge would ordinarily give an instruction that if the jury believed the accused was of good moral character, it should acquit the accused. The Hunter Commission was under no obligation to follow the law. It could, and did, discount the defense character witnesses.[38]

The Incident Witnesses

The defense had to discredit John Lloyd's testimony about the "shooting irons." Joseph Nott, the bartender at the Surrattsville tavern, was called as a defense witness. He testified that Lloyd was drunk on the afternoon of April 14.[39] John Lusby testified that John Lloyd "was very drunk, I think," on the afternoon of April 14, 1865.[40] B. F. Gwynn told the commission that Lloyd had been "drinking right smartly" on the afternoon of April 14.[41] Gwynn also testified he met John Lloyd in Marlborough, Maryland, that afternoon and in Gwynn's opinion Lloyd had been drinking heavily.[42] Lay opinions on the issue of a witness's intoxication were admissible in civilian courts to prove the witness's lack of ability to observe an event and to have accurate recollection of what had occurred.[43] Eliza Holohan, one of Mrs. Surratt's boarders, was called by the defense. She admitted to seeing Powell, known to her as "Mr. Wood," a Baptist preacher, and Atzerodt, known as "Port Tobacco," at Mrs. Surratt's house. She mentioned that both men took rooms with Mrs. Surratt for some period of time.[44]

Poor Eyesight Witnesses

The defense needed to explain why Mrs. Surratt did not recognize Lewis Powell when he turned up on her doorstep on April 17. Eliza Holohan and Honora Fitzpatrick, who boarded with Mrs. Surratt, testified for the defense. Ms. Fitzpatrick stated that Powell (known as Mr. Wood) and Atzerodt had boarded briefly during the winter of 1864–1865 at Mrs. Surratt's and, despite objection from the judge advocate, managed to state that Mrs. Surratt sent Atzerodt away.[45] She testified that Mrs. Surratt could not sew or read at night due to her weak eyes.[46] Ms. Holohan also swore that Mrs. Surratt had bad eyesight.[47] Mrs. Surratt's poor vision was confirmed by the testimony of Augustus S. Howell, an infamous blockade runner, who related a story in which Mrs. Surratt asked him to read a newspaper to her at dusk. Howell denied that he knew Mrs. Surratt had bad eyesight. Howell also testified that he went to the Surratt boardinghouse after dark one evening and Mrs. Surratt failed to recognize him, even though the gaslight was turned up in her hallway. Unfortunately, Howell's responses to cross-examination about his "occupation" that involved trips to Richmond to sell letters of credit were evasive and discredited his testimony.[48]

The Nothey-Calvert Affair

George Calvert was called as a defense witness to authenticate a letter he wrote to Mrs. Surratt concerning a debt due him. The government did not have the letter in court, but promised to produce it for inspection.[49] B. F. Gwynn testified that he met Mrs. Surratt at Surrattsville on April 14 and took a letter from her to deliver to Mr. Nothey.[50] Z. G. Jenkins told the panel under oath that he was present on April 14 when Mrs. Surratt and Louis Weichmann drove up in their buggy. Jenkins remembered seeing the letter from Mr. Calvert that afternoon.[51] Jenkins also stated that he had never heard Mrs. Surratt discuss a plot to kidnap President Lincoln, or a plot to assassinate him.[52] John Nothey testified that he met Mrs. Surratt only once to attempt to settle the payment due her for land sold to him. He stated he did not meet with her on April 14, 1865.[53] Anna Surratt took the stand in her mother's behalf. She testified that her mother had very poor eyesight and often failed to recognize her friends.[54] She testified her mother never talked about kidnapping President Lincoln and no one at the Surratt boardinghouse ever discussed assassinating the president.[55]

Attacking Henry Von Steinacker

Defense counsel attempted to present evidence impeaching the testimony of Henry Von Steinacker. Von Steinacker was a Union deserter who joined the Confederate army and served on the staff of Maj. Gen. Edward Johnson. Von Steinacker testified that he saw John Wilkes Booth in Richmond in 1863. Von Steinacker had been convicted of theft. Unfortunately Aiken and Clampitt did not learn of Von Steinacker's shady past until he was discharged as a witness. They requested the court to recall Von Steinacker for purposes of presenting impeaching evidence.[56] General Hunter refused to permit his recall. The court did allow Gen. Edward Johnson, CSA to testify that he never saw John Wilkes Booth and there was no meeting with his staff to discuss the assassination of Lincoln.[57] Defense counsel were unable to discredit the testimony of Louis Weichmann, whose evidence showed that Mary Surratt aided John Wilkes Booth by taking his binoculars to Surratt's tavern on the afternoon of April 14.

Mary Surratt was condemned to death by hanging on June 30, 1865. The sentences handed down by the Hunter Commission were forwarded by Judge Advocate General Holt to President Johnson for approval. The sentence relating to Mary Surratt was accompanied by a recommendation for clemency for Mrs. Surratt based on her age and sex. The recommendation was signed by five of the nine commission members.[58] President Johnson signed her death warrant despite the recommendation for clemency. Only Holt and Johnson were present when Holt delivered the Hunter Commission's sentences to the president for approval. Joseph Holt maintained that President Johnson saw the clemency recommendation and signed Mrs. Surratt's death warrant despite the recommendation. President Johnson claimed in 1873 that he never saw the clemency recommendation.[59]

Within a decade after Mrs. Surratt was executed, commentators and historians probed the legitimacy of her death sentence. In 1880, Mrs. Surratt's lawyer John W. Clampitt published an article in the *North American Review* in which he revealed a discussion he had with Maj. Gen. David Hunter. Hunter told Clampitt that the commission had initially voted against the death penalty for Mrs. Surratt. Judge Advocate Holt and his assistant John Bingham were allowed to deliberate with the commission. Holt demanded that the testimony against Mrs. Surratt be reread and reinterpreted. He proposed an amended finding of guilt, voting the death penalty for Mrs. Surratt, and attaching to that sentence a clemency recommendation. The commission eventually adopted Holt's proposed findings for Mrs. Surratt.[60]

General Hunter disapproved of Holt's demand to reread and reinterpret the testimony. Although military commission trials were governed by the Articles of War to some extent, the normal procedural safeguards that protected the accused from prosecutorial interference with deliberations simply did not exist at that time.

Mrs. Surratt's case lay dormant until 1895. In 1895, ex-congressman David DeWitt published the *Judicial Murder of Mary E. Surratt*.[61] DeWitt contended that Mary Surratt did not receive a fair and impartial trial. He based his contention on a number of incidents occurring during trial. Senator Reverdy Johnson of Maryland had agreed to represent Mrs. Surratt pro bono. General Harris, one of the members of the commission, objected to Johnson's appearance before the court unless he took a loyalty oath. Senator Johnson, with typical Southern sense of honor, fired back that he was a U.S. senator sworn to uphold the Constitution and a former attorney general of the United States. The demand that he take a loyalty oath was an insult to his dignity.[62] Johnson seldom appeared at trial after the challenge to his loyalty. He left the conduct of the defense of Mrs. Surratt in the hands of Fred Aiken and John Clampitt, very junior members of the bar with limited trial experience. Senator Johnson did file a plea to the jurisdiction of the commission, arguing that as the civilian courts were open and Washington was not under threat of invasion, trial of civilians by military commission was unconstitutional—anticipating the U.S. Supreme Court's decision in *Ex parte Milligan*. General Hunter denied the plea to the jurisdiction of the commission. In 1865, there was no mechanism by which that ruling could be reviewed by an independent judicial officer.

WAS MARY SURRATT GUILTY OF CONSPIRACY TO MURDER LINCOLN?

The evidence showing that Mary Surratt was a knowing member of the conspiracy to assassinate Abraham Lincoln is very weak. The prosecution's testimony established that her boardinghouse was a safe house for Confederate blockade runners, including her son John. There is no direct evidence showing that Mary Surratt was aware of the conspiracy to kidnap or kill President Lincoln, and no direct evidence showing she was a knowing participant in Booth's plot. The evidence did show that Booth made use of her safe house to meet with fellow accomplices in the winter and early spring of 1865. According to Louis Weichmann, Booth and his associates never talked in front of Mrs. Surratt about their plans.

Mrs. Surratt was charged with taking part in a treasonable conspiracy. The government failed to produce two witnesses to any treasonable act that she committed. If she had been tried in a civilian court, the defense would have good grounds for a directed verdict of acquittal. John Lloyd's evidence that Mrs. Surratt told him to have the shooting irons ready on the afternoon of April 14, 1865, is highly suspect and uncorroborated. Granted, if Mrs. Surratt told Lloyd to "have the shooting irons ready" for use either to kidnap Lincoln or to be used by the men who murdered him, she would have committed a treasonable act. It is very difficult to accept Lloyd's evidence at face value. First, Lloyd, a habitual drinker, was intoxicated on the afternoon of April 14. Second, the War Department threatened Lloyd with prosecution for conspiracy if he failed to identify other members of the conspiracy. Third, Louis Weichmann could not overhear the conversation between Lloyd and Mrs. Surratt, hence Lloyd's evidence was not fully corroborated. Fourth, Marshal Cottingham's testimony repeating Lloyd's statement about the shooting irons was contradicted by his earlier out-of-court statement to Aiken that Lloyd said nothing about Mrs. Surratt telling him to have the shooting irons ready.

Louis Weichmann's evidence showed that Mrs. Surratt carried out an errand for John Wilkes Booth on the afternoon of April 11 and a second errand on the afternoon of April 14—delivery of the field glasses to Lloyd. This chore was secondary to her attempt to collect the balance due on land conveyed to Mr. Nothey so that she could pay off Mr. Calvert. Nothey and Calvert testified to the existence of the land indebtedness and Calvert's collection attempt. Weichmann never knew what the package entrusted to her by Booth contained. This is not evidence of treason.

The evidence would at best prove that Mrs. Surratt unintentionally aided and abetted the assassination plot by providing a meeting place for Booth's accomplices and delivering Booth's package to Lloyd. Taking Lloyd's evidence at face value, there was no direct evidence showing that Mrs. Surratt was aware why the "shooting irons" were to be picked up by Lincoln's assassin on the night of April 14–15. Lloyd's testimony about having the shooting irons ready was given under fear of prosecution for conspiracy to kill the president. Lloyd was under the influence of alcohol on April 14 when Mrs. Surratt allegedly made the "shooting irons" statement to him. Lloyd's credibility was suspect. He had both motive and opportunity to make up a story implicating Mrs. Surratt to save himself from prosecution. Mrs. Surratt's statement to the detectives that she did not recognize Lewis Powell may have been at worst a lie to protect herself and her son from arrest by the detectives who came to her boardinghouse on April 17. It may also have been the truth—given the testimony about her poor vision.

Senator Reverdy Johnson's plea to the jurisdiction of the Hunter Commission based on his reading of the constitution would ultimately prevail in 1866 when the U.S. Supreme Court overturned the conviction of Lambdin Milligan, one of the alleged Northwest Conspirators, tried by military commission in Indianapolis in 1865. Justice David Davis, writing for the majority, in *Ex parte Milligan*[63] said that when the civilian courts are open and no threat of invasion exists, a civilian cannot be tried by military commission for a civilian offense.[64] Chief Justice Chase, writing for the minority, concurred in the result, but not in Davis's reasoning. Chase held that the executive branch of the government could not authorize trial by military commission unless Congress passed a statute delegating authority to the president to set up military commissions to try civilians.[65]

In a civilian court, the case against Mary Surratt would have fallen apart. She would have been entitled to the standard good moral character instruction. The prosecution could not prove beyond a reasonable doubt that she was a conspirator or a knowing accessory before the fact to murder.

POSTTRIAL EVIDENCE

Kate Clifford Larson, who drew the conclusion that Mary Surratt was a conspirator, based her conclusion on a posttrial statement made by Richard Smoot in his 1908 book *The Unwritten History of the Assassination of Abraham Lincoln*. Smoot, writing forty-three years after the events of April 1865, said that sometime in 1865, he went to Washington to talk to John Surratt about final arrangements for transporting President Lincoln across the Potomac. He knew Mrs. Surratt slightly, and went to her boardinghouse on H Street to locate her son. John Surratt was not at home. Smoot and Mrs. Surratt allegedly had a conversation about the kidnap conspiracy:

> I asked the old lady where I could see her son John. For a moment her face was a study. She really made me uneasy with her penetrating look of inquiry. She evidently was not satisfied with my appearance, for after a brief silence she informed me that she was unable to tell me of the exact whereabouts of her son, or when and where I could see him. I saw that I was under suspicion, and so told her the object of my visit. In an instant her whole demeanor changed. Her face brightened and she extended me a most cordial greeting. She eagerly inquired if the boat was in place and easily accessible, as it might be called into requisition that night. I informed her what disposition had been made of the boat, and that Bateman was in charge of it. Then she assumed an anxious expression and hurriedly and earnestly importuned me to leave the city at once. She did not vouchsafe me any explanation of her sudden change of disposition, but I inferred that she feared that I had been followed, and that my presence in her house would lead to her arrest as well as my own. She whispered to me that if I would return to the house on Friday I would most likely see John and the boys, and she showed me a letter written by John to a Miss Mitchell, in which he said that he would be in Washington on the following Friday if he possibly could.[66]

Smoot did not testify before the Hunter Commission. Smoot's visit with Mary Surratt is not corroborated by any other witness to the assassination events. It was written four decades after the event by an old man, and to that extent, its truthfulness may be questioned.

The other posttrial evidence against Mary Surratt came from George Atzerodt, who gave a statement to Baltimore provost marshal McPhail that was excluded from evidence at trial and not discovered until the 1990s. Atzerodt said: "Booth told me that Mrs. Surratt went to Surrattsville to get out the guns (Two Carbines) which had been taken to that place by Herold. This was Friday. The carriage was hired at Howard's."[67]

Confessions of an accused that implicate others in the crime that the accused committed are not credible and may not be admitted in a trial where the person who confessed is being tried jointly with other defendants. The Fifth Amendment states the accused may not be forced to testify against himself, which prevents other defendants from cross-examining the defendant who confessed.[68]

MODERN SURRATT APOLOGISTS AND HER MODERN DETRACTORS

The two best studies of the Lincoln assassination by Edward Steers Jr. and Michael Kauffman did not conclude that Mary Surratt was innocent.[69] Each author carefully avoided any judgment relating to her innocence and neither author argued that her trial was unconstitutional, although both found irregularities that occurred during trial.

Mary Surratt's Apologists

Mrs. Surratt has had her champions in the past eighty years. Otto Eisenschiml cast doubt on Mary Surratt's participation in the assassination of Lincoln in 1940 in his second assassination work, *In the Shadow of Lincoln's Death.*[70] Eisenschiml devoted three chapters to his review of the evidence against Mary Surratt and her treatment by her jailors prior to trial. Eisenschiml suggested that Secretary Stanton had assured Mrs. Surratt's brother that her life would be spared if Jenkins gave information on the probable course of Booth's flight through Charles County, Maryland. Eisenschiml cited articles in the *Washington Sunday Gazette* authored by Col. William Wood, the warden of the Old Capitol Prison where Mrs. Surratt was briefly confined before being transferred to the Washington Arsenal Prison. Eisenschiml said that Jenkins received a false promise from Stanton who had no intention of preventing Mrs. Surratt's execution.[71]

Eisenschiml never asserted that Mary Surratt was not guilty of conspiracy to assassinate Abraham Lincoln. Following his successful method of innuendo developed in *Why Was Lincoln Murdered?* he suggested that the government "fixed" the trial to be able to convict and execute Mary Surratt:

> Summarizing the evidence, what is there to show? Mrs. Surratt was promised clemency and was deluded at the last moment; her execution followed the sentence within one day; she was not allowed to proclaim her innocence in public; the attending priest was admonished to keep quiet; her lawyers were not allowed to converse with her in privacy; the leading attorney abandoned his client and was later rewarded politically; two junior lawyers who might have been indiscrete were given government positions.[72]

Otto Eisenschiml never argued that Mary Surratt was not guilty of the crimes charged against her. He suggested that she was given a false promise of executive clemency, was tortured by her keepers, and her lawyers were bought off by the government in order to be sure that she did not get a competent defense.

Elizabeth Steger Trindal published *Mary Surratt: An American Tragedy* in 1996.[73] Trindal argued that Mrs. Surratt was innocent of any involvement in the kidnapping conspiracy or the assassination of Lincoln.[74] Trindal analyzed the case against Mary Surratt as presented by the government at trial. Trindal correctly noted that Louis Weichmann's evidence had not directly implicated Mary Surratt in the assassination plot. She did not accept John Lloyd's testimony about the "shooting irons" because her research indicated that Mrs. Surratt talked to Lloyd only after Bennett Gwynn had pointed out that a spring was broken on her buggy. She noted that John Lloyd had given a prior statement denying that Booth had passed by the Surratt tavern. Lloyd disclaimed any knowledge of the assassination plan.[75] Trindal concluded that Mary Surratt was an innocent victim of a vindictive government.[76]

Al Benson Jr., a twenty-first-century neo-Confederate researcher, maintains a blog that he uses to report on his revisionist findings. Benson is suspicious of the government in Washington and published a two-part blog post on Mary Surratt in 2013. Benson turned Eisenschiml's innuendos into assertions of fact. He did not cite Eisenschiml's *In the Shadow of Lincoln's Death*, even though his blog posts followed the portions of Eisenschiml's book devoted to Mary Surratt's trial and execution, explicitly referring to Colonel Wood's articles in the *Washington Sunday Gazette* and Father Walter's admonition to Mary Surratt not to tell the crowd at her execution that she was innocent.[77]

A common thread runs through Mary Surratt's modern apologists. All assert that Mrs. Surratt was the victim of a vengeful government that maliciously destroyed Reverdy Johnson's morale by claiming that Johnson was disloyal, placing her defense in the hands of two inexperienced young lawyers. All attempt to explain away the "shooting irons" testimony of John Lloyd and Louis Weichmann's testimony about the two trips to Surratt's tavern on April 11 and 14. None of the apologists deal with posttrial documents such as Atzerodt's lost confession and Richard Smoot's memoirs relating to Mary Surratt's knowledge of the kidnapping conspiracy. Her supporters did not argue that she had no knowledge of Booth's kidnapping plot or the plot to murder President Lincoln.

Mary Surratt's Modern Detractors

Not all modern commentators believe that Mrs. Surratt was innocent. H. Donald Winkler evaluated the evidence for and against Mary Surratt in *Lincoln and Booth*, concluding that Mary Surratt was morally responsible for failing to prevent Lincoln's death. He acknowledged that Judge Advocate General Holt and his coprosecutors had the duty to produce John Wilkes

Booth's diary, held by Secretary Stanton. By failing to produce evidence that arguably exculpated Mary Surratt, her conviction was unfair. Nonetheless Winkler noted that Louis Weichmann claimed in his 1898 memoir that Mary Surratt and John Surratt were deeply involved in the assassination conspiracy. Therefore, Mary Surratt was morally responsible for Lincoln's death because she could have prevented it by going to the police or the War Department and exposing Booth and her son as assassins.[78] Kate Clifford Larson's *The Assassin's Accomplice: Mary Surratt and the Plot to Kill Abraham Lincoln* takes the viewpoint that the evidence showed that Mrs. Surratt was a knowledgeable participant in the kidnapping conspiracy.[79] Larson was the historical advisor for Robert Redford's 2011 motion picture *The Conspirator*. That production contains a fictionalized scene in which Mary Surratt tells Frederick Aiken, one of her lawyers, that she knew about Booth's plot to kidnap President Lincoln. Larson concluded that:

> Today, at the beginning of the twenty-first century, the evidence cannot be ignored. Mary Surratt indeed "kept the nest that hatched the egg." She could have chosen not to help Booth, but she decided to assist him in whatever way she could. In providing a war home, private encouragement, and material support to Abraham Lincoln's murderer, she offered more than most of Booth's other supporters. For that Mary Surratt lost her life and must forever be remembered as the assassin's accomplice.[80]

Larson's analysis has not been shared by other authors. She follows Steers in conflating the kidnap conspiracy with the assassination conspiracy. Her conclusion that Atzerodt's confession and Richard Smoot's passage in his 1908 memoir proves that Mary Surratt was one of the conspirators depends on Steers's argument that the Booth kidnapping conspiracy morphed into the assassination conspiracy, making all parties to the kidnapping plot guilty of conspiring with Booth to murder the president, the vice president, and the secretary of state.[81]

The most probable version of Mary Surratt's case, based on known documents and on the testimony of Weichmann, Lloyd, and Mrs. Offutt, Lloyd's sister-in–law, is as follows:

Mary Surratt's husband, John Surratt Sr., was a participant in the Maryland Confederate underground operation. The courier line passed by the Surratt tavern, and Surratt Sr. was a postmaster for mail to and from the Confederacy. At his death, John Surratt Jr. took over his father's services for the Confederate underground from 1862 to 1864, when Maryland passed a constitutional amendment freeing all slaves. Mary Surratt could not run the tavern and the Surratt farm without slaves, so she leased the tavern and farm to John Lloyd, another Confederate underground operative.

When Mrs. Surratt opened her boardinghouse on H Street in Washington, she rented rooms to members of John Wilkes Booth's kidnap plot. Much like the strategy that former president Ronald Reagan employed with the Iran-Contra operation, she did not ask her son and his friends what they were up to. She did support the kidnapping conspiracy indirectly and unknowingly by providing a safe house for Booth's accomplices, not knowing that her son and Booth had agreed to kidnap President Lincoln. She also entertained John Wilkes Booth and enjoyed his attention to herself and her family.

On April 11, she was planning a trip to Surrattsville to collect a debt from Mr. Nothey. Louis Weichmann drove her in a buggy rented with funds from John Wilkes Booth. On the way to Surrattsville, Mrs. Surratt's buggy passed John Lloyd's buggy going south and they exchanged words. Louis Weichmann recalled that Lloyd and Mrs. Surratt spoke about arranging for the release of blockade runner Augustus Howell after Howell took the oath of allegiance. He did not report any conversation about shooting irons, contradicting Lloyd's testimony.[82] On April 14, in response to the demand letter from Mr. Calvert, she planned another trip to collect the Nothey debt. Booth met with her that morning and asked her to take a package to Surrattsville for him to deliver to John Lloyd. She agreed, not knowing what was in the package. Once she arrived at Surrattsville on Good Friday afternoon, she delivered the package to Lloyd's sister and made a fruitless attempt to get Nothey to come to Surrattsville and pay his debt to her. As she was leaving, Bennett Gwynn, who happened to be at the tavern, pointed out that the spring on her rented buddy was broken. John Lloyd, who had been drinking and by his own admission was very drunk, pulled in in his buggy. Mrs. Surratt asked Lloyd to fix the buggy spring. Lloyd was too intoxicated to be much help—he found a rope to tie up the broken spring and Weichmann and Surratt left Surrattsville for home. In the early evening, Booth paid a brief call on Mrs. Surratt at the H Street boardinghouse. What the two talked about is unknown.

Assuming that Booth had given her a message to be delivered to Lloyd about having the two carbines and revolvers ready for that night, there is no evidence that Mary Surratt knew that Booth planned to murder President Lincoln, since the weapons were originally secured for the kidnap plot. In order to be guilty of an accessory before the fact to murder, the accused must be shown to have known that the acts committed were in furtherance of the murder, and that the accused intended to further the homicide.[83] Lloyd's doubtful statement, later retracted in 1867, simply does not carry sufficient weight to establish Mary Surratt's guilty knowledge.

Mary Surratt did not have a fair trial before the military commission. John Lloyd probably gave fabricated evidence hoping to avoid punishment for participation in Booth's kidnap plot.[84] After the failed March 1865 attempt to kidnap President Lincoln, John Surratt rode out to Surrattsville and left two Spencer carbines, pistols, and knives to be called for on the next attempt to capture President Lincoln. Lloyd agreed to hide the weapons in the attic wall. When Booth and Herold came to Surrattsville on April 14 and asked for the weapons, Lloyd fetched the carbines, pistols, and knives from their hiding place for the fugitives. At the Hunter Commission trial, Lloyd accused Mrs. Surratt of leaving the "shooting irons" message—in 1867 during the trial of John Surratt he did not make the accusation that Mary Surratt told him to get the shooting irons ready on April 14.

Louis Weichmann's testimony, standing alone, did not prove that Mrs. Surratt was an accomplice. Lloyd's testimony about the "shooting irons," an uncorroborated assertion that Weichmann could not confirm, convinced the Hunter Commission that Mary Surratt was Booth's accomplice and an accessory before the fact to murder. The incident involving her failure to identify Lewis Powell looked to be her attempt to hide her guilty knowledge that Powell was involved with Booth in the assassination plot. It did not prove that she knew that Powell was ordered to murder Secretary Seward in aid of Booth's attempt to decapitate the government. The evidence against Mary Surratt failed to prove that she knew she was furthering Booth's murder of President Lincoln when she traveled to Surrattsville on April 14, 1865.

NOTES

1. Ben Perley Poore, ed., *The Conspiracy Trial for the Murder of the President, and the Attempt to Overthrow the Government by the Assassination of Its Principal Officers, Edited with an Introduction by Ben. Perley Poore*, 1:115, 122–23 (Boston: J. E. Tilton, 1865).
2. Poore, *Conspiracy Trial*, 1:117–18.
3. Poore, *Conspiracy Trial*, 1:119.
4. Poore, *Conspiracy Trial*, 1:119.
5. See *The Trial of John H. Surratt in the Criminal Court of the District of Columbia (Transcript of the Trial of John H. Surratt, U.S. District Court, District of Columbia)* (Washington: French & Richardson, 1867) 2:275–302.
6. *Trial of John H. Surratt*, 3:281.
7. Poore, *Conspiracy Trial*, 2:193. Cottingham also testified that he searched the Surrattsville tavern and could not find the second Spencer carbine that Booth and Herold had left behind. Finally, a hired man got an axe and broke through the lath and plaster to the place where the Spencer had fallen.
8. Poore, *Conspiracy Trial*, 2:195.
9. Poore, *Conspiracy Trial*, 2:193–94.
10. Poore, *Conspiracy Trial*, 2:215–16.
11. Kate Clifford Larson, *The Assassin's Accomplice: Mary Surratt and the Plot to Kill Abraham Lincoln* (New York: Basic Books, 2008), 161.
12. Larson, *Assassin's Accomplice*, 162.
13. Poore, *Conspiracy Trial*, 1:66–67.
14. Poore, *Conspiracy Trial*, 1:66. Weichmann was wrong about the date. The meeting between Booth, Surratt, and Mudd took place on December 23, 1864.
15. Poore, *Conspiracy Trial*, 1:68. Weichmann estimated that Atzerodt called ten to fifteen times at the Surratt boardinghouse.
16. Lewis Powell used two aliases during the time he worked with Booth. He was known as "Lewis Payne" when he took a loyalty oath in Virginia and is referred to as "Payne" in the Pittman and Poore transcripts. Powell used the alias "Mr. Wood" when he rented a room from Mary Surratt, Powell was the son of a Baptist minister. Powell was not a minister.
17. Poore, *Conspiracy Trial*, 1:70–72.

18. Poore, *Conspiracy Trial*, 1:74–75. See also Poore, *Conspiracy Trial*, 1:352–53 (Weichmann recalled).
19. Poore, *Conspiracy Trial*, 1:75.
20. Poore, *Conspiracy Trial*, 1:69–70.
21. Poore, *Conspiracy Trial*, 1:75, 86.
22. Poore, *Conspiracy Trial*, 1:71–77.
23. Poore, *Conspiracy Trial*, 1:80–81.
24. Poore, *Conspiracy Trial*, 2:5–6.
25. Poore, *Conspiracy Trial*, 2:15.
26. Poore, *Conspiracy Trial*, 1:21–22.
27. Poore, *Conspiracy Trial*, 1:23. Von Steinacker also made reference to Capt. John Y. Beall, who tried unsuccessfully to highjack the USS *Michigan* on Lake Erie in order to free Confederate prisoners on Johnson's Island.
28. Poore, *Conspiracy Trial*, 2:472–73.
29. Poore, *Conspiracy Trial*, 2:473. General Johnson also testified that he had never met John Wilkes Booth.
30. Poore, *Conspiracy Trial*, 2:474.
31. Poore, *Conspiracy Trial*, 2:478–79.
32. Poore, *Conspiracy Trial*, 2:174.
33. Poore, *Conspiracy Trial*, 2:179.
34. Poore, *Conspiracy Trial*, 2:221–22.
35. Poore, *Conspiracy Trial*, 2:180.
36. Poore, *Conspiracy Trial*, 2:219–20.
37. Poore, *Conspiracy Trial*, 2:486.
38. David Miller DeWitt, *The Judicial Murder of Mary E. Surratt* (Baltimore: John Murphy, 1895), 69.
39. Poore, *Conspiracy Trial*, 2:482–83.
40. Poore, *Conspiracy Trial*, 3:65, 67.
41. Poore, *Conspiracy Trial*, 2:191. The witness encountered Lloyd at Marlborough that afternoon.
42. Poore, *Conspiracy Trial*, 2:190–91.
43. Lay opinion evidence relating to someone's intoxication was probably also admissible in courts martial, but there are no precedent cases to rely upon prior to 1865. The Hunter commission allowed lay opinion evidence to be admitted at the trial of Booth's accomplices.
44. Poore, *Conspiracy Trial*, 2:181–83. Frederick Aiken asked the witness, "In all the time you boarded in her house, did you ever hear Mrs. Surratt say any thing with reference to the existence of a conspiracy to assassinate the President?" The judge advocate objected to the question and the objection was sustained.
45. Poore, *Conspiracy Trial*, 2:186.
46. Poore, *Conspiracy Trial*, 2:187.
47. Poore, *Conspiracy Trial*, 2:183–84.
48. Poore, *Conspiracy Trial*, 2:342.
49. Poore, *Conspiracy Trial*, 2:189.
50. Poore, *Conspiracy Trial*, 2:190–91.
51. Poore, *Conspiracy Trial*, 2:486–87.
52. Poore, *Conspiracy Trial*, 2:486–87.
53. Poore, *Conspiracy Trial*, 2:250.
54. Poore, *Conspiracy Trial*, 2:497.
55. Poore, *Conspiracy Trial*, 2:501.
56. Poore, *Conspiracy Trial*, 2:369–71.
57. Poore, *Conspiracy Trial*, 2:270–75.
58. William Hanchett, *The Lincoln Murder Conspiracies* (Urbana-Champaign: University of Illinois Press, 1989), 87.
59. H. Donald Winkler, *Lincoln and Booth* (Nashville: Cumberland House, 2003) 208–9.
60. Winkler, *Lincoln and Booth*, 207.
61. DeWitt, *Judicial Murder of Mary E. Surratt*.

62. DeWitt, *Judicial Murder of Mary E. Surratt*, 41–48, 38 (loyalty oath requirement).
63. Ex parte Milligan, 71 U.S. (4 Wall.) 2 (1866).
64. *Milligan*, 71 U.S. 127.
65. *Milligan*, 71 U.S. 136–37.
66. Richard M. Smoot, *The Unwritten History of the Assassination of Abraham Lincoln* (Clinton, Mass.: W. J. Coulter, 1908), 11–12.
67. Douglas Linder, ed., "George Atzerodt's Confession," Famous Trials Project, University of Missouri, Kansas City, http://law2.umkc.edu/faculty/projects/ftrials/lincolnconspiracy/atzerodtconf.html.
68. See Bruton v. United States, 391 U.S. 123 (1968).
69. See Michael W. Kauffman, *American Brutus: John Wilkes Booth and the Lincoln Conspiracies* (New York: Random House, 2004); Edward Steers Jr., *Blood on the Moon: The Assassination of Abraham Lincoln* (Lexington: University Press of Kentucky, 2001).
70. Otto Eisenschiml, *In the Shadow of Lincoln's Death* (New York: Wilfred Funk, 1940).
71. Eisenschiml, *In the Shadow of Lincoln's Death*, 129–30.
72. Eisenschiml, *In the Shadow of Lincoln's Death*, 147.
73. Elizabeth Steger Trindal, *Mary Surratt: An American Tragedy* (Gretna, LA: Pelican, 1996).
74. See also Elizabeth Steger Trindal, "The Story of Mary Surratt," Confederate Historical Society of Belgium, http://chab-belgium.com/pdf/english/Mary%20Surratt.pdf.
75. Trindal, *Mary Surratt*, 158.
76. Trindal, "Story of Mary Surratt."
77. Al Benson Jr., *Revised History* (blog); two blog posts on Mary Surratt may be found at https://revisedhistory.wordpress.com/2013/12/the-hanging-of-mary-surratt-judicial-murder-and-government-dirty-linen-part-one/ and https://revisedhistory.wordpress.com/2013/12/10/the-hanging-of-mary-surratt-judicial-murder-and-government-dirty-linen-part-two/. Although this citation does not always take the reader directly to the blog posts for December 6 and 10, 2013, a pull-down menu tab on the right side of the screen leads the reader to Benson's December 2013 posts. Since there is no other source for his neo-Confederate thesis relating to Mrs. Surratt, this is the only option for the conscientious reader. A nineteen-minute award-winning short video produced by Chris King and Heather King for Watermark Films is also a twenty-first-century apologia for Mary Surratt's innocence, filled with fictitious courtroom scenes that materially affect the credibility of the documentary. "The Killing of Mary Surratt," Vimeo video, 20:28, 2009, Watermark Films Video, https://vimeo.com/87644667.
78. Winkler, *Lincoln and Booth*, 231–34. Winkler did not think that Mrs. Surratt's unfair trial relieved her of moral responsibility for Lincoln's death.
79. Larson, *Assassin's Accomplice*.
80. Larson, *Assassin's Accomplice*, 230.
81. See Steers, *Blood on the Moon*, 210.
82. Statement of Louis Weichmann to Col. William P. Wood, Old Capitol Prison, dated April 30, 1865, reported in William C. Edwards and Edward Steers Jr., *The Lincoln Assassination: The Evidence* (Urbana-Champaign: University of Illinois Press, 2009), 1318.
83. Joel Prentiss Bishop, *Commentaries on the Criminal Law*, §§ 227, 473, 484 (Boston: Little, Brown, 1856). Bishop stated that anyone who was ignorant of the intent and purpose of an act that furthers the commission of a crime could not be guilty as an accessory before the fact (§§ 241–242).
84. See Poore, *Conspiracy Trial*, 1:106–9, for Lloyd's testimony. See also Poore, *Conspiracy Trial*, 1:286–88, where Mrs. Offutt denies taking the package containing Booth's binoculars from Mary Surratt.

Chapter Six

The Case against Samuel Mudd

> Dr. Samuel R. Mudd had been a medical student in my office; he would be one of the last men to assassinate anybody, but he was a bitter man in the war, and that sullen, sour feeling was not uncommon among us.—Dr. George Mudd, interview with George Alfred Townsend, May 1883

Samuel Mudd was the son of Henry Lowe Mudd and Sarah Ann Reeves. He was born December 20, 1833, on his father's plantation near Bryantown, Charles County, Maryland.[1] Henry L. Mudd, a prosperous, slave-owning planter, had ample resources to see that his son was well educated.[2] He was homeschooled by a governess until age fourteen, then Samuel attended St. John's College in Frederick, Maryland, for two years before matriculating at Georgetown College, then transferring to the University of Maryland School of Medicine where he received his MD in 1856. Samuel Mudd was an accomplished musician who could play the flute, piano, and violin.[3]

Dr. Mudd set up his medical practice in Bryantown, Maryland. About eighteen months after he opened his office, he married Sarah Frances Dyer on November 26, 1857.[4] Two years after his marriage Dr. Mudd bought a substantial farm in Charles County, Maryland, near Bryantown. He purchased several slaves and became a part-time physician and tobacco planter.[5] Samuel Mudd was a pro-slavery, pro-Confederate Marylander, like most of the slave owners of Charles County. Dr. Mudd despised Abraham Lincoln and the Republican Party.

MUDD'S PARTICIPATION IN THE CONFEDERATE UNDERGROUND

No one knows if Dr. Mudd belonged to one of the Copperhead secret societies, although Edward Steers confidently asserts that Dr. Mudd was a member of the Confederate underground. Dr. Mudd's involvement in the Confederate underground was supported by the evidence of two of Mudd's former slaves, Mary Simms and Elzee Eglin. They testified at the Hunter Commission trial that Mudd knew John Surratt and had sheltered escaped Confederate soldiers near his farmhouse.[6] Former slave Melvina Washington testified that men in gray coats had often visited the Mudd farm and sometimes slept in the house as well as in a thicket.[7] Ex-slave Milo Simms testified that Mudd sheltered Confederates and that John Surratt was a visitor to Mudd's house during the war.[8] Rachel Spencer also testified that men visited with Mudd. She identified two of the men whom Mudd sheltered: Bennett Gwynn and Walter "Wat" Bowie.[9] Bennett Gwynn, Mudd's neighbor, testified that in August or early September 1861, he was one of a party of local Confederate militia members whom Mudd sheltered to avoid their arrest by Brig. Gen. Daniel Sickles's men. Gwynn stated that Dr. Mudd was a member of the same militia company.[10]

Figure 6.1. Dr. Samuel Mudd House, near Bryantown, Md. ***Source:*** **Photograph by the author.**

MUDD'S PARTICIPATION IN THE CONSPIRACY TO KIDNAP PRESIDENT LINCOLN

John Wilkes Booth was introduced by John Thompson to Dr. Mudd Sunday, November 23, 1864. Thompson was the son-in-law of Dr. William Queen.[11] Mudd met Booth and Thompson at St. Mary's Church after Catholic Mass.[12] Ostensibly, Booth was interested in buying a horse. That night, Booth returned to Washington. In December 1864, Booth came down to Bryantown a second time, and this time he spent the night at Dr. Mudd's house. Booth also bought a one-eyed gelding from George Gardiner that would later be used by Lewis Powell, one of his accomplices in the assassination. There is no record of their conversations during the November and December meetings at Mudd's house.[13]

On December 23, 1864,[14] Mudd was in Washington, D.C. He introduced Booth to John Surratt, and followed up that introduction with a meeting at Booth's rooms in the National Hotel. Louis Weichmann, a boarder at the Surratt boardinghouse and a longtime friend of John Surratt, was with Surratt when Dr. Mudd hailed him on Seventh Street on December 23, 1864. Weichmann was excluded from the confidential meeting between Surratt, Mudd, and Booth, although he spent part of the time in the same hotel room waiting for the meeting to end. Weichmann saw Booth make a drawing on an envelope that he thought was a map.[15]

Mudd and Booth met three times between November 1864 and April 14, 1865. The last meeting was in the presence of John Surratt and Louis Weichmann. Although Mudd steadfastly maintained that he knew nothing of the plan to kidnap President Lincoln, circumstantial evidence at the time of trial suggests that he knew about the kidnap plot. Posttrial documents, particularly the suppressed confession of George Atzerodt, offered by defense counsel but excluded by the military commission, contains Atzerodt's direct evidence of Mudd's involvement. Dr. Mudd was part of the conspiracy to kidnap Abraham Lincoln.

APRIL 15, 1865: DR. MUDD'S HOUSEGUESTS

About 4:00 a.m. on April 15, John Wilkes Booth and David Herold rode up to the front door of Dr. Mudd's house. Herold dismounted and pounded on the door. Dr. Mudd, in his nightshirt, eventually answered Herold's pounding. Herold told him that his companion had fallen from his horse and injured his left leg. Mudd and Herold then helped Booth dismount and moved him into the parlor. According to Dr. Mudd, the man with the broken leg was named "Tyson" and his companion was named "Henson."[16] A quick examination showed that Booth had broken the small bone (fibula) in his left leg about a third of the way up from his left ankle. Herold and Mudd then trundled Booth up to a second-floor bedroom.[17]

Dr. Mudd fashioned splints for Booth's broken leg from a bandbox and, after cutting off Booth's left riding boot, which was tossed under the bed, Mudd proceeded to stabilize the fracture and wrap the splints. Dr. Mudd insisted that he did not recognize his patient because the injured man wore a beard and covered his head with a shawl. Mudd put the patient to bed and went to the first floor to eat breakfast. David Herold ate breakfast with the Mudd family while waiting for Booth to wake up.[18]

Mudd whittled two crosspieces for crutches for Booth and had one of his hired men attach poles to the crosspieces. Early on the afternoon of the fifteenth, Mudd and Herold rode over to Henry Mudd Sr.'s house to see if Herold could borrow a carriage for Booth. Mudd's brother told Herold that the family carriage was old and unfit to travel any distance. Mudd and Herold started off to Bryantown to see about a carriage, then gave up on finding a carriage for Booth.[19]

Before Herold was halfway there, he turned around and went back to Mudd's house. Mudd rode on to Bryantown on other business. He learned that President Lincoln had been assassinated and according to his own statement, the killer had been identified as "Boyd," an individual with the same last name as a well-known Charles County robber.[20] Mudd returned to his house either around 4:00 p.m. or around 6:00 p.m., depending on whether or not Mudd's statement can be accepted. He told Booth and Herold to leave at once. Booth and Herold mounted up and prepared to leave. Herold asked Mudd about the way to Parson Wilmer's farm on the other side of Zekiah Swamp. Mudd told the two to take a shortcut across the swamp and avoid the road to Beantown. Booth and Herold disappeared.

Dr. Mudd spoke to his cousin George Mudd, a staunch Union man, on Sunday April 16. Dr. Mudd told his cousin that two suspicious strangers had come to his house for a medical emergency, and he asked George Mudd to inform the Union cavalry command at Bryantown that two suspicious strangers had passed through Dr. Mudd's farm to the south.[21] George Mudd told the Union commander at Bryantown, Lieutenant Dana of the Thirteenth New York Cavalry, about the strangers calling on his cousin on Monday April 17.[22] Dana in turn passed the information to Veterans Reserve Corps lieutenant Alexander Lovett, who was ordered by District of Columbia provost marshal O'Beirne to take nine troopers from the Veteran Reserve Corps and two provost marshal's detectives, Simon Gavacan and William Williams, to form a detail to ride out to Charles County to look for Booth and Herold.[23]

Lieutenant Lovett, accompanied by George Mudd and the two detectives, rode out to Mudd's house on Tuesday, April 18. Lovett took a statement from Dr. Mudd in which Mudd told the interrogator that he treated "Tyson," a man with a beard who wore a shawl, for a broken leg, and then allowed the man to rest for several hours. Mudd described "Tyson" as a man with black hair inclined to be curly, about five feet, eight or ten inches in height with fair skin. "Tyson" was accompanied by another man named "Henson" who was much younger and seemed to be carefree and happy go lucky.[24] Mudd noted that "Tyson" took no food and slept most of the day on April 15. Mudd and "Henson" went out to look for a carriage and, unable to obtain one, split up. Mudd said he returned to his farm about 6:00 p.m. Mudd told the interrogators that he then sent them on their way to Reverend Wilmer's farm around that time. Lieutenant Lovett also took a statement from Mrs. Mudd. She informed Lovett that "Tyson's" whiskers were false. Dr. Mudd did not mention that to the interrogators.[25]

Lieutenant Lovett was not satisfied with Mudd's first statement and returned to the Mudd house on April 21 to take a second statement from Mudd. This time, Mudd wrote out a statement that tracked his earlier oral statement to Lovett. Lovett's men searched the premises. Mrs. Mudd recalled that the stranger's left riding boot was left in the bed in the second-floor room where Booth had slept. A soldier fetched the boot and Lovett inspected it. He found "J. Wilkes" written inside the boot. Lovett came to the conclusion that Mudd's mysterious stranger was the man he was looking for. Lovett and his soldiers then escorted Mudd to Bryantown where Col. Henry H. Wells, provost marshal for the District of Maryland including Charles County, interrogated Mudd a third time. Wells wrote out a second statement for Mudd. Mudd admitted that he had met John Wilkes Booth in November or December when J. C. Thompson, Dr. Queen's son-in–law, introduced Booth to Mudd. Mudd said that Booth had stayed with him the night following their meeting before Booth bought a horse from George Gardiner. Mudd lied to Colonel Wells, telling him that he had not seen Booth since that meeting. He also maintained that "Tyson" was not Booth, failing to identify Booth from the photograph carried by the provost marshal.[26] Mudd was arrested on April 24 and taken to the Old Capitol Prison in Washington to await further interrogation and potential charges.[27]

THE PROSECUTION WITNESSES

The prosecution paraded an odd combination of white and African American witnesses to prove that Mudd was a conspirator. Louis Weichmann testified that he met Dr. Mudd on Seventh Street, Washington, D.C., in the company of John Wilkes Booth on January 15, 1864. Weichmann testified that Mudd, John Surratt, and Booth conducted a secret meeting, leaving Weichmann in the same room to amuse himself while he waited for the three to conclude their business.[28] Weichmann's testimony was direct proof that Mudd, Surratt, and Booth were engaged in some kind of common plan involving a map.

Circumstantially, it showed that Mudd was involved in the kidnap plot. According to Weichmann, the meeting concerned Booth's intention to buy Mudd's farm, which sounded like a "cover story." Weichmann on cross-examination also indicated Booth confirmed Mudd's story.[29]

Thomas Gardiner, George Gardiner's nephew, confirmed that Mudd and Booth had visited the Gardiner farm to buy a horse. Gardiner placed the sale date as "the latter part of November."[30] Daniel Thomas also testified before the commission.[31] Thomas related a conversation between himself and Dr. Mudd that Thomas said occurred in March 1865:

> Q. In that conversation, did he speak of the President of the United States?
>
> A. He said that the President, or Abraham Lincoln, was an abolitionist; that the whole Cabinet were such; and that he thought the South would never be subjugated under an abolition doctrine; and he went on stating that all the Cabinet, and every Union man in the State of Maryland besides that, would be killed in six or seven weeks.
>
> Q. Did he speak of the President as embraced in that?
>
> A. He said that the President was an abolitionist, and the whole Cabinet were such.
>
> Q. Did he speak about the President being killed?
>
> A. Yes, sir: he said that the President and the whole Cabinet were abolitionists, and that the whole would be killed in six or seven weeks, and every Union man in the State of Maryland; and then he remarked to me that I was no better.
>
> Q. Was he very violent and excited in the declaration?
>
> A. From his conversation, I would not think he was excited much.[32]

Thomas told the commission that he wrote to the provost marshal of his district about Mudd's declaration before Lincoln was assassinated.[33] General Ewing cross-examined Thomas and got him to admit that he laughed off Mudd's remarks before the assassination.[34] Marcus Norton, a native of Troy, New York, told the commission that he saw Booth, O'Loughlen, and Atzerodt, the latter two of whom he identified in court, just prior to Lincoln's inauguration. Then Ewing turned Norton's attention to Dr. Mudd:

Q. Now, I ask you if you ever saw the man among the prisoners who wears a linen coat [pointing to Samuel A. Mudd, one of the accused].

A. I think I have seen him once.

Q. When and where?

A. It was at the National Hotel.

Q. Under what circumstances?

A. There was a person came to my room, entered it hastily, on the morning of the 3d of March, I think. He appeared somewhat excited, made an apology, and said that he had made a mistake; that he wanted to see Mr. Booth. I told him that Booth's room, perhaps, was on the next floor above; the number I did not know. My room being entered in that way, by a person apparently excited, I left my writing, went into the hall, followed him partly through the hall, and he went down the flight of the stairs to the story below. He turned, and gave a look at me.

Q. Did you, when you first entered the Court-room this morning, recognize that person here?

A. I pointed out to the Hon. Horatio King those three persons.

Q. The man that entered your room was which one of these prisoners?

A. I should say that (pointing to Samuel A. Mudd) was the gentleman. It was either he, or a man exactly like him.

Q. Do you recognize him? and are you satisfied in your own mind that he is the man?

A. I am satisfied myself; but I do not know that I can satisfy others.[35]

The White Witnesses

John H. Ward told the commission that he was in Bryantown on Saturday April 15. Ward said he saw Union soldiers commanded by Lieutenant Dana in town, and a African American told him that President Lincoln had been shot. Ward also told the commission that he had a "faint memory" that Dr. Mudd was in Bryantown that afternoon.[36] Ward was in town from 1:00 to about 2:00 p.m., returned home, and then came into town a second time around 3:00 or 4:00 p.m.[37] Augustus Howell, a notorious blockade runner called by Mary Surratt's lawyer, admitted under cross-examination that he knew George Atzerodt and Samuel Mudd whom he met during his trips through Charles County. He was forced to admit stopping at Mudd's house for an hour or two within the past year.[38]

The African American Witnesses

The prosecution produced several people of color, including Dr. Mudd's former slaves as witnesses against him. Eleanor Boyce was the first to testify before the commission. She was a free person of color living near Bryantown who said she saw Dr. Mudd and another man ride toward Bryantown past her house, around 3:00 or 4:00 p.m. on April 15. She herself went into town and learned that President Lincoln had been assassinated. She then said she saw Dr. Mudd riding away from town by himself.[39] Becky Briscoe also gave evidence corroborating Ms. Boyce. She repeated the hearsay declaration of an unidentified little boy on the side of the road who said that Dr. Mudd was traveling with "Hamilton Southards coming from Virginia."[40] Frank Bloyce had gone to Bryantown on Saturday April 15, and testified he saw Dr. Mudd in Bryantown about three or four in the afternoon that day. Bloyce could not recall if any news of the assassination of President Lincoln had reached Bryantown that day.[41]

Mary Simms, Dr. Mudd's former slave, testified that she heard Mudd talk about the president sneaking into Washington in women's clothes to avoid an assassination plot. She could not give the date of Mudd's exclamation that "he could have killed him right" if he had come in the way that the president was supposed to, implying that Dr. Mudd had some connection with the 1861 Baltimore plot to assassinate President-Elect Lincoln.[42] Simms told the commission that John Surratt had called on Dr. Mudd several times and had stayed over to have dinner with the Mudd family.[43] Former Mudd slave Elzee Eglin testified that Mudd harbored men dressed in gray uniforms in a thicket near his house and fed them. He did not state the date or time of this incident and could not say that Mudd harbored Confederate soldiers on more than one occasion.[44] Sylvester Eglin, a former slave of Mudd's father, testified that Dr. Mudd threatened to send him along with his brother and Elzee Eglin to Richmond to work on fortifications in the summer of 1864.[45] Former slave Melvina Washington told the commission that Dr. Mudd had said sometime in the summer of 1864:

> Q. State whether, while you lived at Dr. Samuel Mudd's, you heard him say any thing about President Lincoln.
>
> A. I heard him say that he would not keep his seat long.
>
> Q. When was it that you heard him say that?

A. I heard him say it the summer before I came away,—the summer before last.

Q. Was there anybody talking with him at the time he said that?

A. There was a heap of gentlemen in the house; but I don't know who they were.

Q. How were the gentlemen that were in the house dressed? and where did they sleep?

A. Some had on gray clothes, and some had on little short jackets, with a little peak to them behind.

Q. Had they any uniform about their clothing?

A. They had black buttons. That was all the uniform they had about them.[46]

This declaration was relevant to Dr. Mudd's motive for associating himself with Booth and the other accomplices. It also showed that he had some knowledge of a plan to do away with the president before he was introduced to Booth in November 1864. Mary Simms and Milo Simms also told the commission that John Surratt had visited the Mudd farm several times.[47] William Marshall, a free person of color, testified that he overheard a conversation between Benjamin Gardiner, his wife's master, and Dr. Mudd in which Gardiner said that Stonewall Jackson would cross the Potomac at Point of Rocks and descend on Washington and burn up President Lincoln in the White House. Mudd said that he would not be surprised if that occurred.[48] Assuming that the conversation was correctly restated by Marshall, it would have been irrelevant to any of the charges against Mudd and improper character evidence. General Ewing objected to Marshall's testimony, and the objection was overruled.[49] Rachel Spencer, another former Mudd slave, told the commission that she overheard Dr. Mudd threaten to send one of his slaves to Richmond.[50] The commission overruled General Ewing's objection to this improper character evidence.

The Detectives

Lieutenant Lovett testified to his two trips to Mudd's farm on April 18 and 21. Lovett's evidence was consistent with the two statements taken from Mudd. Lovett said that on the eighteenth, Mudd had told him that his two strangers were going off in the direction of Allens Fresh when they left the Mudd farm. Lovett stated that he believed Mudd's "directions" to Booth and

Herold were intended to throw him off the fugitives' track.[51] Lovett told the commission that Mudd did not admit that he knew John Wilkes Booth until after he was arrested and on his way to Bryantown. Lovett said:

> He did not mention it until we were on horseback. I do not think he mentioned it until I had arrested him. I had mentioned Booth's name to the other doctor, though.
>
> Q. You say that the doctor seemed very much excited and alarmed?
>
> A. He seemed to turn pale, and blue about the lips, like a man that is frightened at something.
>
> Q. Like what?
>
> A. Like a man that might be frightened at something he had done. I do not mean to say that he was afraid of us.[52]

Lovett also added that Mudd told him he had not heard of the assassination until Sunday, April 16, which was inconsistent with Mudd's two statements that he first heard about the assassination on Saturday, April 15, in the early afternoon.[53]

Detective Joshua Lloyd testified that Mudd told him on April 18 that he had heard about the Lincoln assassination. Lloyd asked Mudd if he knew anything about the whereabouts of Booth and Herold. According to Lloyd, Mudd denied any knowledge of the two fugitives.[54] Colonel Wells testified that he had three conversations with Dr. Mudd on April 21.[55] Wells authenticated Mudd's April 22 written statement. He recited his recollection of Mudd's responses to him in the first interview on April 21. Wells told the commission that Mudd, after studying a photograph of John Wilkes Booth, admitted that the mysterious stranger "Tyson" was John Wilkes Booth.[56] Wells gave the following testimony:

> Q. I understand you to say that Dr. Mudd stated distinctly that he had not seen Booth since that introduction in November last?
>
> A. Yes, sir: until the Saturday morning when he arrived at his house.
>
> Q. And that he did not recognize him?
>
> A. No, sir: he said he did not recognize him at first; but, on reflection, he knew it was the same person.[57]

Wells added that the "strongest evidence of his guilt" was Mudd's attempt to conceal the facts of Booth's visit to his house.[58] Defense counsel made no objection to Wells's improper opinion evidence. Wells continued his examination by telling the judge advocate that he believed Mudd had recognized Booth while Booth was at his house on April 15.[59] General Ewing got Wells to admit he was unsure of the precise time that Mudd came to believe his houseguest was Booth.[60]

William Williams, who accompanied Lieutenant Lovett to Mudd's house on April 18 and April 21, also testified before the commission. He stated that Mudd had denied that either one of the "strangers" was Booth. His evidence corroborated Lieutenant Lovett's and Colonel. Wells's testimony.[61] William A. Evans testified he saw Mudd go into Mrs. Surratt's boardinghouse sometime in March 1865.[62] William A. Evans testified to being nearly run off the road by Dr. Mudd in late February 1865 when Mudd's buggy flew past him, crowding him off the road.[63]

Francis Farrell, a rebuttal witness, testified that Dr. Mudd came to his house around 3:00 or 4:00 p.m. on Saturday, April 15. Farrell said that Mudd and he had a discussion about the assassination of the president:

> Q. [By the Judge Advocate.] Now state to the Court what Dr. Mudd said in regard to the assassination of the President in that conversation with you.
>
> A. When the doctor came to my house, I was in the house; and Mr. Hardey was in my house also. He walked out, and had some talk with the doctor; I do not know what. He hallooed to me directly after he went out, and told me that the President was assassinated, and also Seward and his son, I think. Then I got up and went out to my yard-gate, where the doctor and Mr. Hardey [*sic*] were. I asked if it was so. I understood the doctor to say that it was so; and that the President was assassinated, and also Mr. Seward and his son. I asked the question who assassinated the President; and the doctor replied, and said, "A man by the name of Booth." Mr. Hardey then asked him if it was the Booth that was down here last fall. The doctor said he did not know whether it was or not; that there were three or four men of the name of Booth, and he did not know whether it was that one or not: he said, if it was that one he knew him. That was all he said about it, excepting that he said he was very sorry that this thing had occurred,—very sorry.
>
> Q. Do you remember whether, in the course of that conversation, he spoke of two men having been at his house that morning and during the day?

A. He did not.

Q. He made no allusion to it?

A. No, sir.

Q. How long did he remain at your house?

A. I do not think he staid over fifteen minutes.[64]

John Hardy was present during this conversation and confirmed Farrell's testimony. Hardy's version was as follows:

> Q. Will you state what, if any thing, he said to you on that occasion in regard to the assassination of the President?
>
> A. He said to me that there was terrible news now; that the President and Mr. Seward and his son had been assassinated the evening before. Something was said in connection with Boyle (the man who is said to have killed Captain Watkins) assassinating Mr. Seward. I remember that Booth's name was mentioned in the same connection; and I asked him if Booth was the man who had been down there, and was represented as Booth. His reply was, that he did not know whether it was that man, or some of his brothers: he understood that he had some brothers. That ended the conversation, except that he said it was one of the most terrible calamities that could have befallen the country at this time.[65]

He also recalled a man named "Booth" attending church services in November or December 1864.[66]

THE DEFENSE CASE

Defense witness Dr. John Thomas testified that his brother Daniel Thomas never mentioned the alleged conversation with Dr. Mudd about the president being dead in five or six weeks to him or to any other family member prior to learning of the president's assassination on April 15. John Downing, at whose house Mudd was alleged to have made his claim that Lincoln would be dead in five or six weeks, denied that Mudd ever made any such statement.[67]

Samuel McAllister, the front desk clerk at the Pennsylvania House hotel, testified that Dr. Samuel Mudd's name was not on the register for January 15, 1865. McAllister testified that "Samuel A. Mudd" had registered for a room in December 1864.[68] Jeremiah Mudd told the commission that he had accompanied Samuel Mudd to Washington on December 23, 1864, and left for Bryantown on Christmas Eve. Jeremiah Mudd volunteered that he was separated from Samuel Mudd for a period of time on the afternoon and early evening of December 23, at the National Hotel, providing for the encounter described by Louis Weichmann, even though Weichmann was incorrect about the date of that meeting.[69] Jeremiah Mudd stated that he never heard Samuel Mudd make any disloyal or antigovernmental remarks.[70] Jeremiah Mudd also admitted he knew of the incident where Samuel Mudd shot his slave in the calf.[71] Jeremiah Mudd was recalled to authenticate the signature of Samuel A. Mudd on the register of the Pennsylvania House on December 23, 1864. He was able to do so.[72]

Bennett Gwynn denied being one of a party of men in the summer of 1864 that allegedly were sheltered by Mudd. Gwynn did testify that he and several other former Confederate militia members went to Mudd's house in August 1861 to avoid arrest by Union general Daniel Sickles, whose division was stationed in Prince George's County.[73] Gwynn held a commission as captain of militia issued by Governor Hicks.[74]

Defense witness Frank Lewis testified that Dr. Mudd had asked him to take down a stove for him on Christmas Eve 1864. Lewis was unable to accommodate Mudd.[75] J. H. Montgomery testified that Dr. Mudd asked him to bring down a stove from Washington, just before Christmas 1864. Montgomery told Mudd to get Montgomery's associate Lucas to do the job.[76]

John Thompson testified that he introduced Mudd to John Wilkes Booth in the latter part of October or early November 1864. Thompson testified that Booth had a letter of introduction "from a man named Martin" to show to Mudd.[77] Thompson told the commission that Booth wanted to acquire land somewhere in Charles County. He also said Booth asked him about the roads in Charles County. Booth stayed at the home of Dr. Queen that evening, according to Thompson.[78] He also confirmed that Booth had returned to Charles County in December 1864.[79]

Betty Washington, Mudd's African American maid, told the Hunter Commission that since she was hired around Christmastime 1864 that Dr. Mudd had been away from home three times, first to a party at the Gardiners', second to Giesboro to buy a horse, and third to Washington.[80] Ms. Washington said she saw a small man going to the swamp on April 15, and she was unable to identify John Wilkes Booth as that individual.[81] Thomas Davis, a white farm laborer who worked for Dr. Mudd January through March 1865, corroborated Washington's testimony.[82] Thomas Gardiner and Dr. Charles Allen corroborated Washington's statement with regard to the trip to Washington on March 23, 1865.[83] Henry A. Clark testified that Mudd and Gardiner spent an evening at Clark's house on March 23. Clark said that Mudd spent the night at his house.[84] Dr. Blandford corroborated Mudd's trip to Giesboro.[85] Robert Martin told the commission that Mudd and his companions stopped for dinner at his house before going to buy horses at Giesboro.[86]

He was recalled to clarify his earlier testimony: he placed the dinner on April 14 and also said he saw Dr. Mudd in Washington on December 23, 1864.[87] Henry Mudd Jr. corroborated Washington's evidence that Mudd had gone to Giesboro to buy horses around April 10.[88]

Ben Gwynn told the commission that Dr. Mudd hid him and other members of his Prince George's militia company in August 1861 to avoid arrest by General Sickles.[89] Jeremiah Dyer, Mudd's brother-in-law and a former Charles County slave owner, testified that he never had any conversation with Dr. Mudd and Wat Bowie in August 1863 because he was in Baltimore. This was to refute government evidence that Mudd and Wat Bowie held an August 1863 meeting with Dyer. He also denied having a conversation with Dr. Mudd, Dr. Blandford, and John Surratt at Mudd's house, although Dyer admitted meeting Surratt on the road to Bryantown toward Surrattsville. Dyer gave no date and time for this chance meeting.[90] Dyer stated that he was knocking about in the woods" with Ben Gwynn and other militia members in August 1861, to avoid capture by Colonel Dwight 70th New York regiment part of Gen. Sickles' brigade that was moving through Prince George's County looking for Confederate sympathizers.[91] Dyer was cross-examined about his participation in the Sons of Liberty a.k.a. Order of American Knights a.k.a. Knights of the Golden Circle. Dyer denied belonging to any of these secret societies.[92] General Hunter cross-examined Dyer showing that in July 1861, he was a Confederate sympathizer, rejoicing at the Confederate victory at the First Battle of Manassas. Dyer claimed his sentiments changed before the fall of Richmond and he was now a loyal citizen.[93] Dyer was forced to admit on cross-examination that his militia company was regarded as a disloyal organization by the government.[94] On recall, Dyer acknowledged that he had met John Surratt in 1862 or 1863 at the Surrattsville tavern.[95] He was also extensively questioned by the prosecution about his trip to Richmond in 1861 and when and where he took the loyalty oath to the United States. The cross-examination weakened Dyer's credibility.[96]

Frank Washington, Mudd's former hired hand, testified that he never saw any men camped out in the woods near Mudd's house in 1864.[97] Washington said he could not recognize David Herold, even though he had put up Booth's and Herold's horses on the morning of April 15.[98] He was recalled to state the whereabouts of Dr. Mudd on March 5. Washington said Dr. Mudd was at home working in his tobacco beds.[99] Baptist Washington, another defense witness, told the commission that he never saw Captain White, from Tennessee, Lieutenant Perry, Captain Bennett Gwynn, Andrew Gwynn, or George Gwynn at Dr. Mudd's house during the time he worked at Dr. Mudd's house.[100] Albin Brooke, who had lived with the Mudd family in 1864, was the next defense witness. Brooke denied seeing Captain White, Lieutenant Perry, Captain Bennett Gwynn, Andrew Gwynn, or George Gwynn at Dr. Mudd's house in 1864. Brooke acknowledged that Bennett

Gwynn, Jerry Dyer, and other militia members were hiding out in the thicket behind the Mudd house in 1861. He admitted seeing John Surratt in August 1864 in Prince George's County.[101] Julia Bloyce, the washerwoman for the Mudd family, corroborated Baptist Washington's and Albin Brooke's testimony.[102]

Dr. William J. Bowman, testifying for Mudd, said that he met John Wilkes Booth near Bryantown at church. Booth asked him about the prospects for buying land in Charles County.[103] George Booz, who lived with Dr. Mudd's father, said that he saw Dr. Mudd riding alone toward his home coming from the direction of Bryantown at 3:00 or 4:00 p.m. on April 15.[104] Booz's testimony was consistent with that of Primus Johnson and John Acton who also saw Mudd riding home alone at that time.[105] Mary Jane Simms, Mudd's house servant, testified that she did not see Captain Bennett Gwynn, Andrew Gwynn, or George Gwynn at Dr. Mudd's house during the summer and fall of 1864. She also said that she did not see John Surratt at Dr. Mudd's house during the same time period. Ms. Simms told the commission that she knew all of these men slightly:[106]

> A. Yes, sir.
>
> Q. Did you know John Surratt?
>
> A. I have seen him once.
>
> Q. Did you see any of those parties that I have named at Dr. Mudd's last year?
>
> A. No, sir: never.

Charles Bloyce, another person of color, who knew only Ben Gwynn, corroborated Simms's evidence.[107]

Dr. George Mudd testified on behalf of his cousin. He told the Hunter Commission that his cousin, for whom he had been a medical preceptor, had a good reputation for peace, order, and good citizenship.[108] George Mudd told the commission that he informed the authorities that his cousin had told him that two strange, suspicious men had been at his house.[109] George Mudd told the commission that he accompanied Lieutenant Lovett and the detectives to his cousin's house on April 18. He also said he forgot to tell the detectives that his cousin had told him that he attempted to get a carriage for the two men but was unable to find one.[110] George Mudd was forced to admit that Samuel Mudd was a Southern sympathizer.[111] George Mudd did state that he administered a loyalty oath to his cousin when George Mudd was an election judge for the 1864 constitutional convention, which he believed his cousin made sincerely.[112] John Waters testified that Samuel Mudd's reputation for good character was excellent.[113]

John F. Hardy briefly testified to being present when Lieutenant Lovett and the detectives came to Samuel Mudd's house on April 21 when Booth's boot was discovered.[114] Marcellus Gardiner was not permitted to tell the commission what Dr. Mudd had said to him regarding Lincoln's assassination on Easter Sunday after church.[115] E. D. R. Bean told the commission that he heard about Lincoln's assassination on April 15, 1865. Bean said he had a conversation with Dr. Mudd that afternoon in which he told Mudd about the assassination.[116] William Mudd stated that he had not seen Captain White of Tennessee, Captain Perry, Lieutenant Perry, Andrew Gwynn, Ben Gwynn, or George Gwynn at or near Dr. Mudd's house in 1864.[117]

General Ewing also attacked the government's proof that Mudd knew the president had been assassinated by John Wilkes Booth. Mason McPherson, John McPherson, John T. Langley, and Peter Trotter testified that they were in Bryantown the afternoon of April 15, heard that Lincoln was assassinated, but did not learn that John Wilkes Booth was the assassin until Sunday the sixteenth or Monday the seventeenth.[118] Benjamin Gardiner testified that he went to church on Easter Sunday. He was precluded from stating that Dr. Mudd told him about the two suspicious men who stopped at Mudd's house on April 15.[119] Several days later, Gardiner was recalled and by agreement of counsel made the following statement to the commission:

> Q. And I asked you what he said then about the persons being at his house. Go on now, and state what he said.
>
> A. I heard on Saturday evening that the assassination had taken place; but I heard it in such a way that I did not believe it. Our church generally commences about ten o'clock, or thereabouts, on Sunday. As I got to the church, I saw the people collected together, talking, and apparently in earnest conversation. It turned out to be respecting the assassination of the President of the United States. As I advanced towards the church, I happened to go to where Dr. Samuel Mudd was. I walked up to where he was, and spoke to him, and he spoke to me. I asked him was such the fact that the President had been assassinated. He then turned around to me from the crowd, and said, "Yes, such seems to be the fact;" and he added, "Sir, we ought to raise immediately a home guard, and to hunt up all suspicious persons through our section of country, and arrest them and deliver them up to the proper authorities; for there were two suspicious persons at my house yesterday morning." I paid no attention to what he said about suspicious persons, because, since the war commenced, we have always had in our neighborhood deserted soldiers constantly, and

detectives, and soldiers of the United States; and we could hardly tell who they were.

Q. State the whole conversation.

A. I have given all the conversation I recollect that I had with him on that occasion.

Q. Did he say any thing about the assassination itself?

A. Nothing that I recollect after that. There were so many persons talking about it, that I can hardly tell who did say any thing respecting the assassination after the conversation between me and him; for everybody in church was talking about it until church commenced, and I cannot tell whether he said any thing more, or whether anybody else did.[120]

George Mudd was recalled to state to the commission what his cousin Samuel Mudd said to him after church on Easter Sunday. Samuel Mudd said as they were riding home together that two suspicious men had arrived at his house early on April 15, and one man had a broken leg which Samuel Mudd had set. Samuel Mudd said he fed the two and helped one man search for a carriage to transport his injured companion. Samuel Mudd had said the men were going to Parson Wilmer's farm, and Samuel told George Mudd that he gave them directions to Wilmer's farm. George Mudd asked his cousin if he should tell the authorities about the two men, and Samuel told his cousin to go ahead and inform the authorities.[121]

Betty Washington testified that Dr. Mudd was working in his tobacco beds on March 1 and 2 and was at home March 5.[122] Thomas Davis, Mudd's farm hand, Henry L. Mudd Jr., Dr. Blandford, and Mary Mudd also agreed with Washington that Mudd was at home those three days[123] John F. Davis agreed with his son's testimony; he had gone to Mudd's farm to visit his son who was sick in early March.[124]

General Ewing launched an attack on Daniel Thomas's credibility. Jeremiah Dyer stated that Daniel Thomas's reputation for honesty was poor.[125] Jeremiah Mudd testified that Daniel Thomas's reputation for truthfulness was bad.[126] George Mudd also testified that he considered Daniel Thomas to be insane and further that Thomas's reputation for truthfulness was poor.[127] Leonard Roby testified that Thomas's reputation for truthfulness was bad.[128] Joshua Naylor, James Richards, Mason McPherson, Daniel Orme, Richard Skinner, John H. Baden, Eli Watson, John H. Turner, Polk Deakins, John Waters, Joseph Waters, Frank Ward, Daniel Hawkins and Daniel Monroe testified that Thomas's reputation for truthfulness was poor.[129] Although Dr. Thomas told the commission that he treated his brother for what would today be diagnosed as major depression, he was in his right mind on April 16 when he told the family about Mudd's declaration. Dr. Thomas was a very unhelpful witness.[130] Emily Mudd told the commission that Dr. Mudd went to his father's house to treat him on the second and third of March.[131] One witness, William Watson, testified under cross-examination that Daniel Thomas's reputation for truthfulness was as good as anyone living in his neighborhood. Under stressful cross-examination he changed his evidence and stated that Thomas's reputation for honesty was poor.[132]

General Ewing also attacked the character for truthfulness of Mary Simms. Betty Washington stated that the reputation of Mary Simms for truthfulness was poor.[133] The defense recalled Daniel Thomas to worm out of him testimony that on June 1, 1865, he applied for a reward for giving information leading to the capture of Booth's collaborators. That evidence showed that Daniel Thomas turned in Samuel Mudd for a share of the reward money, suggesting that Thomas's testimony was motivated by an economic benefit.[134] James Richards and William Watson testified that they were present on June 1 when Thomas importuned for reward money.[135] Provost Marshal John C. Holland testified that Daniel Thomas was drafted into the army in and became a special detective for Holland for the Fifth Congressional District. Holland denied receiving a letter from Thomas stating that Samuel Mudd had foretold Lincoln's assassination.[136]

Defense counsel recalled John Davis in an attempt to get into evidence a conversation between Dr. George Mudd and Dr. Samuel Mudd on April 18, 1865. The government objected to the hearsay and the president sustained the objection.[137]

Defense counsel put James Judson Jarboe on the stand to testify that he never saw Samuel Mudd going into the Surratt boardinghouse on H Street in Washington in the winter of 1865.[138]

Anna Surratt testified that she never saw Judson Jarboe or Samuel Mudd at her mother's boardinghouse in 1864–1865.[139] Jane Herold and Mary Nelson, David Herold's sisters, each testified that she had never heard anyone in her house speak of Samuel Mudd.[140] General Ewing's last witness was Father Charles Stonestreet, former president of Frederick College in 1850. Father Stonestreet stated he had the impression that Samuel Mudd was a student at the college in 1850 and 1851, although he was not certain.[141]

George Atzerodt's confession, the most important documentary evidence that would likely have helped to carry the burden of proof in a civilian court, was offered by William E. Doster, Atzerodt's counsel; the reason for doing so is not clear. Assistant Judge Advocate General Bingham promptly objected to its admission and the commission sustained the objection.[142] The exclusion of this document materially aided Dr. Mudd and Mary Surratt.[143]

POSTCONVICTION LEGAL ACTION

Dr. Mudd, Samuel Arnold, Michael O'Loughlen, and Edman Spangler were sent to be incarcerated at Fort Jefferson, Dry Tortuga. The steamer *Florida* delivered the prisoners to Fort Jefferson on July 18.[144] According to Captain George W. Dutton of the Veteran Reserve Corps, part of the prisoners' escort, in the presence of Brig. Gen. Levi A. Dodd, Captain Budd, and Captain Potter the post surgeon,

> Dr. Mudd acknowledged to Capt. Budd, Gen. Dodd and others, that he knew Booth when he came to his house with Herold on the morning after the assassination, but that he was afraid to tell of his having been there, fearing the life of himself and family would be endangered thereby. He knew that Booth would never be taken alive. He also acknowledged that he had been acquainted with Booth for some time, and that he was with Booth at the National Hotel on the evening referred to by Weichmann.[145]

Dutton sent a letter to the *Washington Star*, which was published August 3, 1865. When Dr. Mudd saw the article, he executed an affidavit denying that he told Dutton or anyone else that he recognized John Wilkes Booth on the morning of April 15, 1865. Mudd said:

> August 28, 1865
>
> 1st. That I confessed to having known Booth while in my house; was afraid to give information of the fact, fearing to endanger my life, or made use of any language in that connection—I positively and emphatically declare to be notoriously false.
>
> 2nd. That I was satisfied and willingly acquiesced in the wisdom and decision of the Military Commission who tried me, is again notoriously erroneous and false. On the contrary I charged it (the Commission) with irregularity, injustice, usurpation, and illegality. I confess to being animated at the time but have no recollection of having apologized.
>
> 3rd. I did confess to a casual or accidental meeting with Booth in front of one of the hotels on Pennsylvania Avenue, Washington, D.C., on the 23d of December 1864, and not on the 15th of January, 1865, as testified to by Weichmann. Booth, on that occasion desired me to give him an introduction to Surratt, from whom he said he wished to obtain a knowledge of the country around Washington, in order to be able to select a good locality for a country residence. He had the number, street, and name of John Surratt, written on a card, saying, to comply with his request would not detain me over five minutes. (At the time I was not aware that Surratt was a resident of Washington.) I declined at first, stating I was with a relative and friend from the country and was expecting some friends over from Baltimore, who intended going down with me to spend Christmas, and was by appointment expected to be at the Pennsylvania House by a certain hour—eight o'clock. We started down one street, and then up another, and had not gone far before we met Surratt and Weichmann.[146]

If the alleged statement by Dr. Mudd to Captain Dutton was accurate and authentic, then it undercut his claim to be innocent. If Mudd knew he was harboring a fugitive from justice on April 15, and failed to report to the authorities without an excuse, he became an accessory after the fact. Mudd's affidavit denied that he "confessed" to Captain Dutton. Mudd confirmed most of the details relating to his December 23, 1864, meeting with Booth and Surratt. Mudd declared that Booth was only interested in buying land in Charles County and asked for the map to be drawn for that purpose.[147]

General Thomas Ewing continued to press for Mudd's release from confinement. In July 1865, he had Frances Mudd swear to an affidavit stating that her husband did not know the man he was treating was John Wilkes Booth. The affidavit was submitted to President Andrew Johnson by General Ewing as in the nature of a clemency petition requesting that the president reduce Dr. Mudd's sentence. Johnson never replied to the petition.[148]

Dr. Mudd attempted to escape from Fort Jefferson in September 1865. Mudd persuaded a sailor aboard the *Thomas A. Scott* to allow Mudd to board the government transport. Mudd went below and secreted himself under a plank. When Mudd was reported missing, garrison soldiers searched the *Scott* and located Mudd. Dr. Mudd, who had been assigned as an assistant to the post surgeon, was placed in irons in a dungeon. He lost his prison job and on release from solitary confinement was set to hard labor, cleaning bricks.[149] Meanwhile, the post garrison was rotated, putting Mudd under the guard of a regiment of U.S. Colored Troops, which led Mudd to write a letter in October 1865 telling his wife that "My dear Frank, it is bad enough to be a prisoner in the hands of white men, your equals under the Constitution, but to be lorded over by a set of ignorant, prejudiced and irresponsible beings of the unbleached humanity, was more than I could submit to, when I had every reason to believe my chances of escape almost certain, and would be crowned with success."[150]

Fort Jefferson's garrison was stricken with yellow fever in September 1867. The post surgeon, Dr. Smith, died from the disease. Since Dr. Mudd was the only other physician at the post, he volunteered to treat yellow fever victims. Mudd did get assistance from Dr. Whitehurst who came over from Key West to help with the yellow fever patients.[151] Mudd broke up the quarantined yellow fever patients at a makeshift tent hospital on an adjacent island, which prevented the spread of the disease. He commenced treating all patients according to his own theories. Samuel Arnold and Michael O'Loughlen came down with yellow fever. Arnold survived but O'Loughlen perished.[152] Mudd worked incessantly from late August through the end of September 1867 when the epidemic began to subside.[153]

Meanwhile, General Ewing was given a new way to set aside Mudd's conviction. The Supreme Court decided *Ex parte Milligan*[154] in April 1866, announcing the Supreme Court's majority opinion holding that trial of civilians by military commission was unconstitutional when the civil courts were open and the jurisdiction was not under invasion.[155] Taking this decision as authority for setting aside Dr. Mudd's conviction as unconstitutional, Ewing prepared and filed a habeas corpus petition in the District of Florida, arguing that Mudd's conviction should be set aside following *Milligan*. Judge Thomas Jefferson Boynton, a Lincoln appointee, denied the writ.[156] Boynton's unpublished opinion held that *Ex parte Milligan* did not apply to Booth's alleged accomplices because the president was the commander in chief and his murder was committed when the District of Columbia was under martial law. Judge Boynton held that the murder of the commander in chief of the army was a military offense subject to trial by military commission:

> The President was assassinated not from private animosity nor any other reason than a desire to impair the effectiveness of military operations and enable the rebellion to establish itself into a government: the act was committed in a fortified city which had been invaded during the war and to the northward as well as to the southward of which battles had many times been fought, which was the headquarters of all the Armies of the United States from which daily and hourly went military orders. The President is the Commander in Chief of the Army and the President who was killed had many times made distinct military orders under his own hand. . . . It was not Mr. Lincoln who was assassinated but the commander-in-chief of the Army for military reasons. I find no difficulty in classifying the offense as a military one and with this opinion arrive at the necessary conclusion that the proper tribunal for the trial of those engaged in it was a military one.[157]

Before a writ of error could be taken to the U.S. Supreme Court, President Johnson pardoned Dr. Mudd. The pardon was carefully drawn to show that Mudd was pardoned for his work during the yellow fever epidemic at Fort Jefferson, not because he was innocent.[158] President Johnson also pardoned Arnold and Spangler, averting a writ of error from Judge Boynton's court to the U.S. Supreme Court.

POSTTRIAL DISCLOSURES

According to Edward Steers who relied on Dutton's letter, after Mudd returned from Bryantown with news of Lincoln's assassination, Mudd ordered Booth and Herold to leave his house and scolded them for putting himself and his family under suspicion of aiding the fugitives.[159] Dutton's letter and the *Washington Star* article do not mention Mudd saying anything about chastising Booth and Herold and ordering them away. Mrs. Frances Mudd told Osborn Oldroyd in 1901 that her husband knew that the man with the broken leg was John Wilkes Booth and had told Booth that his act had inflicted an irreparable injury to the Southern cause.[160] She did not tell Oldroyd when she discovered that the man her husband treated for a leg fracture was John Wilkes Booth nor when Dr. Mudd admonished Booth.

In 1877 when Mudd was running for a seat in the Maryland General Assembly, he told Samuel Cox Jr. that he had met with Booth twice before April 15. Mudd told Cox that he knew the man he treated was John Wilkes Booth and the crime that Booth was guilty of.[161] Cox did not reveal that Dr. Mudd knew Booth was an escaped felon on the morning of April 15. All sources agreed that Mudd knew Booth was President Lincoln's assassin by the afternoon of April 15, learning the truth at Bryantown sometime that afternoon.

Dr. Mudd's many letters to his wife and other family members from Fort Jefferson contained statements asserting his innocence and denying he knew anything about the plan to kidnap President Lincoln. The suppressed confession of George Atzerodt, offered by William E. Doster on behalf of his client but excluded by the military commission, contains Atzerodt's direct evidence of Mudd's involvement in the kidnap plot. Atzerodt said: "I am certain that Dr. Mudd knew all about it, as Booth sent (as he told me) liquor & provisions for the trip with the President to Richmond about two weeks before the murder to Dr. Mudd's."[162] Atzerodt had no firsthand knowledge that Mudd was one of the kidnap conspirators. He was allegedly repeating Booth's statement. Atzerodt was trying to save his own life. He was motivated to accuse other people of complicity in the conspiracy to bargain for his own life. His "confession" was unreliable and his accusation about Dr. Mudd was equally unreliable.

Dr. George Mudd consented to an interview with George Alfred Townsend in May 1881 that was published on June 3, 1881, in the *Cleveland Leader*. George Mudd said that:

> Dr. Samuel R. Mudd had been a medical student in my office; he would be one of the last men to assassinate anybody, but he was a bitter man in the war, and that sullen, sour feeling was not uncommon among us. There is no question but that he knew Booth some time before the tragedy, and was in the plan to abduct the President. Nor is there any doubt but that Booth had long selected this country as the region through which he meant to operate.[163]

Townsend interviewed Dr. George Mudd two years later, after Dr. Samuel Mudd's death. He repeated his earlier statement that Samuel Mudd was involved in the kidnap conspiracy, without stating the factual basis for his opinion. George Mudd asserted that

> there is no question that Sam Mudd immediately knew Booth, and that Booth had told him that he had murdered the President. If he had possessed the moral courage to have said at once: "I will have nothing to do with assassination; I will give this man up to his Government," he would have stood very different-

> ly toward himself, his family and his fame. But you see those rebel views he had held, that obstinacy of character, his prejudices, his false sense of honor, made him secrete his information till he had actually made himself an accessory after the fact.[164]

George Mudd did not disclose the factual basis for this statement, either. He also accused his cousin of a "want of moral courage" that prevented him from turning Booth and Herold in to the authorities in Bryantown.[165] George Mudd also opined that his cousin's life had been saved because the evidence against him was muddled, otherwise he would have been the fifth accomplice to be given the death sentence.[166] Townsend also interviewed Thomas Harbin in 1883. Harbin told Townsend about his involvement in the kidnap plot and in protecting Booth and Herold after they had crossed the Potomac into Virginia in April 1865. Harbin told Townsend that he met for the first time with John Wilkes Booth and Samuel Mudd in October 1864:

> Mr. Harbin says that in Mudd's presence in October, six months before the murder, Booth acquainted him with the fact that he had a plot to run President Lincoln out of Washington, and wanted Mr. Harbin's cooperation.
>
> Dr. Mudd entered into the conversation and favored the scheme. Harbin listened to it, thought it over, but hardly believed it feasible; and yet, having heart and soul for the Confederacy, he did not discourage it; but the idea of bloodshed never entered into the talk.
>
> Booth described Lincoln, said he knew him well, and expressed hatred for him. Harbin said he would render any assistance in his line of operations.
>
> Booth made three visits to the vicinity of Bryantown, in October, in November, and in December, and each time stayed four or five days, invariably at Dr. Mudd's, though he would spend a day or two, perhaps, at the hotel in the village. Harbin met him on each of these visits.[167]

Harbin's statement is partially incorrect: Booth did not meet Mudd until November. If Harbin was called as a prosecution witness by the Hunter Commission and had he told the truth about Booth's three trips to Charles County to plot the abduction of President Lincoln with Harbin and Mudd as accomplices, Dr. Mudd may very well have been given a death sentence, since the Hunter Commission made up "the law of war" as it went along.

CONCLUSION

The government proved that Samuel Mudd was part of the Charles County Confederate underground in 1861. It proved that he knew John Surratt, a major blockade runner and messenger. It proved that Mudd was introduced to John Wilkes Booth in November 1864 at Bryantown. It proved that Booth was an overnight guest at Mudd's house in November or December 1864.

The government showed that Mudd, Booth, and Surratt engaged in a secret conference at Booth's hotel room in the National Hotel in January 1865, although that date was incorrect. That was sufficient circumstantial evidence to show that Mudd was a member of the conspiracy to abduct President Lincoln. The government proved that Dr. Mudd had helped the escape of Booth and Herold in three ways: (a) by harboring the two for a day, (b) directing Booth and Herold to their next rendezvous point, and (c) failing to promptly report to federal authorities on April 15 that he had encountered Booth and Herold and that the two were at his house where they could be arrested. The government failed to prove that Dr. Mudd knew that John Wilkes Booth had murdered President Lincoln and was fleeing to avoid capture and prosecution for that crime. Dr. Mudd's statements to Lieutenant Lovett and Colonel Wells, and his wife's statement to Lieutenant Lovett showed that Mudd helped Booth and Herold under assumed names and in disguise until Mudd returned from Bryantown around 4:00 p.m. on the fifteenth, learning from townspeople that Booth had assassinated President Lincoln. Dr. Mudd maintained his innocence until his death and the evidence supports his stand.

In General Thomas Ewing's closing argument at the trial of the alleged Booth accomplices, he cited the correct law with respect to accessories and principals as it was in 1865.

"If a person supply a felon with food, or other necessaries for his sustenance, or professionally attend him sick or wounded, though he know him to be a felon, these acts will not be sufficient to make a party an accessory after the fact."[168] General Ewing also argued that Dr. Mudd was not an accessory even if he knew that Booth was a felon fleeing from justice when he set his leg, fed him, and sent him on his way south.[169]

The government produced no credible evidence that Dr. Mudd had known his patient was John Wilkes Booth and that Booth told him that he had murdered President Lincoln prior to Dr. Mudd's trip to Bryantown on the afternoon of April 15. Mudd should have been acquitted, but the prosecution's strategy to charge all the Booth accomplices as conspirators to murder the president worked to ensure that Mudd would be convicted of conspiracy to commit treason, despite the specification that limited his participation to postassassination actions as an accessory after the fact.

The defense was based on Dr. Mudd's good moral character. Had the case been tried in a civil court, the judge would have given the standard good character instruction and would have left it to the jury to determine if Dr. Mudd's general good character created a reasonable doubt as to his guilt. The Hunter Commission did not abide by civilian rules on the burden of proof and weight of the evidence.

The defense demonstrated that Daniel Thomas was seriously mentally ill and had a very poor reputation for truthfulness. Thomas's testimony that Dr.

Mudd had said before the assassination that President Lincoln would be killed was seriously compromised, but Thomas's evidence was not supportive of any of the charges against Mudd. Thomas's evidence would at best have been circumstantial proof that Mudd was involved in the Booth conspiracy and knew weeks before the assassination that Lincoln was to be murdered. Thomas's credibility was shredded by the reputational evidence, by Thomas's importuning for reward money in June 1865, and by Dr. Thomas's testimony that his brother had a serious mental illness.

The government also introduced bad character evidence in its case in chief to show that Mudd treated his slaves brutally by shooting one and threatening to send others to work on Confederate fortifications in Richmond. The civil courts would not permit the prosecution to offer bad character evidence against the accused in its case in chief, and in rebuttal only when the accused raised the issue of good character.[170] Since Dr. Mudd made an issue of his good character, the government's anticipatory bad character evidence was not very prejudicial.

The government also brought up irrelevant evidence about the Confederate attempt to spread yellow fever among the civilian population in New York City.[171] Much of the testimony taken from former prisoners of war relating to prison atrocities, as well as evidence about the Confederate plot to burn down New York City, was both irrelevant and highly prejudicial to all the defendants.

Dr. Mudd was involved in the Lincoln kidnapping conspiracy. If one adopts the prosecution's erroneous theory that the kidnapping conspiracy was from the outset a conspiracy to assassinate the president, then one could find that Samuel A. Mudd, a coconspirator, was guilty of all the substantive crimes committed by Booth and Powell. He helped John Wilkes Booth's flight to avoid prosecution,[172] but no evidence showed that he knew Booth had murdered the president until Booth and Herold were leaving his house for their next stop. The government never proved that he was a knowing accessory after the fact.

The most likely scenario that explains Mudd's behavior on April 15–16 is as follows:

At 4:15 a.m. John Wilkes Booth and Herold turn up at Mudd's house. Mudd recognizes Booth, whom he had met with several times before when plotting the Lincoln kidnap conspiracy. Booth does not tell Mudd that he murdered Lincoln six hours earlier and gives Mudd a cover story for his left leg injury. Mudd treats Booth and agrees to help Herold find a carriage to take his wounded companion to Washington. The two ride over to Dr. Mudd's father's house and find out that Henry Mudd's carriage is unavailable. They decide to go to Bryantown. Herold senses danger, perhaps even sees men in blue in the distance near Bryantown and returns to the farm while Mudd picks up his mail and finds out that his houseguest is an assassin.

He returns home trying to remain calm and finds that Booth and Herold are about to leave. Mudd is angry that Booth has put Mudd and his family in danger of arrest for aiding him, tells the two how to get to Parson Wilmer's house, and tries to resume his normal daily activities. On Sunday he asks his cousin to tell the authorities in Bryantown that two strange men had shown up at his house on April 15. Mudd could have told his cousin that John Wilkes Booth was one of those strangers, but he fears arrest and does not come forward with the information that would have sent the Union soldiers at Bryantown on Booth's trail.

Mudd did not believe that the aid he furnished Booth and Herold made him morally responsible for the death of Lincoln. To this day, his descendants are convinced that Samuel A. Mudd was not guilty of any crime. It is certain that the Hunter Commission found Mudd guilty on grounds other than his assistance to Booth and Herold. Mudd should have been acquitted.

NOTES

1. Biography of Dr. Samuel Mudd, available at http://rogerjnorton.com/Lincoln29.html .
2. Nettie Mudd, ed., *The Life of Dr. Samuel A. Mudd: Containing His Letters from Fort Jefferson, Dry Tortugas Island, Where He Was Imprisoned Four Years for Alleged Complicity in the Assassination of Abraham Lincoln. . . .* (New York: Neale, 1906), 23.
3. Nettie Mudd, *Life of Dr. Samuel A. Mudd*, 25.
4. See Nettie Mudd, *Life of Dr. Samuel A. Mudd*, 25–26. Samuel Mudd referred to his wife as "Frank" in his correspondence. She was a graduate of the Visitation Convent School, Frederick, Md.
5. Nettie Mudd, *Life of Dr. Samuel A. Mudd*, 27–28. Nettie Mudd was the youngest child of Samuel and Frances Mudd, born in 1878. She was not a witness to her father's activities relating to John Wilkes Booth. Her biography apparently was based on a series of conversations with her mother.
6. Edward Steers Jr., *Blood on the Moon: The Assassination of Abraham Lincoln* (Lexington: University Press of Kentucky, 2001), 145. During the Hunter Commission trial at least two of Dr. Mudd's former slaves testified for the government that Mudd knew John Surratt who had called at Mudd's house while escorting Confederate soldiers on the reverse underground railroad to the Confederacy. See testimony of Mary Simms, in Ben Perley Poore, ed., *The Conspiracy Trial for the Murder of the President, and the Attempt to Overthrow the Government by the Assassination of Its Principal Officers, Edited with an Introduction by Ben. Perley Poore* (Boston, J. E. Tilton, 1865), 1:150–53; also available at http://www.surrattmuseum.org/ben-perley-poore-the-conspiracy-trial-tr . Simms's brother Elzee Eglin also testified that Dr. Mudd sheltered Confederate escapees in a thicket near his house. Eglin also testified that Mudd shot him in the leg for disobedience and threatened to send Eglin to Richmond to dig trenches. Poore, *Conspiracy Trial*, 1:157–59.
7. Poore, *Conspiracy Trial*, 1:161–63.
8. Poore, *Conspiracy Trial*, 1:164–66.
9. Poore, *Conspiracy Trial*, 1:171. Walter "Wat" Bowie was a member of the Forty-Third Virginia Battalion, better known as Mosby's Rangers. See Jeffrey D. Wert, *Mosby's Rangers: The True Adventures of the Most Famous Command of the Civil War* (New York: Simon & Schuster, 1990), 300 (appendix).
10. Poore, *Conspiracy Trial*, 1:291–300.
11. Nettie Mudd, *Life of Dr. Samuel A. Mudd*, 29 (statement of Mrs. Frances Mudd).
12. Steers, *Blood on the Moon*, 75.

13. Mudd told Lieutenant Lovett that he met Booth only once on November 23 and also told Lovett that Booth bought the one-eyed horse in December 1864. See statement of Samuel A. Mudd, in William C. Edwards and Edward Steers Jr., eds., *The Lincoln Assassination: The Evidence* (Urbana-Champaign: University of Illinois Press, 2009), 948.

14. Louis Weichmann gave January 15, 1865, as the meeting date in his testimony before the Hunter Commission. Michael Kauffman points out that Weichmann erred and General Ewing produced a witness to show that the meeting occurred on December 23, 1864. Weichmann later admitted his mistake in 1866 after the Hunter Commission trial. See Michael Kauffman, "Process versus Truth in the Case of the Lincoln Conspiracy," in *The Lincoln Assassination: Crime and Punishment, Myth and Memory*, ed. Harold Holzer, Craig L. Symonds, and Frank J. Williams (New York: Fordham University Press, 2010), 198–99.

15. Louis Weichmann, statement to Col. W. P. Wood, dated April 30, 1865, in Edwards and Steers, *Lincoln Assassination: The Evidence*, 1316–17.

16. Statement of Samuel A. Mudd, dated April 22, 1865, in Edwards and Steers, *Lincoln Assassination: The Evidence*, 940.

17. Voluntary statement of Samuel Mudd, dated April 21, 1865, in Edwards and Steers, *Lincoln Assassination: The Evidence*, 942–43.

18. Edwards and Steers, *Lincoln Assassination: The Evidence*, 943.

19. Edwards and Steers, *Lincoln Assassination: The Evidence*, 945.

20. Edwards and Steers, *Lincoln Assassination: The Evidence*, 942–43.

21. Edwards and Steers, *Lincoln Assassination: The Evidence*, 946.

22. Steers, *Blood on the Moon*, 146.

23. Steers, *Blood on the Moon*, 146.

24. Statement of Samuel A. Mudd, dated April 22, 1865, in Edwards and Steers, *Lincoln Assassination: The Evidence*, 947.

25. Steers, *Blood on the Moon*, 147.

26. Statement of Samuel A. Mudd, dated April 22, 1865, in Edwards and Steers, *Lincoln Assassination: The Evidence*, 940.

27. Steers, *Blood on the Moon*, 178.

28. Poore, *Conspiracy Trial*, 1:70–71.

29. Poore, *Conspiracy Trial*, 1:98, 104.

30. Poore, *Conspiracy Trial*, 1:361–62.

31. Poore, *Conspiracy Trial*, 1:435–47.

32. Poore, *Conspiracy Trial*, 1:436.

33. Poore, *Conspiracy Trial*, 1:444.

34. Poore, *Conspiracy Trial*, 1:447. Frederick Stone was the first lawyer to cross-examine Thomas. His cross-examination did not obtain any admissions from the witness that the witness did not take Mudd's statement seriously. At the time Thomas was a candidate to represent his district in the Maryland State House. See Poore, *Conspiracy Trial*, 1:439–40.

35. Poore, *Conspiracy Trial*, 3:198.

36. Poore, *Conspiracy Trial*, 2:62–67. He identified Charles Bloyce as the African American who told him about the assassination.

37. Poore, *Conspiracy Trial*, 2:62–67.

38. Poore, *Conspiracy Trial*, 2:360. Howell told the commission that he had not had much contact with Dr. Mudd in recent years.

39. Poore, *Conspiracy Trial*, 2:47–50.

40. Poore, *Conspiracy Trial*, 2:50–55.

41. Poore, *Conspiracy Trial*, 2:60–61.

42. Poore, *Conspiracy Trial*, 2:150.

43. Poore, *Conspiracy Trial*, 2:155–56. Elzee Eglin, another former slave, gave evidence that Mudd had threatened to send him to Richmond to work on fortifications for his bad behavior. This was, of course, irrelevant to the case against Dr. Mudd, pure bad character evidence that would have been inadmissible in a civilian court. See Poore, *Conspiracy Trial*, 2:156–57.

44. Poore, *Conspiracy Trial*, 2:156, 158–59.

45. Poore, *Conspiracy Trial*, 2:159–60. General Ewing's objection to the question put to Eglin and his answer was overruled by the commission. It was offered only to show the bad moral character of Dr. Mudd and would have been excluded in a civilian court.
46. Poore, *Conspiracy Trial*, 2:161.
47. Poore, *Conspiracy Trial*, 2:152. Milo Simms's testimony is at Poore, *Conspiracy Trial*, 2:164–66.
48. Poore, *Conspiracy Trial*, 2:169.
49. Poore, *Conspiracy Trial*, 2:169.
50. Poore, *Conspiracy Trial*, 2:170–74.
51. Poore, *Conspiracy Trial*, 1:243. Lovett also said that he made up his mind to arrest Dr. Mudd at the April 18 meeting.
52. Poore, *Conspiracy Trial*, 1:244–45.
53. Poore, *Conspiracy Trial*, 1:269.
54. Poore, *Conspiracy Trial*, 1:273.
55. Poore, *Conspiracy Trial*, 1:282.
56. Poore, *Conspiracy Trial*, 1:283–86.
57. Poore, *Conspiracy Trial*, 1:286.
58. Poore, *Conspiracy Trial*, 1:287.
59. Poore, *Conspiracy Trial*, 1:290. Wells either lied or inadvertently misstated Mudd's admission that on April 21 after reflection, he recognized that "Tyson" was really John Wilkes Booth.

> Q. Can you state what time Dr. Mudd professed to have recognized Booth as the man to whom he had been introduced? Was it during their stay at his house, or after they left?
>
> A. It was during their stay at the house.
>
> Q. You understood him to admit that he recognized him as Booth before he left.
>
> A. Yes, sir: his expression was, that he did not recognize him at first; but, on reflecting, he remembered him as the person. I think that was about the expression.

60. Poore, *Conspiracy Trial*, 1:292–93.
61. Poore, *Conspiracy Trial*, 2:295. Detective Simon Gavacan also corroborated Lovett and Wells. See Poore, *Conspiracy Trial*, 1:282–83.
62. Poore, *Conspiracy Trial*, 3:222–39.
63. Poore, *Conspiracy Trial*, 3:235–38.
64. Poore, *Conspiracy Trial*, 3:394–96.
65. Poore, *Conspiracy Trial*, 3:406–11.
66. Poore, *Conspiracy Trial*, 3:410.
67. Poore, *Conspiracy Trial*, 2:424–27.
68. Poore, *Conspiracy Trial*, 2:255.
69. Poore, *Conspiracy Trial*, 2:259–61.
70. Poore, *Conspiracy Trial*, 2:265.
71. Poore, *Conspiracy Trial*, 2:266.
72. Poore, *Conspiracy Trial*, 2:286–87.
73. Poore, *Conspiracy Trial*, 2:295.
74. Poore, *Conspiracy Trial*, 2:299.
75. Poore, *Conspiracy Trial*, 2:267.
76. Poore, *Conspiracy Trial*, 2:438–39.
77. Poore, *Conspiracy Trial*, 2:270. General Hunter asked Thomas if he had seen Booth's letter of introduction. Thomas said he did, and Hunter asked him if he remembered who signed it. Thomas said, " A man named Martin." Poore, *Conspiracy Trial*, 2:271, 273.
78. Poore, *Conspiracy Trial*, 2:270–71.
79. Poore, *Conspiracy Trial*, 2:271–72.
80. Poore, *Conspiracy Trial*, 2:282–86.

81. Poore, *Conspiracy Trial*, 2:285.
82. Poore, *Conspiracy Trial*, 2:375–80. Davis stated the party with the Gardiner family occurred on January 26, and Dr. Mudd's trip to Washington accompanied by Llewelyn Gardiner took place on March 23. Davis denied seeing two men at the Mudd house on April 15, although he did notice that two horses were in the barn that did not belong to Dr. Mudd.
83. Poore, *Conspiracy Trial*, 1:340. For Dr. Allen's testimony see Poore, *Conspiracy Trial*, 1:329–31.
84. Poore, *Conspiracy Trial*, 3:312–13.
85. Poore, *Conspiracy Trial*, 2:434–35.
86. Poore, *Conspiracy Trial*, 2:435–37.
87. Poore, *Conspiracy Trial*, 2:434–46.
88. Poore, *Conspiracy Trial*, 2:429–33. Henry Mudd also corroborated Samuel Mudd's visit to Washington on December 23, 1864.
89. Poore, *Conspiracy Trial*, 2:299–300.
90. Poore, *Conspiracy Trial*, 2:303.
91. Poore, *Conspiracy Trial*, 2:304.
92. Poore, *Conspiracy Trial*, 2:308–9.
93. Poore, *Conspiracy Trial*, 2:310.
94. Poore, *Conspiracy Trial*, 2:312.
95. Poore, *Conspiracy Trial*, 2:330.
96. Poore, *Conspiracy Trial*, 2:447–49.
97. Poore, *Conspiracy Trial*, 2:313. Washington was a plowman, working every day in Mudd's fields. Washington also said he had never seen anyone who looked like John Surratt at the Mudd farm. Poore, *Conspiracy Trial*, 2:314.
98. Poore, *Conspiracy Trial*, 2:316.
99. Poore, *Conspiracy Trial*, 3:265–66. Washington also said Mudd was at home on Ash Wednesday 1865.
100. Poore, *Conspiracy Trial*, 2:322–23.
101. Poore, *Conspiracy Trial*, 2:325–29.
102. Poore, *Conspiracy Trial*, 2:381–82. She also volunteered that the reputation of Mary Simms and Milo Simms for truthfulness was bad. Poore, *Conspiracy Trial*, 2:383–84.
103. Poore, *Conspiracy Trial*, 2:334–36.
104. Poore, *Conspiracy Trial*, 2:337–40.
105. Poore, *Conspiracy Trial*, 3:179, 268–70.
106. Poore, *Conspiracy Trial*, 2:341–42.
107. Poore, *Conspiracy Trial*, 3:181–83.
108. Poore, *Conspiracy Trial*, 2:385.
109. Poore, *Conspiracy Trial*, 2:391. This testimony was preceded by a lengthy legal argument about allowing George Mudd to state what Samuel Mudd told him on Sunday April 16. Samuel Mudd's statement would establish the reason George Mudd went to Lieutenant Dana in Bryantown on Tuesday. It would not be offered for the truth of the matter contained and would not have been hearsay. General Ewing tried to introduce Samuel Mudd's statement as an exception to the hearsay rule, and his proffer was rejected by the commission on the ground that it was a self-serving declaration rather than an admission.
110. Poore, *Conspiracy Trial*, 2:397.
111. Poore, *Conspiracy Trial*, 2:400–401.
112. Poore, *Conspiracy Trial*, 2:401.
113. Poore, *Conspiracy Trial*, 3:433–35.
114. Poore, *Conspiracy Trial*, 3:406–11.
115. Poore, *Conspiracy Trial*, 3:451–52. The court's ruling was correct: Mudd's declaration was a self-serving statement and hearsay.
116. Poore, *Conspiracy Trial*, 3:198–200. Bean said that it was his impression that local outlaw Boyle was one of the assassins.
117. Poore, *Conspiracy Trial*, 2:456.
118. Poore, *Conspiracy Trial*, 2:270–72 (Mason McPherson), 3:273–74 (John McPherson), 3:275–76 (John T. Langley), 3:276–77 (Peter Trotter).

119. Poore, *Conspiracy Trial*, 3:281.
120. Poore, *Conspiracy Trial*, 3:451–59.
121. Poore, *Conspiracy Trial*, 3:459–60. Ewing called L. A. Gobright, an Associated Press reporter, who told the commission that he was not sure that John Wilkes Booth was the assassin until April 15 when he saw the War Department official bulletin.
122. Poore, *Conspiracy Trial*, 3:258–59.
123. Poore, *Conspiracy Trial*, 3:282–83. For Henry L. Mudd. see Poore, *Conspiracy Trial*, 3:307–8. For Blandford see Poore, *Conspiracy Trial*, 3:310. For Mary Mudd see Poore, *Conspiracy Trial*, 3:425–26.
124. Poore, *Conspiracy Trial*, 3:287.
125. Poore, *Conspiracy Trial*, 2:306.
126. Poore, *Conspiracy Trial*, 2:287.
127. Poore, *Conspiracy Trial*, 2:398.
128. Poore, *Conspiracy Trial*, 3:195–96.
129. Poore, *Conspiracy Trial*, 2:453. For McPherson see Poore, *Conspiracy Trial*, 2:289–91. For Richards see Poore, *Conspiracy Trial*, 3:297. For Orme see Poore, *Conspiracy Trial*, 3:305–6. For Skinner see Poore, *Conspiracy Trial*, 3:319–20. For Baden see Poore, *Conspiracy Trial*, 3:392–93. For Watson see Poore, *Conspiracy Trial*, 3:412. For Turner see Poore, *Conspiracy Trial*, 3:430. For Deakins see Poore, *Conspiracy Trial*, 3:432. For John Waters see Poore, *Conspiracy Trial*, 3:433–34. For Joseph Waters see Poore, *Conspiracy Trial*, 3:435. For Frank Ward see Poore, *Conspiracy Trial*, 3:436. For Hawkins see Poore, *Conspiracy Trial*, 3:439. For Monroe see Poore, *Conspiracy Trial*, 3:464.
130. Poore, *Conspiracy Trial*, 2:250–51. Dr. Thomas also testified that he had treated his brother for a nervous condition. This was not particularly effective impeachment of his brother's story.
131. Poore, *Conspiracy Trial*, 3:251–53.
132. Poore, *Conspiracy Trial*, 3:445, 446–47.
133. Poore, *Conspiracy Trial*, 3:260.
134. Poore, *Conspiracy Trial*, 3:289, 291–92. General Ewing also brought out the fact that Thomas did not tell the story of Mudd's knowledge of the president's murder to George Moran before the assassination. Poore, *Conspiracy Trial*, 3:292.
135. Poore, *Conspiracy Trial*, 3:297–98. Richards related that Thomas stated that "he had called on Mr. William Watson and Mr. Benjamin J. Naylor for a certificate certifying that he was entitled to the reward, or a portion of the reward, that was offered for Booth and his accomplices; and thought, if he could get a certificate from them to that effect, he would be entitled to a portion of the reward, as Dr. Mudd was considered one of Booth's accomplices; and if Dr. Mudd was convicted, he would be entitled to the reward."
136. Poore, *Conspiracy Trial*, 3:389–90.
137. Poore, *Conspiracy Trial*, 3:303–5.
138. Poore, *Conspiracy Trial*, 3:368–69.
139. Poore, *Conspiracy Trial*, 3:384–85.
140. Poore, *Conspiracy Trial*, 3:442–43.
141. Poore, *Conspiracy Trial*, 3:467–68.
142. Poore, *Conspiracy Trial*, 2:511–12.
143. Atzerodt's confession could not be offered in a civil court today because Atzerodt, a defendant in the same prosecution, could not be compelled to testify against himself by reason of the Fifth Amendment privilege against self-incrimination. Admitting his confession against Dr. Mudd and Mary Surratt would violate the Sixth Amendment confrontation clause. See Bruton v. United States, 391 U.S. 123 (1968).
144. *Washington Evening Star*, August 3, 1865, available from Samuel Mudd Research, April 24, 2014, http://www.samuelmudd.com/html .
145. *Washington Evening Star*, August 3, 1865.
146. Nettie Mudd, *Life of Dr. A. Samuel Mudd*, 42.
147. Nettie Mudd, *Life of Dr. A. Samuel Mudd*, 44–45.
148. General Ewing's appeal to President Johnson, Samuel A. Mudd Pardon File B-596, U.S. National Archives, College Park, Md. RG 204, available at http://www.samuelmudd.com/ .

149. Maj. George Wentworth to Capt. F. C. Woodruff, September 27, 1865, in Nettie Mudd, *Life of Dr. Samuel A. Mudd*, 121–22. See also Dr. Samuel Mudd to Jere Dyer, September 30, 1865, in Nettie Mudd, *Life of Dr. Samuel A. Mudd*, 123–24. Mudd went on to tell his brother-in-law that he did not regret losing his medical steward's job because he would no longer witness prisoners starving to death for want of rations.

150. Nettie Mudd, *Life of Dr. Samuel A. Mudd*, 131–32. The letter was cited by Steers as proof of Mudd's racism.

151. Nettie Mudd, *Life of Dr. Samuel A. Mudd*, 255–59.

152. Nettie Mudd, *Life of Dr. Samuel A. Mudd*, 255–59, Samuel Mudd to Frank Mudd, dated September 17, 1867 (Arnold & O'Loughlen come down with fever); Nettie Mudd, *Life of Dr. Samuel A. Mudd*, 267, Samuel Mudd to Frank Mudd dated September 23, 1867 (O'Loughlen died).

153. See "Dr. Samuel A. Mudd's Guide to Health," *Baltimore Sun*, March 10, 1883, available at Samuel Mudd Research, April 24, 2014, http://www.samuelmudd.com/ . Mudd described his work at Fort Jefferson in detail in this excerpt from his unpublished manuscript on contagious diseases.

154. Ex parte Milligan, 71 U.S. (4 Wallace) 2 (1866).

155. Ex parte Milligan, 71 U.S. 127.

156. Ex parte Mudd, 17 Fed. Cas. 954 (S.D. Fla. 1868). Boynton's opinion is not in LEXIS or Westlaw but is available from the author from the personal papers of Gen. Thomas Ewing copied in 1997 by Candida Ewing Staempfli Steel for the author. It was part of the record of proceedings before the Army Board for Correction of Records in January 1992.

157. Ex parte Mudd, opinion of Boynton, J., 2.

158. Pardon of Samuel A. Mudd, February 8, 1869. Dr. Samuel A. Mudd Pardon, File # B-596, National Archives Annex, College Park, Md..

159. Steers, *Blood on the Moon*, 234.

160. Steers, *Blood on the Moon*, 234–35.

161. Steers, *Blood on the Moon*, 235.

162. Douglas Linder, ed., "George Atzerodt's Confession," dated May 1, 1865, taken down by Provost Marshal McPhail, Famous Trials Project, University of Missouri, Kansas City, http://law2.umkc.edu/faculty/projects/ftrials/lincolnconspiracy/atzerodtconf.html .

163. George Alfred Townsend, interview of Dr. George Mudd, May 1881, published in the *Cleveland Leader*, June 3, 1881, reprinted from *New York Tribune*, available at Samuel Mudd Research, April 24, 2014,http://www.samuelmudd.com/.

164. George Alfred Townsend, interview of Dr. George Mudd, *Cincinnati Enquirer*, April 16, 1883, available at Samuel Mudd Research, http://www.samuelmudd.com/george-mudd.htm .

165. Townsend, interview of Dr. George Mudd, *Cincinnati Enquirer*.

166. Townsend, interview of Dr. George Mudd, *Cincinnati Enquirer*.

167. George Alfred Townsend, interview of Thomas Harbin, *Cincinnati Enquirer*, August 3, 1884, available at Samuel Mudd Research, http://www.samuelmudd.com/thomas-harbin.htm .

168. Francis Wharton, *The Criminal Law of the United States Comprising a Digest of the Penal Statutes of the General Government and of Massachusetts. . . .* (Philadelphia: James Kay, Jun. and Brother, 1846), 37–38.

169. Wharton, *Criminal Law*, 37–38.

170. Simon Greenleaf, *A Treatise on the Law of Evidence*, vol. 1, 12th ed., ed. Isaac F. Redfield (Boston: Little, Brown, 1866; orig. pub. 1858), § 55.

171. Poore, *Conspiracy Trial*, 2:407–18, testimony of Godfrey Hyams.

172. Townsend, interview of Dr. George Mudd, *Cincinnati Enquirer*.

Chapter Seven

An Unconstitutional, Unfair Trial

> Our fathers thought, and taught us, to believe, that we lived under a government of law—that it was possible that Law might be a rule of government for a nation, as well as a rule of action for a man. But now, the first law officer of the government assures us that this is all a mistake—That "in time of war"—war with any body, great or small—the laws are silenced, and the military at its own caprice, can inflict whatever punishment it pleases, upon any person supposed (by "the Military") to be guilty of some offense against the (unknown) Laws of war, or some offence committed by them as a public enemy.—*The Diary of Edward Bates*

Some scholars, notably Edward Steers Jr., have argued that the assassination of President Lincoln, the attempted murder of Secretary Seward, and the failed attempt to murder Vice President Johnson were acts in furtherance of the original kidnap conspiracy that failed to capture President Lincoln on March 17, 1865.[1] Steers asserts that the assassination was an act furthering the original conspiracy and admonishes the reader that only those unfamiliar with the law of conspiracy would conclude that two separate conspiracies existed: the kidnap plot and the assassination plot.[2] Steers quotes an *American Criminal Law Review* 1997 student note summarizing federal conspiracy law under 18 U.S. Code § 371 a statutory crime.[3] This statute was not enacted in 1865 and the common law of conspiracy controlled the definition and elements of conspiracy. Francis Wharton's 1846 treatise on *The Criminal Law of the United States*, a source available to the Hunter Commission and the prosecution and defense counsel, described the offense at common law in detail, but contained no text relating to the termination of or abandonment of a conspiracy.[4] Twentieth-century law has confirmed that a conspiracy may be terminated by failure of its intended objective or by abandonment.[5]

THE TWO CONSPIRACIES

Applying this rule to the conspiracy to kidnap President Lincoln, the object was to take the president hostage in order to free Confederate prisoners of war and gain other advantages from the Union for freeing their chief executive. Murdering the president, the vice president, and the secretary of state would not have furthered the original conspiracy in any way. Assassination would have destroyed the possible benefits to be gained by using President Lincoln as a bargaining chip. The kidnapping conspiracy terminated March 17, 1865, when Booth and his accomplices failed to capture President Lincoln on the Seventh Street road.

The assassination conspiracy was thrown together by Booth and a handful of his former accomplices sometime between mid-March and April 14, 1865. Proof that one of the defendants was a party to the kidnapping conspiracy would not prove that individual participated in or was included in the conspiracy to assassinate President Lincoln. It is true that the people who were part of the kidnapping conspiracy were potentially indictable for attempt to kidnap the president, but the judge advocate general did not charge any of the defendants with conspiring to kidnap President Lincoln. No civil indictments were issued against any of Booth's accomplices except for John Surratt. The punishment for attempting to kidnap the president would be very light: a prison sentence of confinement from six months to one year.[6]

From this perspective, Samuel Arnold, Samuel Mudd, Michael O'Loughlen, Edman Spangler, and Mary Surratt were tried on charges and specifications that did not apply to their activities, if any, in the kidnap plot. George Atzerodt, David Herold, and Lewis Powell were members of both conspiracies.

TRIAL BY MILITARY COMMISSION WAS UNLAWFUL

John Wilkes Booth's alleged accomplices were tried by military commission. The trial was unconstitutional and contrary to an act of Congress calling for a different venue for the trial. The Hunter Commission trial was based on an oral opinion from Attorney General Speed condoning this process under the supposed laws of war, disregarding the will of Congress and denying to the accused accomplices the fundamental right to a fair and impartial jury trial.

THE RIGHTS OF THE ACCUSED THAT WERE NOT EXTENDED TO THE ALLEGED BOOTH ACCOMPLICES

Although the law of criminal procedure has changed a great deal from what it was in Lincoln's time, the basic constitutional rights of an accused date all the way back to the adoption of the Bill of Rights. To summarize:

Probable Cause to Arrest

Before a federal peace officer was entitled to arrest anyone, the peace officer needed probable cause, a legal justification normally established by applying for an arrest and search warrant to a federal magistrate who passed on the information the peace officer had obtained to show the accused may have committed a federal offense. The magistrate would then issue a warrant and require the peace officer to return the accused and any evidence seized to the magistrate for a hearing. As an emergency alternative, a peace officer could arrest without a warrant if an offense was committed in his presence, or the peace officer had independent probable cause to believe the accused had committed a felony.[7] However, a warrantless arrest was suspect, and the accused had to be produced before a magistrate within twenty-four hours for a hearing on whether there was probable cause to detain the accused.[8] No arrest warrants were issued by any judge or magistrate for any of Booth's accomplices. None of the alleged accomplices were taken before a U.S. magistrate or a state justice of the peace within twenty-four hours after arrest without warrant.

Notice and Hearing on Charges

The Sixth Amendment to the U.S. Constitution required that an accused in federal court was entitled to notice of the charges against him, the right to present a defense to those charges, and the right to legal counsel.[9] State constitutions contained similar provisions.[10] The way this was accomplished was by a hearing on probable cause and let to bail. If evidence was seized by the peace officer, the peace officer was required to show that the search that turned up the evidence was reasonable under the Fourth Amendment or the evidence would be returned to the accused. Although the federal justice system did not provide for free legal counsel, the magistrate permitted the accused to hire a lawyer to speak for him at the preliminary hearing and thereafter. None of the alleged accomplices were given notice of the charges against them prior to the first day of the Hunter Commission trial.

Habeas Corpus

If an accused believed he was wrongfully and unlawfully detained contrary to law, and he was not brought before a magistrate promptly, he could file a writ of habeas corpus in U.S. District or U.S. Circuit Court. The court would order the United States to produce the prisoner in court to show cause why the prisoner should not be released. This was an evidentiary hearing on the merits of probable cause to confine the accused. It was available before trial and after trial. All states had similar provisions for issuing a writ of habeas corpus.[11] President Lincoln anticipated the authority to issue a nationwide proclamation in September 1862. At the time of the arrest of Booth's alleged accomplices and some two hundred other men and women believed to have some knowledge of the conspiracy, the writ of habeas corpus had been suspended by presidential proclamation for "prisoners of war, spies or aiders and abettors of the enemy" throughout the United States by authority of section 1 of the Habeas Corpus Act of 1863 in September 1863. This second proclamation was handed down after passage of the Habeas Corpus Act of 1863. President Lincoln never issued a proclamation suspending the writ of habeas corpus for all citizens in the District of Columbia and never issued a proclamation that martial law was to be imposed on the District of Columbia, contrary to the statements of Lincoln assassination scholars such as Edward Steers Jr. Lincoln did declare martial law in Kentucky for the duration of the war in 1864.[12] Booth's alleged accomplices could be classified as aiders and abettors of the enemy, barring the issuance of a writ of habeas corpus to test the lawfulness of their confinement. In any case, defense counsel did not file any habeas corpus petitions in the District of Columbia during the trial. Frederick Aiken filed a posttrial writ petition on behalf of Mary Surratt that was reviewed by District of Columbia Supreme Court justice Wylie, who issued the writ to Maj. Gen. Winfield S. Hancock, commanding general of the Union army forces in the District of Columbia. Before Hancock could respond to the show cause order, President Johnson suspended the writ of habeas corpus for Mrs. Surratt.

Trial by Jury

The Sixth Amendment also guaranteed that the accused was entitled to a speedy public trial before a jury of his peers in open court. Secret proceedings and involuntary nonjury trials were unconstitutional. Further, an accused could not be convicted unless the charges against the accused were proved beyond a reasonable doubt. Booth's alleged accomplices were not tried before a jury, and the requirement that guilt be proved beyond a reasonable doubt did not apply to their trial by military commission. At that time the

Articles of War and the standard manual for trial by court-martial did not provide for any burden of proof requirement to establish guilt.

Judicial Review of Conviction

If the jury found the accused was guilty and the trial judge issued a judgment of conviction, the conviction could be challenged by writ of error to the U.S. Circuit Court or to the U.S. Supreme Court. Suing out a writ of habeas corpus after conviction was an alternative means of obtaining judicial review of a conviction. President Lincoln would ultimately suspend all these rights by the midpoint of the war throughout the nation for one class of citizens: "aiders and abettors" of the Confederacy, that is, spies and those who opposed the draft and argued for a negotiated settlement with the Confederacy. The alleged accomplices could not petition for a writ of error to the U.S. Supreme Court after their convictions were released on July 6, 1865.

THE SPECIOUS RATIONALE FOR TRIAL BY MILITARY COMMISSION

Attorney General Speed's posttrial opinion supporting trial of the alleged accomplices by military commission without congressional authorization has been analyzed in chapter 4.[13] Congress alone has the constitutional power to enact laws governing offenses against the law of nations.[14] The Articles of War authorized trial of noncitizens for espionage and spying by general court-martial but did not authorize trial by military commission.[15] Congress could have provided for trial of Booth's alleged accomplices by military commission, but the Johnson administration never sought congressional approval for the establishment of the Hunter Commission. This same fallacy surfaced in 2003 when the Bush administration justified the establishment of military commissions that did not adhere to Article 36 of the Uniform Code of Military Justice to try Guantanamo detainees without seeking congressional authorization for these special tribunals.[16] The Supreme Court held that the president's power to wage war under Article II of the Constitution did not authorize him to set up military commissions that failed to follow Article 36 of the Uniform Code of Military Justice without an enabling act.[17]

The U.S. District for the District of Florida invoked a similar specious argument in *Ex parte Mudd*.[18] As noted in chapter 6, Samuel Mudd, Samuel Arnold, and Edman Spangler filed a joint petition for writ of habeas corpus in the District of Florida in 1867. Judge Boynton, a Lincoln appointee, presented his rationale for denying a writ of habeas corpus in his three-page opinion, which is not part of the Federal Reporter system. He asserted that the petitioners were properly tried by military commission because at the time of trial, President Lincoln was the commander in chief of all United States forces, living in Washington, D.C., a heavily fortified city when hostilities had not ceased. Therefore, there was nothing in *Ex parte Milligan*, the U.S. Constitution, nor in the Habeas Corpus Act of 1863 that would compel the conclusion that Mudd and his copetitioners were unfairly tried. According to Judge Boynton, *Milligan* was a case limited to a situation where the state was not invaded and "there is nothing to lead to the conclusion that if an army had been encamped in the State of Indiana . . . and any person a resident of Indiana or any other state (enlisted soldier or not) had not from private animosity but from public reasons, made his made his way into the Army lines and assassinated the Commanding General"[19] that the offender could not have been tried by military commission. Without stating the grounds for this rhetorical flourish, Judge Boynton's hypothetical implicitly relied on the presidential power to wage war derived from Article II of the Constitution to justify President Johnson's appointment of the Hunter Commission in May 1865.

Judge Boynton's conclusion was wrong. First, he distorted the military conditions in Washington, D.C., at the time of President Lincoln's assassination. The relevant date for making the determination of the presidential power to appoint a military commission was May 6, 1865, not April 14, as Judge Boynton alleged. Washington, D.C., was not under any threat of attack in May 1865. Although Confederate armies were in the field in Texas, they were no threat to the security of Washington, D.C.[20] The civilian courts were open for business. Although the writ of habeas corpus had been suspended in the District of Columbia in 1862, criminal trials were held in the D.C. Court of General Sessions and in the D.C. Circuit Court. The *Milligan* majority specifically held that when the civilian courts were open for business and the trial location was under no threat of invasion, the Constitution forbade trying civilians by military tribunals.[21]

Judge Boynton failed to note that Congress alone had the power to authorize the trial of anyone by military commission according to the laws of war or the law of nations. If Congress had authorized such trials, the president could appoint military commissions to try such cases. Article II § 8 did not grant the president unilateral power to try anyone before a military commission. He failed to note that all the justices of the Supreme Court in *Milligan* held that Congress had not authorized trial of civilians by military commission. The court has never overruled *Milligan* on this point. The World War II Nazi saboteur case, *Ex parte Quirin*,[22] did not overrule *Milligan*. The Supreme Court held that Congress had authorized the president to try saboteurs by military commission when it amended the Articles of War after World War I.[23]

THE HUNTER COMMISSION CONVICTED THE ACCOMPLICES USING PERJURED TESTIMONY

Sanford Conover a.k.a. Charles A. Dunham, Richard Montgomery and Dr. James B. Merritt gave false evidence connecting Jacob Thompson, Clement Clay, George N. Sanders, and President Jefferson Davis with the plot to assassinate President Lincoln. The government's case was based on a conspiracy between these individuals and John Wilkes Booth's accomplices that was supposed to have been agreed upon in February 1865 if not earlier, months before the assassination. The conspiracy charge allowed the prosecution to use evidence against the accomplices consisting of atrocities committed by agents of Clay and Thompson, that would be chargeable against the accomplices as if they had committed those crimes themselves. The Hunter Commission considered the atrocity evidence and may very well have used it to convict Samuel Arnold, Michael O'Loughlen, Dr. Samuel Mudd, and Mary Surratt since the case against these alleged accomplices was circumstantial and weak.

A judgment of conviction based in part on perjured testimony is void.[24] It is also a judgment contrary to due process of law.[25] Since the perjured testimony of Conover a.k.a. Dunham, Merritt, and Montgomery was admitted against all the defendants, the Hunter Commission judgments of conviction should have been set aside, if only a disinterested judge could have reviewed the transcript and the decision after Conover's perjury was detected in June 1865. At least the defendants were entitled to a new trial that did not include the perjured testimony.

FIFTH AND SIXTH AMENDMENT DUE PROCESS OF LAW AND RIGHTS OF THE ACCUSED

Traditional scholarship has focused on the Hunter Commission's refusal to grant the basic rights of the accused to the alleged accomplices. As far back as 1895, David DeWitt denounced the trial of the Booth accomplices as unconstitutional on the basis that Mary Surratt was not afforded her Fifth and Sixth Amendment rights.[26]

Booth's alleged accomplices were denied a fair trial guaranteed by the due process clause of the Fifth Amendment.[27] The Hunter Commission did not extend the commonly recognized elements of procedural due process of law to the defendants. The defendants were entitled to exclusion of inadmissible evidence. The commission repeatedly rejected defense objections to evidence inadmissible in a civil court.[28] The commission did not convict the accomplices by the constitutional standard of proof beyond reasonable doubt. The voluminous record of proceedings does not show what standard of burden of proof was applied during the trial. The government's prosecutors sat in with the panel of officers during deliberation and advised the panel on the law and on interpretation of the facts.[29]

FAILURE TO PROVE TREASON

All the alleged accomplices were charged with committing treason and conspiracy to commit treason. The Treason Act required proof from two witnesses of a treasonable act to convict.[30] The evidence submitted by the prosecution proved that it was more probable than not that Samuel Arnold, George Atzerodt, Samuel Mudd, Michael O'Loughlen, Lewis Powell, and John Surratt were members of a group organized by John Wilkes Booth to kidnap President Lincoln that involved assistance from Confederate commissioners Clement Clay and Jacob Thompson. The evidence proving the association from sources other than the accomplices consisted of:

1. The December 1864 meeting in the National Hotel testified to by Lewis Weichmann, linking Booth to Mudd and Surratt.
2. The testimony of John Lloyd that John Surratt brought Spencer carbines and ammunition to Surrattsville to be held for the kidnapping.
3. Sanford Conover's testimony that Booth met with Confederate commissioners Clay and Thompson in Montreal in the fall of 1864.[31]

All the accomplices were charged with committing treason. Treason was defined by Article III § 3 of the Constitution and the 1790 Treason Act as levying war against the United States, adhering to the enemies of the United States, or giving aid and comfort to the enemies of the United States. Conviction required the eyewitness testimony of two witnesses, assuming the alleged traitor did not confess to treason in open court.[32] In April 1865, treason was punishable according to the Second Confiscation Act of 1862 as death, or in the alternative, five years' imprisonment and confiscation of the offender's slaves.[33] The District of Columbia Code contained a prohibition on treason that referenced the Treason Act of 1790 as amended.[34]

The Hunter Commission failed to follow the Constitution and the Treason Act of 1790. It convicted Edman Spangler of treason on Jake Ritterspaugh's uncorroborated testimony:

> Q. State where you were at the time, and what you did when you heard that cry, "Stop that man!"
>
> A. I was standing on the stage behind the scenes. Some one cried that the President was shot. Then I saw a man running that had no hat on.

Q. Which way was he running?

A. Towards the back door. He had a knife in his hand, and I ran to stop him, and ran through the last entrance; and as I came up to him he tore the door open. I made for him, and he struck at me with the knife; and I jumped back then. He then ran out, and slammed the door shut. I then went to get the door open. In a moment afterwards, I opened the door, and the man had just got on his horse, and was running down the alley; and then I came in. I came back on the stage where I had left Edward Spangler, and he hit me on the face with the back of his hand, and he said, "Don't say which way he went." I asked him what he meant by slapping me in the mouth; and he said, "For God's sake shut up!" and that was the last he said.

Q. Is the Edward Spangler to whom you refer the prisoner at the bar?

A. Yes, sir.[35]

Samuel Arnold was convicted on the strength of his letter to Booth unsupported by any eyewitness testimony connecting Arnold with the failed March 17, 1865, kidnapping attempt or with the assassination plot.

The evidence against Dr. Samuel Mudd did not meet the Treason Act standard of proof. Knowingly harboring Booth and Herold on April 15 was his alleged treasonable act. Colonel Wells, the officer who interrogated Mudd, testified that he forced Mudd to admit that he recognized the patient he treated for a leg fracture as Booth. The evidence given by Mudd's former slaves and hired hands failed to prove that Mudd knowingly harbored the fugitives. Weichmann's evidence of the meeting between Booth and Mudd at the National Hotel in December 1864 was circumstantial evidence that he was a member of the kidnap conspiracy, but did not corroborate Colonel Wells's evidence relating to Mudd's harboring of the fugitives. The Hunter Commission allowed Sanford Conover and two other witnesses to repeat hearsay implicating Booth and the Confederate commissioners to Canada and their agents as coconspirators and coperpetrators without producing the person who made the statement in court, or explaining why the utterer was not available to be cross-examined. Most of the hearsay admitted went to prove that the Confederate leadership, Jefferson Davis, Judah Benjamin, Clement Clay, and Jacob Thompson, were behind the conspiracy to assassinate President Lincoln.[36] The prosecution produced no evidence that Mudd knew that John Wilkes Booth had murdered President Lincoln until the afternoon of April 15 when he learned about the assassination in Bryantown. Dr. Mudd was unconstitutionally convicted.

The treason case against Michael O'Loughlen was also weak: he was identified by two witnesses as loitering about the reception for General Grant and expressing a wish to meet him. No witness put O'Loughlen aboard Grant's train as the Grants departed Washington, or at any other location where O'Loughlen could assault Grant. Disregarding O'Loughlen's alibi, the prosecution failed to show O'Loughlen had committed treason. His conviction was unconstitutional.

Finally, the Hunter Commission took evidence showing that Mary Surratt had instructed John Lloyd to have "the shooting irons ready" for the night of April 14. It had evidence from Louis Weichmann that Mrs. Surratt had met with John Wilkes Booth on the afternoon of April 14 and had a package from Booth to deliver to Lloyd. Neither Lloyd's nor Weichmann's evidence was corroborated by another eyewitness. The Hunter Commission conviction of Mary Surratt for treason was unconstitutional. The secretary of war, Judge Advocate General Holt, and the Hunter Commission committed numerous Sixth Amendment violations. The alleged accomplices were entitled to a speedy trial before a jury of their peers. Trial by military commission was not a jury trial. The alleged accomplices were not given the right to notice of the charges against them until the first day of trial. The notice clause of the Sixth Amendment required sufficient advance notice to permit the defendant to prepare a defense. The government did not give notice of intent to use uncharged misconduct evidence: that is, the testimony of ex-prisoners of war relating to atrocities committed by the Confederate States against prisoners of war, or testimony from Godfrey Hyams about the yellow fever plot.[37]

PRESIDENT JOHNSON'S FAILURE TO COMPLY WITH THE HABEAS CORPUS ACT OF 1863

Booth's alleged accomplices were tried by a military commission appointed by President Johnson without any ratifying act of Congress. The constitutionality of the military commission therefore depended on the power of the president under Article II sections 2 and 3 of the Constitution to act unilaterally in the case of the men and woman accused of being Booth's accomplices. President Johnson and the War Department ignored the Habeas Corpus Act of 1863 by setting up the military commission.

The Civil War commenced without a congressional declaration of war, which would have recognized the existence of the Confederate States of America as a sovereign state. During the war, President Lincoln carried out policies that treated the Confederate States as if they were a juridical state without conceding the Confederate States' sovereignty over the eleven former states that seceded from the Union in 1861.[38] In 1863, the Supreme Court had conceded that the Confederate States were to be treated as if sovereign for the purpose of supporting President Lincoln's blockade of Southern ports without congressional authorization and a formal declaration of war. Lewis Powell was a Florida citizen. He could be treated as if he were the agent of a foreign power if the holding of the *Prize Cases* could be applied outside the narrow scope of approving President Lincoln's blockade of Southern ports during the war before receiving congressional authority to impose the blockade.[39] All the other defendants were District of Columbia or Maryland citizens. Neither jurisdiction seceded from the Union, and the District of Columbia and Maryland federal and state courts never ceased functioning due to the three Confederate invasions of western Maryland.[40] The defendants were entitled to be disposed of according to the Habeas Corpus Act of 1863, which guaranteed them the protection afforded defendants by the Fifth and Sixth Amendments to the Constitution. Speed tried to argue that the Fourth, Fifth, and Sixth Amendments did not apply to Booth's alleged accomplices because they were enemy belligerents. Had the alleged accomplices been disposed of in accordance with the Habeas Corpus Act of 1863, their names would have been sent to the Supreme Court for the District of Columbia sitting as Criminal District Court for potential indictment. The alleged accomplices would then have been indicted by grand jury, been informed of the charges against them, and would be afforded a speedy public trial by a jury of twelve on those charges. The civilian rules of evidence and of criminal procedure should have been followed, in particular the criminal burden of proof beyond a reasonable doubt and the rule barring most forms of hearsay. If the jury returned a verdict of guilty, the defendants could file a writ of error to seek judicial review of the conviction by the Supreme Court. Since Speed never considered that the president and secretary of war were bound to follow the Habeas Corpus Act of 1863 with regard to Booth's alleged accomplices, they were not accorded the treatment specified by Congress. Speed gave no reason for ignoring the act.

The duty to send the list of prisoners to the appropriate federal magistrate did not call for any discretion on the part of the president, Secretary of War Stanton, or his civilian or military subordinates. The War Department had a ministerial duty to turn over the names of Booth's alleged accomplices to the District of Columbia courts for potential indictment. That issue was settled in 1805 in *Marbury v. Madison*.[41] President John Adams had signed a Justice of Peace Commission appointing William Marbury justice of the peace for the District of Columbia, just before he left office and turned the presidency over to Thomas Jefferson. The incoming secretary of state, James Madison, refused to forward the commission to Marbury who filed an original action for a writ of mandamus in the Supreme Court under section 13 of the Judiciary Act of 1789 authorizing the court to entertain writs in aid of its processes.[42] The court's decision, denying the petitioners' mandamus on the ground that section 13 was unconstitutional,[43] also dealt with Article II and the duty of the president to carry out acts of Congress. The court held that Secretary of State Madison had no right to withhold Marbury's commission because he was acting under an act of Congress requiring him to deliver the commission.[44] After discussing the difference between discretionary duties, which a private citizen could not compel an executive branch officer to perform, and nondiscretionary duties, which allowed for a private person to seek a civil remedy for failure to perform that duty, the court said:

> But when the legislature proceeds to impose on that officer other duties; when he is directed peremptorily to perform certain acts; when the rights of individuals are dependent on the performance of those acts; he is so far the officer of the law; is amenable to the laws for his conduct; and cannot at his discretion sport away the vested rights of others.
>
> ***
>
> But where he is directed by law to do a certain act affecting the absolute rights of individuals, in the performance of which he is not placed under the particular direction of the President, and the performance of which the President cannot lawfully forbid, and therefore is never presumed to have forbidden; as for example, to record a commission, or a patent for land, which has received all the legal solemnities; or to give a copy of such record; in such cases, it is not perceived on what ground the courts of the country are further excused from the duty of giving judgment that right be done to an injured individual, than if the same services were to be performed by a person not the head of a department.[45]

The Marbury court did not specifically reference Article II section 2. The court's characterization of the secretary of state's duty was premised on the duty laid on the president to faithfully execute the laws specified by Article II. Thirty-five years later, the Supreme Court was required to construe Article II section 2 in *Kendall v. United States*.[46] Four contractors who carried the U.S. mail applied to the postmaster general for credits due them under their contracts.[47] Postmaster General Barry allowed the credits amounting to $122,000, but his successor, Postmaster General Amos Kendall, reexamined the claim and disallowed it.[48] Solicitor for the Treasury William T. Maxey reviewed the postmaster general's report and found that the contractors were entitled to $169,000 as a credit against their accounts.[49] The president then submitted the contractors' claim without comment to Congress for a special act of Congress directing the postmaster general to pay the contractors' claims. The Senate replied with a resolution that the postmaster general pay the contractors according to the solicitor's report, but Postmaster General Kendall did not comply with the act. The contractors filed a petition for mandamus directing the postmaster general to post the credit on the contractors' accounts in the Circuit Court for the District of Columbia, which issued a rule to show cause from which the postmaster general took a writ of error to the Supreme Court.[50] The Supreme Court affirmed the issuance of the mandamus.[51] The court dealt with Article II section 2's mandate to the president to enforce the laws of the United States. It held that the postmaster general could be compelled to credit the contractors' accounts in accordance with the opinion of the solicitor of the treasury. That was true because the crediting on the books of the post office department was a nondiscretionary ministerial act.[52] The court said:

> The act required by the law to be done by the postmaster general is simply to credit the relators with the full amount of the award of the solicitor. This is a precise, definite act, purely ministerial; and about which the postmaster general had no discretion whatever. The law upon its face shows the existence of accounts between the relators and the post office department. No money was required to be paid; and none could have been drawn out of the treasury without further legislative provision, if this credit should overbalance the debit standing against the relators. But this was a matter with which the postmaster general had no concern. He was not called upon to furnish the means of paying such balance, if any should be found. He was simply required to give the credit. This was not an official act in any other sense than being a transaction in the department where the books and accounts were kept; and was an official act in the same sense that an entry in the minutes of a court, pursuant to an order of the court, is an official act. There is no room for the exercise of any discretion, official or otherwise: all that is shut out by the direct and positive command of the law, and the act required to be done is, in every just sense, a mere ministerial act.[53]

The court held that the All Writs Act[54] granted the circuit court power to issue writs of mandamus.[55] *Kendall* stands for the proposition that an official of the executive branch of the United States government may be compelled to perform a ministerial duty prescribed by Congress. The president and his cabinet officers may not willfully disregard an act of Congress imposing a nondiscretionary duty on the executive branch of the government. There is an academic argument that the president may refuse to enforce an act of Congress if he believes in good faith that the act is unconstitutional.[56] That argument does not extend to the situation in *Kendall*. Postmaster General Kendall had no discretion to refuse to enter the credits to the contractors' accounts.

John Surratt, apprehended in Egypt in 1867, was not tried by military commission for conspiracy to assassinate President Lincoln. By that time the U.S. Supreme Court's decision in *Ex parte Milligan*[57] had been handed down. The court unanimously overturned the conviction of Northwest Conspirator Lambdin Milligan as inconsistent with the Habeas Corpus Act of 1863, which allowed the military to arrest suspected traitors, but required the military commander responsible for the arrest to turn over the names of those arrested to the relevant federal magistrate for potential indictment by grand jury and civil trial. The court demolished Speed's argument raised before it that Milligan and his fellow conspirators were subject to and should be tried according to the law of war and not to domestic law.[58] The court also demolished Speed's contention that Indianapolis, Indiana, was subject to martial law, permitting trial of suspected traitors by military commission. The court held that martial law could be imposed on a city only when the city was under invasion and the civil courts were closed.[59] The majority also held that civilians could not be tried by a military commission when the site of the trial was not under invasion and the civilian courts were open as a matter of due process of law.[60] All the justices agreed that President Lincoln was not free to disregard the Habeas Corpus Act of 1863, and his failure to submit the names of Milligan and his coconspirators was a fatal flaw requiring that Milligan's conviction and death sentence be set aside.[61]

Justice Davis never addressed the constitutionality of the executive branch disregarding an act of Congress. Since 1866, the courts have dealt with claims by the executive branch to be able to refuse to follow an act of Congress. It is generally conceded that the president may refuse to follow a statute if the president finds the statute to be unconstitutional. In *Myers v. United States*[62] decided in 1926, the court held that President Wilson could dismiss a postmaster without complying with the Tenure of Office Act that might have precluded the postmaster's dismissal without the advice and consent of the Senate. President Wilson believed that the Tenure of Office Act was an unconstitutional infringement on his Article II powers. The court sustained Myers's dismissal and did not expressly pass on Wilson's constitutional law issue. The Supreme Court sustained the dismissal without suggesting that the president had acted improperly in refusing to abide by the statute.[63] The court also determined in 1935 that President Roosevelt's failure to comply with the Federal Trade Commission Act's provision for removing commissioners was a violation of his obligation under Article II § 3 of the Constitution in *Humphrey's Executor v. United States*.[64] Neither case sustained the president's power to disregard an act of Congress that was deemed constitutionally permissible. Both decisions cited *Marbury*. In *Freytag v. Commissioner*,[65] the four justices who took up the issue of obedience to an act of Congress agreed that the president has "the power to veto encroaching laws . . . or even to disregard them when they are unconstitutional."[66]

Article I section 9 of the Constitution authorizes Congress to suspend the writ of habeas corpus in time of national emergency. Congress acted in accordance with this grant of authority in 1863 when it passed the Habeas Corpus Act. The statute prescribed that the War Department, acting through its district commanders, had to turn over a list of its prisoners of state for indictment and trial. This duty was not discretionary, and President Johnson, Secretary Stanton, and Gen. Winfield Scott Hancock, the commanding general with oversight over prisoners held in the District of Columbia, failed to comply with the act.

Attorney General Speed counseled President Johnson that Booth's alleged accomplices could be tried by military commission because they were enemy belligerents. Speed relied on the provisions of General Order 100 relating to trial of irregular combatants. Article 13 states that "cases which do not come within the Rules and Articles of War, or the jurisdiction conferred by statute on courts-martial, are tried by military commissions." Article 82 states that irregulars who "commit hostilities, whether by fighting, or inroads for destruction or plunder, or by raids of any kind, without commission, without being part and portion of the organized hostile army," have divested "themselves of the . . . appearance of soldiers . . . are not public enemies, and therefore, if captured, are not entitled to the privileges of prisoners of war, but shall be treated summarily as highway robbers or pirates."[67] How Speed could have drawn the conclusion that Booth and his accomplices were subject to trial by military commission based on General Order 100 is unclear: Professor Lieber, the author of General Order 100, intended that irregulars should be treated as common criminals, not subject to military jurisdiction. Mary Surratt and the other defendants should not have been tried by a military commission. They were not enemy belligerents. The defendants were entitled to the protection afforded defendants by the Fifth and Sixth Amendments to the Constitution. The alleged accomplices should have been indicted by grand jury, been informed of the charges against them, and should have been afforded a speedy public trial by a jury of twelve on those charges. The civilian rules of evidence and of criminal procedure should have been followed, in particular the criminal burden of proof beyond a reasonable doubt and the rule barring most forms of hearsay.

THE ACCOMPLICES AND CRIMINAL STATUTES

Federal jurisprudence never recognized common-law crimes.[68] All federal crimes must be defined by statute. In 1865, the United States had no statutes defining "conspiracy" and making conspiracy a federal crime. The statutes at large also had no law defining "murder" or "assassination" as crimes. Booth and his associates were subject to the statutory criminal law of the District of Columbia. The District of Columbia recognized the common law as a source of rules in civil and criminal cases, including common-law conspiracy. Following Maryland case law, common-law conspiracy was a misdemeanor.[69] It is not clear that pre-1865 Maryland law recognized the doctrine of merger of the substantive offense and the conspiracy.[70] If the alleged accomplices of John Wilkes Booth were to be tried for conspiracy to commit murder, assault with intent to kill, and attempted murder, that indictment would have to be issued by the Supreme Court of the District of Columbia sitting as a Criminal District Court.

The District of Columbia Code prescribed the death penalty for premeditated murder in 1865.[71] Assault with intent to murder carried a penalty of imprisonment from two to fifteen years.[72] Accessories before the fact were considered to be the same as principals in the first degree.[73] Conspiracy was a common-law misdemeanor, and substantive crimes that were felonies did not merge into the conspiracy. Some of the alleged accomplices would have been punished as principals in the first degree because they were accessories before the fact. Maryland law inherited by the District of Columbia would permit sentencing accessories before the fact to death.[74] Powell committed an assault with intent to commit murder, punishable by imprisonment from two to fifteen years.[75] Atzerodt also attempted to murder Vice President Johnson, although the evidence against him was thin.[76] Mary Surratt could have been indicted as an accessory before the fact if John Lloyd's evidence is to be accepted as true.[77] If their guilt was established beyond a reasonable doubt by a jury empaneled in the Supreme Court of the District of Columbia sitting as a Criminal District Court, all four could be sentenced to death. The prosecution case against Mrs. Surratt was so weak that a motion for directed verdict of acquittal would have been granted.

Although the Booth accomplices could be indicted for treason, the District of Columbia would follow the federal statute and the Constitution in requiring proof of treason from two eyewitnesses. The treason case against Arnold, O'Loughlen, and Spangler would fail for want of two witnesses to any treasonable act. The case against Dr. Mudd would also collapse, since the prosecution could not produce two witnesses who would testify that Mudd knowingly aided and abetted Booth's and Herold's escape. The case against Mary Surratt would also fail, since only John Lloyd's uncorroborated evidence related to an arguably treasonable act.

Samuel Arnold and Michael O'Loughlen had withdrawn from the kidnapping conspiracy in March 1865 and never took part in the assassination plot. They would probably not be indicted. Dr. Samuel Mudd and Edman Spangler would at worst be accessories after the fact. If convicted they would have received a sentence of confinement for one year and a fine of up to $500.[78]

The Supreme Court of the District of Columbia sitting as a Criminal District Court could have issued an indictment against the alleged Booth accomplices for conspiring to kidnap President Lincoln. If found guilty, the accessories before the fact, that is, Arnold, Atzerodt, O'Loughlen, Herold, Mudd, Powell, and Mary Surratt, would have drawn sentences of imprisonment of from one to five years, or a fine and only one year's imprisonment.[79]

The penalties served up by the Hunter Commission were not based on the criminal law of the District of Columbia, nor on any known body of federal law. The penalties were arbitrary and capricious and in the case of Arnold, Mudd, O'Loughlen, and Spangler, bordering on cruel and unusual punishment.

CONCLUSION

The alleged accomplices of John Wilkes Booth were tried before a military tribunal not authorized by Congress and in defiance of the Habeas Corpus Act of 1863. The Hunter Commission received perjured testimony from Sanford Conover, Dr. Merritt, and Richard Montgomery that the judge advocate general knew before the commission reached its judgment was probably

Figure 7.1. The Execution of George Atzerodt, David Herold, Lewis Powell, and Mary Surratt, July 7, 1865. *Source:* Library of Congress.

perjurious. Booth's alleged accomplices were tried on the theory that the murder of President Lincoln had been plotted early in 1865, denying that the assassination plot was a separate, distinct plot initiated by John Wilkes Booth after his failed kidnap plot had ended. The civilian courts were open for business in the District of Columbia, and Washington was under no immediate threat of Confederate invasion in May 1865. *Ex parte Milligan* held that the military had no business trying civilians when the civil courts were open for business. The same argument that prevailed in *Milligan* was made to the Hunter Commission by Senator Johnson and General Ewing. Booth's alleged accomplices were unlawfully and unconstitutionally convicted.

The Hunter Commission allowed irrelevant, uncharged misconduct evidence of maltreatment of Union prisoners of war to be used against the alleged accomplices, and permitted a parade of witnesses to testify about Confederate atrocities such as the fire raid on New York City, the yellow fever plot, and the raid on St. Albans, Vermont, all of which were irrelevant to the conspiracy as charged and not shown by any evidence to relate to the accomplices on trial. The government never gave advance notice of intent to use the uncharged misconduct evidence.

The evidence against Samuel Arnold and Michael O'Loughlen did not show they participated in the assassination plot. Neither man was ever shown to be a member of any assassination conspiracy. Although one government witness stated that he saw O'Loughlen hovering about Secretary Stanton's house the night before April 14 during the reception for General Grant, there was no evidence that O'Loughlen was assigned to murder General Grant. O'Loughlen also had an alibi for the night of April 14, 1865. There was no evidence that Edman Spangler had anything to do with the kidnap plot or the assassination plot. These people should have been acquitted. They were unjustly convicted.

The evidence received by the Hunter Commission proving that Mary Surratt was a knowing participant in the conspiracy to murder President Lincoln was not strong. No witness for the prosecution testified that Mary Surratt knew that John Wilkes Booth and his cohorts planned to kidnap President Lincoln, or that the object of the plot had shifted to assassination on April 14. Louis Weichmann's evidence showed that her house was a meeting place for Booth and his accomplices and that she undertook an errand to Surrattsville for Booth on the afternoon of April 14. No evidence other than the self-serving declaration of John Lloyd showed that Mary Surratt was an accessory before or after the fact to the assassination of President Lincoln. Lloyd's evidence was not corroborated by any other witness who was present at Surrattsville on the afternoon of April 14.

No evidence showed that Dr. Samuel Mudd knew that John Wilkes Booth had murdered the president on the morning of April 15, 1865, when he treated Booth for a leg fracture. Mudd's statements, used against him by the prosecution, showed that he recognized the mysterious Mr. Tyson as John Wilkes Booth when Colonel Wells produced a photograph of John Wilkes Booth during interrogation. If Mudd recognized Booth on the morning of April 15 and aided Booth not knowing that he was an assassin fleeing justice, he was not an accessory after the fact and should have been acquitted.

The evidence against George Atzerodt, David Herold, and Lewis Powell was strong enough to carry the burden of proof beyond a reasonable doubt with respect to their participation in Booth's assassination plot. A civilian court would have indicted these men and a civilian jury would have in all probability found them guilty as charged. That said, these men did not receive a fair trial and were unconstitutionally convicted.

The trial of the alleged accomplices of John Wilkes Booth failed to meet the basic constitutional standards for a fair trial. The trial was conducted in defiance of an act of Congress. It also spawned 150 years of challenges to the Hunter Commission's conduct of the trial carried on by descendants of the alleged accomplices, lawyers, scholars, and interested amateurs. The murder of President Lincoln and the attempted murder of Secretary Seward were atrocious crimes. The heinousness of Booth's attacks was not an excuse to ignore the Constitution and the laws of the United States to ensure that Lincoln and the Union were avenged. The Hunter Commission's palpably unfair and unconstitutional trial of Booth's alleged accomplices did nothing to enhance the standards for fair and impartial criminal justice.

NOTES

1. Edward Steers Jr., *Blood on the Moon: The Assassination of Abraham Lincoln* (Lexington: University Press of Kentucky, 2001), 209–11.

2. Steers, *Blood on the Moon*, 210.

3. See Robert R. Arreola, Angela R. Brown, Isabelle Ord, and Norman Minnear, "Federal Criminal Conspiracy," *American Criminal Law Review* 34 (1997): 617, 619–20.

4. Francis Wharton, *The Criminal Law of the United States Comprising a Digest of the Penal Statutes of the General Government and of Massachusetts. . . .* (Philadelphia: James Kay, Jun. and Brother, 1846), 486.

5. In Krulewitch v. United States, 336 U.S. 440 (1949) the U.S. Supreme Court reversed the defendant's conspiracy conviction because the trial court allowed the admission of a statement by one of the women that Krulewitch had allegedly transported to Florida for immoral purposes after the end of the conspiracy. In reaching this conclusion the court stated that the statement was inadmissible because the conspiracy had either ended by failure or by accomplishment of its purpose when the woman made her statement to the police (*Krulewitch*, 442–443). See also Justice Oliver Wendell Holmes's opinion in United States v. Kissell & Harned, 218 U.S. 601, 610 (1910). Without citing to authorities Holmes said: "Under the general issue all defenses, including the defense that the conspiracy was ended by success, abandonment, or otherwise more than three years before July 1, 1906, will be open and unaffected by what we now decide."

6. The attempt to kidnap President Lincoln was committed in the District of Columbia. The District of Columbia Criminal Court had statutory jurisdiction to try the kidnap attempt, assuming that Arnold, Atzerodt, Herold, O'Loughlen, Powell, and Mary Surratt were indicted for attempted kidnapping and were convicted. Since the kidnap attempt was unsuccessful, the

accomplices could be found guilty of attempted kidnapping. The 1857 District of Columbia Code did not contain any conspiracy statute. The penalty for kidnapping was imprisonment from one to five years, or, in the discretion of the court, a fine not exceeding $1,000 and one year's confinement in jail. Robert Ould and W. B. B. Cross, eds., *The Revised Code of the District of Columbia Prepared under the Authority of the Act of Congress entitled "An Act to Improve the Laws of the District of Columbia and to Codify the Same," Approved March, 1855*, Part IV Title II Ch. 129 § 28 (Washington, D.C.: A.O.P. Nicholson, 1857) (hereafter "D.C. Code") The punishment for attempted kidnapping was specified by Part IV Title II ch. 129 § 11 as confinement for not less than six months nor more than twelve months. No fine was authorized. Any accessory after the fact (e.g., Dr. Mudd, Samuel Cox, Thomas Jones, Thomas Harbin, Elizabeth Quesenberry , Dr. Stuart) if convicted would be sentenced to six months' to one year's imprisonment.

7. See "Law of Arrest without Warrant," *Albany Law Journal* 1 (1870): 149.

8. See, e.g., Harvey Cortlandt Voorhees, *The Law of Arrest in Civil and Criminal Actions*, (Boston: Boston Book, 1904), 1:§ 121 (arrest without warrant); Henry R. Dearsley, *Criminal Process; or, A View of the Whole Proceedings Taken in Criminal Prosecutions from Arrest to Execution Intended as an Introduction to the Study and Practice of Crown Law* (Philadelphia: T. & J. W. Johnson, 1854), 11–12 (person arrested must be taken before magistrate within a reasonable time after arrest).

9. U.S. Const. amend. VI.

10. See, e.g., Ala. Const. Declaration of Rights art. I, § 10 (1861); Ark. Const. art. II, § 11 (1836); Calif. Const. art. I, § 8 (1849); Conn. Const. art. I, § 9 (1821); Del. Const. art. I, § 9 (1837); Fla. Const. art. I, § 10 (1861); Ill. Const. art. XIII, § 9 (1848); Ind. Const. art. I, § 13 (1852); Iowa Const. art. I, § 10 (1857); Kans. Const. Bill of Rights § 10 (1857); Ky. Const. art. XIII, § 12 (1850); La. Const. art. CIII (1861); Maine Const. art. I, § 7 (1819); Md. Const. Declaration of Rights art. XIX (1851); Mich. Const. art. II, § 28 (1851); Minn. Const. art. I, § 6 (1857).

11. For a description of habeas corpus at the time of the Civil War see Horace Binney, *Privilege of the Writ of Habeas Corpus under the Constitution*, 2nd ed. (Philadelphia: C. Sherman & Son, 1862).

12. See An Act relating to Habeas Corpus, and regulating Judicial Proceedings in Certain Cases, 12 Stat. 755 § 1 (1863). See also Presidential Proclamation 104 of September 15, 1863. See Steers, *Blood on the Moon*, 324 (note 7). See Presidential Proclamation 133 dated July 5, 1864, for the martial law proclamation for Kentucky.

13. See chapter 4, notes 16–23, in this volume for the development of the argument against Speed's opinion.

14. U.S. Const. art. I, § 8, cl. 10.

15. See *Military Laws and Rules and Regulations for the Government of the Army of the United States* (Washington, D.C.: E. DeKraft, 1806) (rev. Sept. 1817), 24, Articles of War § 2 (1806), which reads: "That in time of war, all persons not citizens of, or owing allegiance to, the United States of America, who shall be found lurking as spies in or about the fortification or encampments of the armies of the United States, or any of them, shall suffer death, according to the law and usage of nations, by sentence of a general courts-martial."

16. The Bush administration based its assertion that it had the inherent power to set up military commissions that lacked a uniform set of procedures on a memo written by Prof. John Yoo based on his 1996 law review article supporting a claim of executive authority to convene military commissions without congressional authorization. See John Yoo, "Memorandum Opinion: The President's Constitutional Authority to Conduct Military Operations against Terrorists and Nations Supporting Them," U.S. Department Justice, Opinions of the Office of Legal Counsel, September 25, 2001, http://www.justice.gov/sites/default/files/olc/opinions/2001/09/31/op-olc-v025-p0188_0.pdf.

17. See Hamdan v. Rumsfeld, 548 U.S. 557, 594–605 (2006); see also concurring opinion of Breyer, J. at 636. 10 U.S.C. § 836 in 2005 stated that:

(a) "Pretrial, trial, and post-trial procedures, including modes of proof, for cases arising under this chapter [10 USCS §§ 801 et seq.] triable in courts-martial, military commissions and other military tribunals, and procedures for courts of inquiry, may be prescribed by the President by regulations which shall, so far as he considers practicable, apply the principles of law and the rules of evidence generally recognized in the trial of criminal cases in the United States district courts, but which may not be contrary to or inconsistent with this chapter [10 USCS §§ 801 et seq.]."

(b) "All rules and regulations made under this article shall be uniform insofar as practicable."

In 2006 Congress authorized military commission trials adding to Art. 36 the following in subsection (a), "except as provided in chapter 47A of this title," and in subsection (b) "except insofar as applicable to military commissions established under chapter 47A of this title."

18. Fed. Cas. 9899 Dist. Fla. 1868 (text of opinion from the archives of the Fifth Circuit Court of Appeals retrieved in 1996 by Candida Ewing Steel, Esq., copy in author's possession).

19. Ex parte Mudd, Fed. Cas. 9899.

20. Confederate general E. Kirby Smith surrendered his Texas command on June 2, 1865. John S. Bowman, ed., *The Civil War Almanac* New York: World Almanac Publications, 1983), 268–69.

21. Ex parte Milligan, 71 U.S. 121–22.

22. Ex parte Quirin, 317 U.S. 1 (1942) (Held: U.S. citizen acting as a Nazi German spy in World War II not entitled to trial by jury because Articles of War passed by Congress authorized trial by military commission.) See also Hamdi v. Rumsfeld, 542 U.S. 507 (2004) (Held: U.S. citizen apprehended in Afghanistan and alleged to be Taliban fighter could not be tried by military commission because did not authorize trials by military commission for U.S. detainees.)

23. Ex parte Quirin, 317 U.S. 1 (1942).

24. See, e g., Chaney v. Brown, 730 F.2d 1334 (10th Cir. 1984), cert. denied, 469 U.S. 1090 (1984): "First, where the prosecutor has knowingly used perjured testimony, the judgment must be set aside 'if there is any reasonable likelihood that the false testimony could have affected the judgment of the jury.'"

25. People v. Alfano, 420 N.E.2d 1114 (Ill. App. 1981).

26. David Miller DeWitt, *The Judicial Murder of Mary E. Surratt* (Baltimore: John Murphy, 1895), 126–30, 258.

27. U.S. Const. amend. V. "Nor deprive any citizen of the United States of life, liberty or property, except by due process of law."

28. See John W. Clampitt, "The Trial of Mrs. Surratt," *North American Review* 131, 1880, 233–34; DeWitt, *Judicial Murder of Mary E. Surratt*, 58–59 (Ewing's objection); William E. Doster, *Lincoln and Episodes of the Civil War* (New York: Putnam, 1915), 260.

29. DeWitt, *The Judicial Murder of Mary E. Surratt*, 91–92.

30. See U.S. Const. art. III, § 3; 18 U.S.C. § 1 now compiled as 18 U.S.C. § 2381.

31. Conover's testimony was later proved to have been fabricated. He was indicted and convicted of perjury. Seymour J. Frank, "The Conspiracy to Implicate the Confederate Leaders in Lincoln's Assassination," *Mississippi Valley Historical Review* 40 (1954): 629.

32. "[I]f any person or persons, owing allegiance to the United States of America, shall levy war against them, or shall adhere to their enemies, giving them aid and comfort within the United States or elsewhere, and shall be thereof convicted, on confession in open court, or on the testimony of two witnesses to the same overt act of treason whereof he or they shall stand indicted, such person or persons shall be adjudged guilty of treason against the United States, and shall suffer death." 1 Stat. 112 (1790).

33. 12 Stat. 589 Thirty-Seventh Congress Sess. II Ch. 195 § 1 (1862).

34. D.C. Code Part IV, Title II Ch. 129 §1 (1857).

35. Ben Perley Poore, ed., *The Conspiracy Trial for the Murder of the President, and the Attempt to Overthrow the Government by the Assassination of Its Principal Officers, Edited with an Introduction by Ben. Perley Poore* (Boston: J. E. Tilton, 1865), 2:457 (Ritterspaugh testimony for prosecution); also available at http://www.surrattmuseum.org/ben-perley-poore-the-conspiracy-trial-tr . See also Poore, *Conspiracy Trial*, 3:47 (testimony of Jake Ritterspaugh for defendant).

36. See Benn Pitman, ed., *The Trials for Treason at Indianapolis: Disclosing the Plans for Establishing a Northwest Confederacy* (Cincinnati: Moore, Wilstach & Baldwin, 1865), 24–64.

Note the summarized version of the testimony of Montgomery, 24–26; Merritt, 34–35; Conover, 28–33.

37. Current practice requires advance notice of intent to use uncharged misconduct evidence at trial. See Fed. R. Evid. 404(b).

38. The Confederate States were Alabama, Arkansas, Florida, Georgia, Louisiana, Mississippi, North Carolina, South Carolina, Tennessee, Texas, and Virginia. The Confederate States also recognized Kentucky and Missouri, two nonseceding states, as Confederate States. Mark M. Boatner III, *The Civil War Dictionary* (New York: David McKay, 1959), 171.

39. Lincoln's actions, sustained in the Prize Cases, supported President John F. Kennedy's imposition of a blockade of Cuba in 1962 during the Cuban missile crisis. A blockade has been traditionally viewed as an act of war in international law.

40. In September 1862, the Confederate Army of Northern Virginia led by General Robert E. Lee invaded western Maryland, fighting two pitched battles at South Mountain and Antietam. In June and July 1863, Lee's army invaded Maryland on its way to Pennsylvania. In July 1864, Lt. Gen. Jubal A. Early's Corps of Lee's army crossed into western Maryland and fought a pitched battle at Monocacy, south of Frederick, and threatened the Washington, D.C., defense perimeter. Boatner, *Civil War Dictionary*, 17–21 (Antietam); 331–40 (Gettysburg); 255–57 (Washington raid).

41. Marbury v. Madison, 5 U.S. 137 (1803).

42. 5 U.S. 153.

43. 5 U.S. 179–180.

44. 5 U.S. 166.

45. 5 U.S. 166.

46. Kendall v. United States, 37 U.S. 524 (1838).

47. The four contractors were William B. Stokes, Richard C. Stockton, Lucius W. Stockton, and Daniel Moore. Kendall, 1838 U.S. Lexis ***1.

48. 37 U.S. 609.

49. 37 U.S. 611.

50. 37 U.S. 608.

51. 37 U.S. 628.

52. 37 U.S. 618.

53. 37 U.S. 613–614.

54. 37 U.S. 621–22. The All Writs Act is currently codified as 28 U.S.C. § 1651 (2013).

55. *Kendall*, 37 U.S. 625.

56. The power known as "executive disregard" has been put forth in a very articulate article by Prof. Saikrishna Prakash arguing that the president has the duty to disregard acts of Congress he believes to be unconstitutional, with or without judicial review. See Saikrishna Bangalore Prakash, "The Executive's Duty to Disregard Unconstitutional Laws," *Georgetown Law Journal* 96, no. 1613 (2008).

57. 71 U.S. (4 Wall.) 2 (1866).

58. 71 U.S. 122. Lincoln was murdered and Seward was attacked in the District of Columbia. The courts in the District of Columbia were open and no invasion threatened the courts in May 1865. The Hunter Commission was not authorized to try Booth's alleged accomplices by any act of Congress.

59. It follows, from what has been said on this subject, that there are occasions when martial rule can be properly applied. If, in foreign invasion or civil war, the courts are actually closed, and it is impossible to administer criminal justice according to law, then, on the theater of active military operations, where war really prevails, there is a necessity to furnish a substituted for the civil authority, thus overthrown, to preserve the safety of the army and society; and as no power is left but the military, it is allowed to govern by martial rule until the laws can have their free course. As necessity creates the rule, so it limits its duration; for, if this government is continued after the courts are reinstated, it is a gross usurpation of power. Martial rule can never exist where the courts are open, and in the proper and unobstructed exercise of their jurisdiction. It is also confined to the locality of actual war. Because, during the late Rebellion it could have been enforced in Virginia, where the national authority was overturned and the courts driven out, it does not follow that it should obtain in Indiana, where that authority was

never disputed, and justice was always administered. And so in the case of a foreign invasion, martial rule may become a necessity in one state, when, in another, it would be "mere lawless violence." 71 U.S. 127.

60. 71 U.S. 126.

61. 71 U.S. 122–123 (majority opinion); 133–134 (Chase, C.J., concurring and dissenting opinion).

62. Myers v. United States, 272 U.S. 52 (1926).

63. 272 U.S. 52.

64. Humphrey's Executor v. United States, 295 U.S. 602 (1935).

65. Freytag v. Commissioner, 501 U.S. 868 (1991).

66. 501 U.S. 906 (Scalia, J., concurring). see also Youngstown Sheet & Tube Co. v. Sawyer, 343 U.S. 579, 635–638 (1952) (Jackson, J., concurring).

67. Gen. Order 100 article 82. This paragraph categorizes any person who commits hostilities without commission, without being part of an organized hostile army as people who "are not public enemies, and therefore, if captured, are not entitled to the privileges of prisoners of war, but shall be treated summarily as highway robbers or pirates."

68. United States v. Hudson & Goodman, 11 U.S. (7 Cranch) 32–33 (1812).

69. An Act Concerning the District of Columbia § 1 (1801), laws which were in force in Maryland on February 27, 1801, should continue in force within the District of Columbia. Conspiracy was a common-law misdemeanor in Maryland. See State v. Buchanan, 5 H. & J. 317 (Md. Ct. App. 1821). See also D.C. Code Part I Title I § 4: "The common law of England and the principles of equity jurisprudence, so far as the same are not repugnant to the constitution of the United States, shall continue in force in this District, and be the rule of decision, except in those respects wherein the same are or may be altered by Congress."

70. Current Maryland law does not recognize the doctrine of merger. See Jones v. State, 259 A.2d 807 (Md. 1969). The Court of Special Appeals cited no cases in its decision, but did cite Wharton on criminal law. Arguably, merger did not apply in 1865, but there are no cases in Maryland holding that merger does not apply prior to April 1865.

71. D.C. Code Part IV Title II Ch. 130 §1.

72. D.C. Code Part IV Title II Ch. 130 § 21.

73. D.C. Code Part IV Title II Ch. 139 §8.

74. Current Maryland case law made this perfectly clear. See, e.g., Gary v. State, 671 A.2d 495 (Md. 1996).

75. D.C. Code Part IV Title II Ch. 130 § 21.

76. D.C. Code Part IV Title II Ch.139 § 9.

77. D.C. Code Part IV Title II Ch. 139 § 8.

78. D.C. Code Part IV Title II Ch. 139 § 8.

79. D.C. Code Part IV Title II Ch. 130 § 28 and Ch. 139 § 8.

Bibliography

MANUSCRIPTS

Birth Certificate of Frederick A. Aiken, Town of Shrewsbury, Mass.

"Consolidated Enrollment Lists, Compiled 1863–1865," 620 vol., District of Columbia at 15. National Archives Catalog ID: 4213514 / MLR Number NM-65 172.

Illinois Marriage License David Clendenin to Sophia Ford, Knox County Court Record, Film #1404972, 1411909–1411921, and 1412045–1412060.

Reed, Thomas J. "Black Davey: The Life of Maj. Gen. David Hunter." Unpublished manuscript, 1997.

Pardon of Samuel A. Mudd, February 8, 1869. Dr. Samuel A. Mudd Pardon, File # B-596, National Archives Annex, College Park, Md.

Service Records of 43rd Virginia Bn, NARA microfilm 324-207-11 RG 94.

CENSUS RECORDS

U.S. Census 1850, Whiteside, Cook Co., Ill., HH 64 FAM 64.

U.S. Census 1860, Coomes, Charles Co., Md., p. 7, HH 52 FAM 52.

U.S. Census 1860, Lyndon, Whiteside, Cook Co., Ill., p. 874, HH 1821 FAM 1799.

U.S. Census 1880, Deerfield, Lake Co., Ill., p. 417D.

U.S. Census 1880, Washington, D.C., p.245A, HH 185 FAM 228.

U.S. Census 1900, Deerfield, Lake Co., Ill., ED 132, p.14B, HH 237 FAM 264.

U.S. Census 1900, Manhattan, New York, ED 103, p. 6B, HH 49 FAM 83.

PERIODICALS

Arreola, Robert R., Angela R. Brown, Isabelle Ord, and Norman Minnear. "Federal Criminal Conspiracy." *A merican Criminal Law Review* 34 (1997): 617–44.

Beckett, Katherine, and Steve Herbert. "Penal Boundaries: Banishment and the Expansion of Punishment." *Law & Social Inquiry* 35, no. 1 (2010): 1–38.

"Biography of Sen. Reverdy Johnson." *Baltimore Barrister*, Summer 1979.

Clampitt, John W. "The Trial of Mrs. Surratt." *North American Review* 131, 1880, 223–40.

Columbian College Catalog 1858–59. Washington, D.C.: Thomas McGill, 1859.

"Death of John W. Clampitt." *Washington Post*, July 18, 1906.
Farrell, Brian. "Habeas Corpus in Time of Emergency: A Historical and Comparative View." *Pace International Law Review Online Companion*, April 2010.
Frank, Seymour J. "The Conspiracy to Implicate the Confederate Leaders in Lincoln's Assassination." *Mississippi Valley Historical Review* 40 (1954): 629–56.
Kelly, John. "A Tip of the Hat to a Former *Post* Editor." *Washington Post*, June 13, 2012, B2.
"Law of Arrest without Warrant." *Albany Law Journal* 1 (1870): 149.
"Marriage Notice: Frederick A. Aiken to Sarah Olivia Weston, June 1, 1857." *Danville (Vt.) North Star*, June 2, 1857.
New York Times, July 14, 1863; July 15, 1863; July 16, 1863; April 2, 1864; May 15, 1865; June 28, 1865; August 1, 1865; February 16, 1905.
"Obit. David Ramsey Clendenin." In *Memorials of Deceased Companions of the Commandery of the State of Illinois Military Order of the Loyal Legion of the United States from July 1 1901 to December 31, 1911*. Vol. 2. Chicago: Military Order of the Loyal Legion of the United States, 1912.
"Obit. Dr. Thomas Maley Harris." *West Virginia Medical Journal* 1 (1907): 237–38.
Obituary of Frederick A. Aiken. *Washington Post*, December 2, 1878.
Prakash, Saikrishna Bangalore. "The Executive's Duty to Disregard Unconstitutional Laws." *Georgetown Law Journal* 96, no. 1613 (2008).
Toronto Daily Globe, July 7, 1865.
Yoo, John C. "The Continuation of Politics by Other Means: The Original Understanding of War Powers." *California Law Review* 84, no. 2 (1996): 167–305.
Yoo, John, and Robert J. Delahunty. "The President's Constitutional Authority to Conduct Military Operations against Terrorist Organizations and the Nations That Harbor or Support Them." *Harvard Journal of Law and Public Policy* 25 (2002).

BOOKS

Arnold, Samuel Bland. *Memoirs of a Lincoln Conspirator*. Edited by Michael W. Kauffman. Bowie, Md.: Heritage Books, 1995.
Articles of War, Military Laws and Regulations for the Army of the United States. Washington, D.C.: U.S. Adjutant General's Office, 1817.
Bancroft, Frederick A. *The Life of William A. Seward*. New York: Harper & Bros., 1899.
Bates, Edward. *The Diary of Edward Bates 1859–1866*. Edited by Howard K. Beale. Washington, D.C.: Government Printing Office, 1933.
Benet, S. V., Capt. *A Treatise on Military Law and the Practice of Courts-Martial*. New York: D. Van Nostrand, 1863.
Binney, Horace. *Privilege of the Writ of Habeas Corpus under the Constitution*. 2nd ed. Philadelphia: C. Sherman & Son, 1862.
Bishop, Joel Prentiss. *Commentaries on the Criminal Law*. Boston: Little, Brown, 1856.
———. *Criminal Procedure; or, Commentaries on the Pleading and Evidence in Criminal Practice*, 3rd rev. ed. Boston: Little, Brown, 1880.
Boatner, Mark M., III. *The Civil War Dictionary*. New York: David McKay, 1959.
Bowman, John S., ed. *The Civil War Almanac*. New York: World Almanac, 1983.
Clampitt, John W. *Echoes from the Rocky Mountains: Reminiscences and Thrilling Incidents of the Romantic and Golden Age of the Great West, with a Graphic Account of Its Discovery, Settlement and Grand Development*. Chicago: Belford, Clarke, 1889.
Conrad, Thomas Nelson. *The Rebel Scout: A Thrilling History of Scouting Life in the Southern Army*. Washington, D.C.: National, 1904.
Cooling, Benjamin Franklin. *Monocacy: The Battle That Saved Washington*. Shippensburg, Pa.: White Mane, 1997.
Crook, William H. *Through Five Administrations: Reminiscences of Colonel William H. Crook Bodyguard of President Lincoln*. Edited by Margarita Spalding Gerry. New York: Harper & Bros., 1910.

Dearsley, Henry R. *Criminal Process; or, A View of the Whole Proceedings Taken in Criminal Prosecutions from Arrest to Execution Intended as an Introduction to the Study and Practice of Crown Law*. Philadelphia: T. & J. W. Johnson, 1854.

DeWitt, David Miller. *The Judicial Murder of Mary E. Surratt*. Baltimore: John Murphy, 1895.

Donald, David Herbert. *Lincoln*. New York: Simon & Schuster, 1995.

Doster, William E. *Lincoln and Episodes of the Civil War*. New York: Putnam, 1915.

Dyer, Frederick H. *A Compendium of the War of the Rebellion Compiled and Arranged from Official Records of the Federal and Confederate Armies Reports of the Adjutant Generals of the Several States, the Army Registers and Other Reliable Documents and Sources*. Des Moines, Iowa: By the author, 1908. Republished by Internet Archives, https://archive.org/details/08697590.3359.emory.edu .

Edwards, William C., and Edward Steers Jr., eds. *The Lincoln Assassination: The Evidence*. Urbana-Champaign: University of Illinois Press, 2009.

Eicher, John H., and David J. Eicher. *Civil War High Commands*. Palo Alto, Calif.: Stanford University Press, 2001.

Eisenschiml, Otto. *In the Shadow of Lincoln's Death*. New York: Wilfred Funk, 1940.

Fairman, Charles W. *History of the Supreme Court of the United States: Reconstruction and Reunion, 1864–1888*. New York: Macmillan, 1971.

Fehrenbacher, Don E., ed. *The Speeches of Abraham Lincoln*. New York: Library of America, 1999.

Freedman, Eric M. *Habeas Corpus: Rethinking the Great Writ of Liberty*. New York: New York University Press, 2001.

Goodspeed, Weston A., and Daniel D. Healy, eds. *Cook County, Illinois: Being a General Survey of Cook County Including a Condensed History of Chicago and Special Accounts of Districts Outside the City Limits; From the Earliest Settlement to the Present*. Chicago: Goodspeed Historical Association, 1909.

Greenleaf, Simon. *A Treatise on the Law of Evidence*. Vol. 1, 12th ed. Edited by Isaac F. Redfield. Boston: Little, Brown, 1866. Originally published 1858.

Hanchett, William. *The Lincoln Murder Conspiracies*. Urbana-Champaign: University of Illinois Press, 1989.

Harris, Leslie M. *In the Shadow of Slavery: African-Americans in New York City 1626–1863*. Chicago: University of Chicago Press, 2003.

Harris, Thomas M. *Assassination of Lincoln: A History of the Great Conspiracy; Trial of the Conspirators by a Military Commission and a Review of the Trial of John H. Surratt*. Boston: American Citizen, 1892.

———. *Rome's Responsibility for the Assassination of Abraham Lincoln*. Pittsburgh: Williams, 1897.

Hodgkins, William H. *The Battle of Fort Stedman, Petersburg, Virginia March 25, 1865*. Boston: By the author, 1889.

Jones, John P., ed. *Dr. Mudd and the Lincoln Assassination: The Case Re-opened—The Proceedings of a Moot Court of Military Appeal to Hear the Case of Dr. Samuel A. Mudd with Contributions by F. Lee Bailey, John Jay Douglass, Candida Ewing Steel, John S. Jenkins and Others*. Conshohocken, Pa.: Combined Books, 1997.

Kauffman, Michael W. *American Brutus: John Wilkes Booth and the Lincoln Conspiracies*. New York: Random House, 2004.

Kautz, Lawrence G. *August Valentine Kautz, USA: Biography of a Civil War General*. Jefferson, N.C.: McFarland, 2008.

Kline, Michael J. *The Baltimore Plot: The First Conspiracy to Assassinate Abraham Lincoln*. Yardley, Pa.: Westholme, 2008.

Langbein, John H. *The Origins of Adversary Criminal Trial*. New York: Oxford University Press, 2003.

Larson, Kate Clifford. *The Assassin's Accomplice: Mary Surratt and the Plot to Kill Abraham Lincoln*. New York: Basic Books, 2008.

Leech, Margaret. *Reveille in Washington 1860–1865*. New York: Harper & Bros., 1941. Reprint, New York: Time, 1962.

Leonard, Elizabeth. *Lincoln's Forgotten Ally: Judge Advocate General Joseph Holt*. Chapel Hill: University of North Carolina Press, 2011.

Lieber, Francis. *Instructions for the Government of Armies of the United States in the Field, Sect. I Art. 3 & 4. Originally promulgated as Gen. Order 100*, 1863. Washington, D.C.: Government Printing Office, 1898.

Macomb, Alexander. *The Practice of Courts Martial*. New York: Harper & Bros., 1841.

Magliocca, Gerard N. *American Founding Son: John Bingham and the Invention of the Fourteenth Amendment*. New York: New York University Press, 2013.

Matheny, H. E. *Major General Thomas Maley Harris: A Member of the Military Commission That Tried the President Abraham Lincoln Assassination Conspirators*. Parsons, W.V.: McClain, 1963.

Miller, Edward A., Jr. *Lincoln's Abolitionist General: The Biography of David Hunter*. Columbia: University of South Carolina Press, 1997.

Mudd, Nettie, ed. *The Life of Dr. Samuel A. Mudd: Containing His Letters from Fort Jefferson, Dry Tortugas Island, Where He Was Imprisoned Four Years for Alleged Complicity in the Assassination of Abraham Lincoln. . . .* New York: Neale, 1906.

Neely, Mark E., Jr. *The Fate of Liberty: Abraham Lincoln and Civil Liberties*. New York: Oxford University Press, 1992.

Oldroyd, Osborn H. *The Assassination of Abraham Lincoln: Flight, Pursuit, Capture, and Punishment of the Conspirators*. Washington, D.C.: By the author, 1891.

Phillipson, Coleman, ed. *Wheaton's Elements of International Law: Fifth English Edition Revised Throughout, Considerably Enlarged and Re-written by Coleman Phillipson, M.A., LL.D., Litt. D., of the Inner Temple, Barrister-at-Law with an Introduction by the Rt. Hon Sir. Frederick Pollock, Bt., D.C.L., LL. D.* London: Stevens & Sons, 1916.

Pitman, Benn, ed. *The Assassination of President Lincoln and the Trial of Conspirators: David E. Herold, Mary E. Surratt, Lewis Payne, George A. Atzerodt, Edward Spangler, Samuel A. Mudd, Samuel Arnold, Michael O'Laughlin*. Cincinnati: Moore, Wilstach & Baldwin, 1865.

———, ed. *The Trials for Treason at Indianapolis: Disclosing the Plans for Establishing a Northwest Confederacy*. Cincinnati: Moore, Wilstach & Baldwin, 1865.

Poore, Ben Perley, ed. *The Conspiracy Trial for the Murder of the President, and the Attempt to Overthrow the Government by the Assassination of Its Principal Officers, Edited with an Introduction by Ben. Perley Poore*. 3 vols. Boston: J. E. Tilton, 1865.

Rehnquist, William H. *All the Laws but One: Civil Liberties in Wartime*. New York: Knopf, 1998.

Scott, Winfield. *Memoirs of Lt. Gen. Winfield Scott Written by Himself*. 2 vols. New York: Sheldon, 1864.

Smith, Charles W. *The Life and Military Service of Brevet Major General Robert S. Foster Preface*. Indianapolis: Indiana Historical Society, 1915.

Smith, Ronald D. *Thomas Ewing, Jr.: Frontier Lawyer and Civil War General*. Columbia: University of Missouri Press, 2008.

Smoot, Richard M. *The Unwritten History of the Assassination of Abraham Lincoln*. Clinton, Mass.: W. J. Coulter, 1908.

Starr, Steven Z. *The Union Cavalry in the Civil War*. 3 vols. Baton Rouge: Louisiana State University Press, 1981.

Stashower, Daniel. *The Hour of Peril: The Secret Plot to Murder Lincoln before the Civil War*. New York: Minotaur, 2013.

Steers, Edward, Jr. *Blood on the Moon: The Assassination of Abraham Lincoln*. Lexington: University Press of Kentucky, 2001.

Steiner, Bernard C. *Life of Reverdy Johnson*. Baltimore: Norman Remington, 1914.

Swanson, James. *Manhunt: The Twelve-Day Chase for Lincoln's Killer*. New York: Harper Perennial, 2007.

Swanson, James, and Daniel Weinberg. *Lincoln's Assassins: Their Trial and Execution; An Illustrated History*. New York: Harper Perennial, 2008.

Tidwell, William. *April '65: Confederate Covert Operations in the American Civil War*. Kent, Ohio: Kent State University Press, 1995.

Tidwell, William A., James O. Hall, and David W. Gaddy. *Come Retribution: The Confederate Secret Service and the Assassination of Lincoln.* Oxford: University of Mississippi Press, 1988.

Townsend, George A. *The Life, Crime, and Capture of John Wilkes Booth with a Full Sketch of the Conspiracy of Which He Was the Leader and the Pursuit, Trial and Execution of His Accomplices*. New York: Dick & Fitzgerald, 1865.

Tredway, Gilbert M. *Democratic Opposition to the Lincoln Administration*. Indianapolis: Indiana Historical Bureau, 1973.

The Trial of John H. Surratt in the Criminal Court of the District of Columbia (Transcript of the Trial of John H. Surratt, U.S. District Court, District of Columbia). Washington, D.C.: French & Richardson.

Trindal, Elizabeth Steger. *Mary Surratt: An American Tragedy*. Gretna, La.: Pelican, 1996.

Vandiver, Frank. *Jubal's Raid: General Early's Famous Attack on Washington in 1864*. New York: McGraw-Hill, 1960. Reprint, Lincoln: University of Nebraska Buffalo Books,1988.

Vattel, Emmerich de. *The Law of Nations or the Principles of Natural Law.* 4 books. Edited by Joseph Chitty. Philadelphia: T. & J. W. Johnson, 1853. Reprint, Lonang Institute, 2003. (Originally published in French, 1758.)

Voorhees, Harvey Cortlandt. *The Law of Arrest in Civil and Criminal Actions*. Vol. 1. Boston: Boston Book, 1904.

Wallace, Lewis. *Lew Wallace: An Autobiography*. 2 vols. New York: Harper & Bros., 1906.

Warner, Ezra. *Generals in Blue*. Baton Rouge: Louisiana State University Press, 1964.

Welles, Gideon. *Diary of Gideon Welles, Secretary of the Navy under Lincoln and Johnson.* Vol. 2. Boston: Houghton Mifflin, 1911.

Wert, Jeffrey D. *Mosby's Rangers: The True Adventures of the Most Famous Command of the Civil War.* New York: Simon & Schuster, 1990.

Weyl, Nathaniel. *Treason: The Story of Disloyalty and Betrayal in American History.* Washington, D.C.: Public Affairs Press, 1950.

Wharton, Francis. *The Criminal Law of the United States Comprising a Digest of the Penal Statutes of the General Government and of Massachusetts, New York, Pennsylvania, and Virginia with the Decisions on Cases Arising upon Those Statutes Together with the English and American Authorities upon Criminal Law in General.* Philadelphia: James Kay, Jun. and Brother, 1846.

Whitman, James Q. *The Origins of Reasonable Doubt.* New Haven, Conn.: Yale University Press, 2008.

Winkler, H. Donald. *Lincoln and Booth.* Nashville: Cumberland House, 2003.

ANTHOLOGIES

Basler, Roy E., ed. *Collected Works of Abraham Lincoln.* Bloomington, Ind.: American Historical Review, 1953.

Brennan, J. Fletcher, ed. *The American Annual Encyclopaedia and Register of Important Events of the Year 1865*. New York: D. Appleton, 1866.

———. *Biographical Cyclopaedia and Portrait Gallery of Distinguished Men with a Historical Sketch of the State of Ohio*. 6 vols. Cincinnati: John C. Yorkston, 1880.

Donnelley, Reuben H., compiler. *Chicago City Directory 1887*. Chicago: Chicago Directory, 1887.

Grant, Ulysses S. "The Battle of Shiloh." In *Battles and Leaders of the Civil War*, vol. 1., edited by Robert Underwood Johnson and Clarence Clough Buel. New York: Century, 1888. Reprint, T. Y. Yoseloff, 1956.

Johnson, Bradley T. *Confederate Military History: Maryland.* Vol. 2 of *Confederate Military History: A Library of Confederate States History, in Twelve Volumes, Written by Distinguished Men of the South, and Edited by Gen. Clement. A. Evans of Georgia.* Atlanta: Confederate, 1899. Reprint, Secaucus, N.J.: Blue & Grey, 1981.

Johnson, Rossiter, and John Howard Brown, eds. *The Twentieth Century Biographical Dictionary of Notable Americans*. 4 vols. Boston: Biographical Society, 1904.

Kauffman, Michael. "Biography of Thomas Ewing." In *Bench and Bar of Ohio*, edited by George Irving Reed, Emilius Oviatt Randall, and Charles Theodore Greve. Chicago: Century, 1897.

———. "Process versus Truth in the Case of the Lincoln Conspiracy." In *The Lincoln Assassination: Crime and Punishment, Myth and Memory*, edited by Harold Holzer, Craig L. Symonds, and Frank J. Williams, 195–215. New York: Fordham University Press, 2010.

Perry, Oran. *Indiana in the Mexican War*. Indianapolis: Office of the Adjutant General, 1908.

U.S. War Department. *The Official Record of the War of the Rebellion*. John Sheldon Moody, Calvin Duvall Cowles, Frederick Caryton Ainsworth, Robert N. Scott, Henry Martyn Lazelle, George Breckenridge Davis, Leslie J. Perry, and Joseph William Kirkley, eds. Series 1, 1–53; Series 2, 1–8; Series 3, 1–5; Series 4, 1–4. Washington, D.C.: Government Printing Office, 1880–1901.

Wallace, Lewis. "The March of Lew Wallace's Division to Shiloh." In *Battles and Leaders of the Civil War*, vol. 1., edited by Robert Underwood Johnson and Clarence Clough Buel. New York: Century, 1888. Reprint, T. Y. Yoseloff, 1956.

INTERNET SITES

Badeau, Adam. *Grant in Peace: From Appomattox to Mount McGregor*. Hartford, Conn.: S. S. Scranton, 1887. Available at http://www.perseus.tufts.edu/hopper/text?doc=Perseus%3Atext%3A2001.05.0262%3Achapter%3D41%3Apage%3D358 .

Benson, Al, Jr. *Revised History* (blog). https://revisedhistory.wordpress.com .

Biography and list of works of George Caleb Bingham. http://www.georgecalebbingham.org/bio.htm .

Biography of Rep. John A. Bingham. Biographical Directory of the United States Congress. http://bioguide.congress.gov/scripts/biodisplay.pl?index=b000471.

Biography of David Clendenin. http://www.geni.com/people/Brevet-Brig-General-David-Clendenin-USA/6000000012654235989 .

Biography of David Wallace. Biographical Directory of the United States Congress. http://bioguide.congress.gov/scripts/biodisplay.pl?index=W000076 .

Biography of Frederick Stone. Biographical Directory of the United States Congress. http://bioguide.congress.gov/scripts/biodisplay.pl?index=S000957 .

Biography of Henry L. Burnett. In *The National Cyclopedia of American Biography Being the History of the United States as Illustrated in the Lives of the Founders, Builders and Defenders of the Republic, and of the Men and Women Who Are Doing the Work and Moulding the Thoughts of the Present Time Edited by Distinguished Biographers from Each State Revised and Approved by the Most Eminent Historians, Scholars and Statesmen of the Day*, 14:272–73. New York: James T. White, 1910. Republished in http://www.iment.com/maida/familytree/burnett/bioportrait.htm .

Biography of James A. Ekin. New Albany, Indiana, Public Library. http://nafclibrary.org/wp-content/uploads/2013/08/Ekin-James-Adams.pdf .

Biography of Joseph Holt. http://www.mrlincolnswhitehouse.org/inside.asp?ID=135&subjectID=2 .

Biography of Reverdy Johnson. Biographical Directory of the United States Congress. http://bioguide.congress.gov/scripts/biodisplay.pl?index=j000169 .

Biography of Dr. Samuel Mudd. http://rogerjnorton.com/Lincoln29.html .

Biography of Walter Cox. Biographical Directory of the United States Congress. http://bioguide.congress.gov/scripts/biodisplay.pl?index=S000957 .

Biography of William E. Doster. http://civilwarcavalry.com/?p=704 .

"Burnett, Henry L." National Park Service, Civil War Soldiers and Sailors profile. http://www.nps.gov/civilwar/search-soldiers-detail.htm?soldierId=EDF03989-DC7A-DF11-BF36-B8AC6F5D926A .

Cauchon, Barry. "The Washington, D.C. Arsenal Penitentiary (Part 1 of 3)." *A Little Touch of History* (blog). July 2, 2009. https://awesometalks.wordpress.com/tag/washington-dc-arsenal-penitentiary/ .

Christensen, Christine R. "Finding Frederick." http://media.virbcdn.com/files/7a/70ad398a865a12f8-Aiken_05252012.pdf .

Civil War Trust. "Attack on Fort Stedman." http://www.civilwar.org/battlefields/fortstedman.html .

"Clampitt, John W." National Park Service, Civil War Soldiers and Sailors profile. http://www.nps.gov/civilwar/search-soldiers-detail.htm?soldierId=DE583A8D-DC7A-DF11-BF36-B8AC6F5D926A .

"Confederate States of America." http://www.history.com/topics/american-civil-war/confederate-states-of-america .

"Confederate States of America." *Encyclopedia Britannica Online*. http://www.britannica.com/EBchecked/topic/131803/Confederate-States-of-America .

Cooling, B. F., and Wally Owen. "Washington's Civil War Defenses and the Battle of Fort Stevens." http://www.civilwar.org/battlefields/fortstevens/fort-stevens-history-articles/washingtons-civil-war.html .

Crook, William. Crook's account of Lincoln's visit to City Point. http://www.mrlincolnandfreedom.org/inside.asp?ID=84&subjectID=3 .

Dahlgren, Ulric. Address to his men. http://www.mdgorman.com/Written_Accounts/Sentinel/1864/richmond_sentinel_351864.htm .

"Dr. Samuel A. Mudd's Guide to Health." *Baltimore Sun*, March 10, 1883. Samuel Mudd Research. April 24, 2014. http://www.samuelmudd.com/ .

Federal Judicial Center, "Cox, Walter Smith." Biographical Directory of Federal Judges. http://www.fjc.gov/servlet/nGetInfo?jid=525&cid=999&ctype=na&instate=na .

General Ewing's appeal to President Johnson. Samuel A. Mudd Pardon File B-596, U.S. National Archives, College Park, Md., RG 204. Available at http://www.samuelmudd.com/ .

History of the 13th Indiana Infantry. http://www.nps.gov/civilwar/search-battle-units-detail.htm?battleUnitCode=UIN0013RI .

History of the 140th Indiana Infantry. http://www.civilwarindex.com/armyin/140th_in_infantry.html .

Interment record. Oak Hill Cemetery. http://www.oakhillcemeterydc.org/Burials/cowie.html .

Johnson, Patricia Carley, transcriber. *The Selected Diaries and Papers, 1858–1866, of Frances Adeline (Fanny) Seward.* http://www.lib.rochester.edu/index.cfm?page=1420&Print=436 .

King, Chris, and Heather King. "The Killing of Mary Surratt." Vimeo video, 20:28. 2009. Watermark Films Video. https://vimeo.com/87644667 .

Kline, Fred R. "George Caleb Bingham: Artist of Missouri and the American Frontier." George Caleb Bingham: Catalogue Raisonné Supplement of Paintings and Drawings. http://www.georgecalebbingham.org/bio.htm .

Lang, Theodore F. *Loyal West Virginia from 1861 to 1865 with an Introductory Chapter on the Status of Virginia for Thirty Years Prior to the War*. Baltimore: Deutsch, 1895. Republished by Internet Archive. http://www.archive.org/stream/loyalwestvirgin00langgoog/loyalwestvirgin00langgoog_djvu.txt .

Leale, Charles A. "Lincoln's Last Hours." Address delivered before the Commandery of the State of New York Military Order of the Loyal Legion of the United States at its regular meeting February 1909. Available at Project Gutenberg. h ttp://www.gutenberg.org/files/24088/24088.txt .

Letter of Maj. Gen. Geo. G. Meade to H. Cram dated April 18, 1864. http://clevelandcivilwarroundtable.com/articles/comment/meade.htm .

Lieber, Francis. Gen. Order 100 (1863). Yale Law School Avalon project. http://avalon.law.yale.edu/19th_century/lieber.asp .

Linder, Douglas, ed. "Biography of Lewis Wallace." Famous Trials Project, University of Missouri, Kansas City. http://law2.umkc.edu/faculty/projects/ftrials/Wirz/BIO3.htm .

———. "Chronology of Lincoln Assassination Conspirators Trial." Famous Trials Project, University of Missouri, Kansas City. http://law2.umkc.edu/faculty/projects/ftrials/lincolnconspiracy/lincolnchronology.html .

———. "George Atzerodt's Confession." Famous Trials Project, University of Missouri, Kansas City. http://law2.umkc.edu/faculty/projects/ftrials/lincolnconspiracy/atzerodtconf.html .

———. "James Speed, Opinion on the Constitutional Power of the Military to Try and Execute the Assassins of the President." July 1865, Washington, D.C. Famous Trials Project, University of Missouri, Kansas City. http://law2.umkc.edu/faculty/projects/ftrials/lincolnconspiracy/commissionorder.html .
———. "Order of the President: Proceedings of a Military Commission." May 1, 1865. Famous Trials Project, University of Missouri Kansas City. http://law2.umkc.edu/faculty/projects/ftrials/lincolnconspiracy/commissionorder.htm .
Liston, Amy. "Ben Hur." *Humanities* 30, no. 6 (2009). http://www.neh.gov/humanities/2009/novemberdecember/feature/ben-hur .
Obit. David Clendenin. *Galesburg Republican-Register*, March 1895. Republished in *Rich Hanson's Civil War Stories* (blog). August 31, 2013. http://monmouthrlhcw.blogspot.com/2013/08/general-david-ramsey-clendenin.html .
Regimental History of the 2nd Ohio Cavalry in Civil War Soldiers and Sailors Index. http://www.nps.gov/civilwar/search-regiments-detail.htm?regiment_id=UOH0002RC .
Spragg, Joanne. "Lewis Wallace (1827–1905)." http://www.thelatinlibrary.com/chron/civilwarnotes/wallace.html .
Surratt, John. Lecture delivered on December 6, 1870, Rockville, Md. http://rogerjnorton.com/Lincoln55.html .
Swift, Beth. "Lew Wallace and the Elstons." *Dear Old Wabash* (blog). December 6, 2010. http://blogs.wabash.edu/dear-old-wabash/2010/12/06/lew-wallace-and-the-elstons/ .
Taylor, Tom. *Our American Cousin.* 1858. http://www.gutenberg.org/ebooks/3158 .
"Thomas Ewing, Jr." Missouri Civil War Sesquicentennial. http://mocivilwar150.com/history/figure/295 .
"Tompkins, Charles H." Congressional Medal of Honor Society. http://www.cmohs.org/recipient-detail/1385/tompkins-charles-h.php .
Townsend, George Alfred. Interview of Dr. George Mudd, May 1881. *Cleveland Leader*, June 3, 1881. Reprinted from *New York Tribune.* Available at Samuel Mudd Research. April 24, 2014. http://www.samuelmudd.com/ .
———. Interview of Dr. George Mudd, *Cincinnati Enquirer* , April 16, 1883. Available at Samuel Mudd Research. http://www.samuelmudd.com/george-mudd.htm .
———. Interview of Thomas Harbin. *Cincinnati Enquirer*, August 3, 1884. Available at Samuel Mudd Research. http://www.samuelmudd.com/thomas-harbin.htm .
Trindal, Elizabeth Steger. "The Story of Mary Surratt." Confederate Historical Society of Belgium. http://chab-belgium.com/pdf/english/Mary%20Surratt.pdf .
Warshauer, Michael. "Andrew Jackson and the Constitution." Gilder Lehrman Institute of American History. http://www.gilderlehrman.org/history-by-era/age-jackson/essays/andrew-jackson-and-constitution .
Washington Evening Star, August 3, 1865. Samuel Mudd Research. http://www.samuelmudd.com/html .
Wittenberg, Eric. "Bvt. Brig. Gen. William E. Doster." *Rantings of a Civil War Historian* (blog). March 6, 2008. http://civilwarcavalry.com/?p=704 .
Yoo, John. "Memorandum Opinion: The President's Constitutional Authority to Conduct Military Operations against Terrorists and Nations Supporting Them." U.S. Department of Justice, Opinions of the Office of Legal Counsel, September 25, 2001. http://www.justice.gov/sites/default/files/olc/opinions/2001/09/31/op-olc-v025-p0188_0.pdf .

LEGAL SOURCES

Cases

Bourjaily v. United States, 483 U.S. 171 (1987).
The Brig Amy Warwick; The Schooner Crenshaw, the Barque Hiawatha and the Schooner Brillitante (The Prize Cases) 67 U.S. 635 (1863).
Bruton v. United States, 391 U.S. 123 (1968).
Chaney v. Brown, 730 F.2d 1334 (10th Cir. 1984).

Commonwealth v. Webster, 5 Cush. (59 Mass.) 285, 320 (1850).
Donnelly v. State, 26 N.J.L.601, 615 (1857).
Ex parte Merryman, 17 Fed. Cas. 144 (C.Ct. Md. 1861).
Ex parte Milligan, 71 U.S. (4 Wallace) 2 (1866).
Ex parte Mudd, 17 Fed. Cas. 954 (S.D. Fla. 1868).
Ex parte Quirin, 317 U.S. 1 (1942).
Ex parte Vallandigham, 68 U.S. 243 (1863).
Freytag v. Commissioner, 501 U.S. 868 (1991).
Gary v. State, 671 A.2d 495 (Md. 1996).
Giles v. State, 6 Ga. 276, 285 (1849).
Glasser v. United States, 315 U.S. 60 (1944).
Griffin v. Wilcox, 21 Ind. 370 (1863).
Hamdan v. Rumsfeld, 548 U.S. 557 (2006).
Hamdi v. Rumsfeld, 542 U.S. 507 (2004).
Humphrey's Executor v. United States, 295 U.S. 602 (1935).
In re Kemp, 16 Wis. 359 (1863).
Jones v. State, 259 A.2d 807 (Md. 1969).
Kendall v. United States, 37 U.S. 524 (1838).
Krulewitch v. United States, 336 U.S. 440 (1949).
Marbury v. Madison, 5 U.S. 137 (1803).
Mudd v. Caldera, 26 F. Supp.2d113 (1998).
Mudd v. White, 309 F.3d 819 (D.C. App. 2002).
Myers v. United States, 272 U.S. 52 (1926).
Pennsylvania v. Wheeling Belmont Bridge Co., 50 U.S. (9 How.) 649 (1850).
People v. Alfano, 420 N.E.2d 1114 (Ill. App. 1981).
Seymour v. McCormick, 60 U.S. (19 How.) 96 (1857).
State v. Buchanan, 5 H. & J. 317 (Md. Ct. App. 1821).
State v. King, 20 Ark. 166 (1859).
Trop v. Dulles, 356 U.S. 86 (1958).
United States v. Beddo, 24 Fed. Cas. 1061 (4 Cranch Crim. Rep.664) (D.C. Cir. 1835).
United States v. Dow, 25 F. Cas. 901 (1 Taney 23) (Cir. Ct. D. Md. 1840).
United States v. Hudson & Goodman, 11 U.S. (7 Cranch) 32 (1812).
United States v. Kissell & Harned, 218 U.S. 601, 610 (1910).
Youngstown Sheet & Tube Co. v. Sawyer, 343 U.S. 579 (1952).

Constitutional Provisions

Alabama Constitution art. I, §§ 10, 17, 27 (1861).
Arkansas Constitution art. II, § 11 (1836).
California Constitution art. I, §§ 5, 8 (1849).
Connecticut Constitution art. I, §§ 9, 14 (1818).
Delaware Constitution art. I, §§ 7, 9 (1837).
Florida Constitution art. I, §§ 10–11 (1861).
Illinois Constitution art. XIII, §§ 9, 13, 18 (1848).
Indiana Constitution art. I, § 13 (1852).
Iowa Constitution art. I, § 10 (1857).
Kansas Constitution Bill of Rights, §§ 10, 12 (1857).
Kentucky Constitution art. XIII, § 12 (1850).
Louisiana Constitution art. CIII (1861).
Maine Constitution art. I § 7 (1819).
Maryland Constitution Declaration of Rights, art. XIX (1851).
Massachusetts Constitution Declaration of Right art. XII (1780).
Michigan Constitution art. II, § 28 (1851).
Minnesota Constitution art. I, § 6 (1857).
Mississippi Constitution art. I, § 27 (1861).
New York Constitution art. I, § 1 (1846).

North Carolina Const. Declaration of Rights, § 12 (1776).
Ohio Constitution art. I, § 12 (1851).
Rhode Island Constitution art. I, § 10 (1843).
South Carolina Constitution art. IX, § 2 (1861).
Tennessee Constitution art. I, § 9 (1796).
Texas Constitution art. I, § 16 (1845).
Virginia Declaration of Rights, § 8 (1776).
United States Constitution art. I, § 8; art. III, § 3; amend. V–VI, XIV.
Wisconsin Constitution art. I, § 7 (1848).

Statutes

1 Stat. 112 (1790).
12 Stat. at Large, Ch. 74 (1863).
12 Stat. at Large, Ch. 81 (1863).
12 Stats. 755 (Ch. 81 3 Mar. 1863).
18 U.S.C. § 1.
28 U.S.C. § 1651.
Judicial Code of 1789 §§ 13, 22 1 Stat. 73.
Ould, Robert, and W. B. B. Cross, eds. *The Revised Code of the District of Columbia Prepared under the Authority of the Act of Congress entitled "An Act to Improve the Laws of the District of Columbia and to Codify the Same," Approved March, 1855*. Part IV Title II Ch. 129 (Washington, D.C.: A.O.P. Nicholson, 1857).

Miscellaneous

Fed R. Evid. 404.
H.R. Report 104 39th Cong. 1st Sess. 39 (1866).
Military Laws and Rules and Regulations for the Government of the Army of the *United States* (Washington, D.C.: E. DeKraft, 1806)(rev. Sept. 1817)
Presidential Proclamation 104 of September 15,1863, Presidential Proclamation 133 dated July 5, 1864, for the martial law proclamation for Kentucky.

Index

About the Author

Thomas J. Reed is professor emeritus of law, Widener University School of Law, Wilmington, Delaware. He received his undergraduate BA from Marquette University in 1962 and his JD from Notre Dame Law School in 1969. He served in the U.S. Marine Corps from 1962 to 1966, winning an Air Medal for combat action in the Dominican Republic in 1965. His teaching career began at Western New England College School of Law, Springfield, Massachusetts, in 1976. In 1981, he accepted a position at Widener University School of Law, and served as associate dean of the law school from 1984 to 1992 in addition to teaching a broad spectrum of law courses. He was the director of the Veterans Law Clinic from 1997 to 2010. He is the author of two Civil War books, *Tibbits' Boys: A History of the 21st New York Cavalry Regiment* (1997) and *The Original Iron Brigade* (2011), and coauthor with Andrew McKay and Rev. Anthony Wade of *Untying the Political Knot: Delaware during the War between the States* (2001). Professor Reed edited the diaries and letters of Orderly Sergeant John F. C. Hartwell with Prof. Ann H. Britton, published as *To My Beloved Wife and Boy at Home* (1997).

Professor Reed has written more than twenty articles for law journals and is the coauthor of *Ross & Reed on Will Contests*. He lives with his wife and two cats in New Castle, Delaware, in a house built in 1872 by a Civil War veteran.

www.ingramcontent.com/pod-product-compliance
Ingram Content Group UK Ltd.
Pitfield, Milton Keynes, MK11 3LW, UK
UKHW041125071026
15587UKWH00009B/206